Overcoming
Our Racism

Derald Wing Sue

Overcoming Our Racism

The Journey to Liberation

JOSSEY-BASS
A Wiley Imprint
www.josseybass.com

Published by Jossey-Bass
A Wiley Imprint
989 Market Street, San Francisco, CA 94103-1741   www.josseybass.com

Jossey-Bass books and products are available through most bookstores.
To contact Jossey-Bass directly call our Customer Care Department within the
U.S. at 800-956-7739, outside the U.S. at 317-572-3986, or fax 317-572-4002.

Jossey-Bass also publishes its books in a variety of electronic formats.
Some content that appears in print may not be available in electronic books.

"Fatigue: An Essay," by Don C. Locke, has been adapted and is reprinted by permission
of the author. © 1994 Don C. Locke.

"Internment Films Lack Perspective" and "Dissecting the Flawed Thinking" are
reprinted by permission of the publisher. © 1999 Contra Costa/Hills Newspapers, Inc.

Quotes from "Rooting Out Our Racism" by Sara K. Winter from *Issues in Radical
Therapy* are reprinted by permission of the author. © 1977 IRT Collective.

Library of Congress Cataloging-in-Publication Data
Sue, Derald Wing.
  Overcoming our racism : the journey to liberation / by Derald Wing
Sue.
    p. cm.
Includes bibliographical references and index.
  ISBN 0-7879-6744-0 (alk. paper)
  1. United States—Race relations. 2. Racism—United States. I.
Title.
  E185.615S84 2003
  305.8'00973—dc21   2003000401

Printed in the United States of America
FIRST EDITION
HB Printing   10 9 8 7 6 5 4 3 2 1

Contents

This book is dedicated to my wife, son, and daughter:
Paulina, Derald Paul, and Marissa

Preface

Overcoming Our Racism will not be an easy book to read or digest. It is written mainly for White folks, but people of color may also find it helpful. You probably selected it from a bookstore with curiosity, some trepidation, and ambivalence. Or your professor might have made it required reading for your class.

I know how difficult it must be to entertain the notion that you harbor racist beliefs and need to overcome them. Yet despite your negative feelings and inclination to find something more pleasant to read, you still chose this book. Congratulations on having the courage to start a painful, yet potentially liberating, journey.

I hope you will read this book from start to finish and not allow the unpleasantness of the topic and feelings of defensiveness to abort your journey to enlightenment and action. If you are even reading this Preface, I know that a part of you realizes that racism exists not only in others but also in you!

The book is likely to evoke defensiveness, resentment, and anger because it may appear accusatory and because it goes against your belief that you do not discriminate on the basis of race. I implore you not to allow those feelings to interfere with your ultimate aim of overcoming personal racism. In reality, you see, racism is an ugly cancer in the heart of most White Americans. It threatens to tear us apart as a nation, unless you and your fellow White citizens face the issue with honesty and integrity.

That is my main purpose in writing this book. People of color need your help. Overcoming racism in our society cannot occur without the help of many well-intentioned White folks, such as you.

Because of our continuing battle against terrorism, I have been told that a book on racism is not what this country needs, that it is unpatriotic for me to question our way of life in America, and that I would best serve the country by stressing all that is good and just about it. Although the spirit of patriotism can bring us together as a nation, give us feelings of comfort and pride, and reaffirm cherished democratic ideals, it can also be applied in an ethnocentric and oppressive manner.

In some educational circles, for example, there is a suggestion that discussions of racism are unpatriotic and that the study of other cultural groups inside and outside the United States is un-American. Those of you who marched with us and were in the forefront of civil rights and who dissent or protest against unfair practices in our society, especially those dealing with racial/cultural differences, now encounter increased accusations of being disloyal.

Nothing could be further from the truth. It is precisely my belief in the racial/cultural mosaic of America and in your willingness to help that has resulted in the production of this book. Squelching dialogue on race and racism will prove to be a hindrance or burden to mutual understanding. Only if you are open to dialogue about such a "hot topic" will we be able to provide answers to society's polarizing perceptions of racial, ethnic, religious, and sociodemographic differences. Only dialogue and critical thinking, for example, will help us distinguish between terrorists and our law-abiding Muslim citizens and lay the seeds to combat all forms of prejudice, stereotyping, and discrimination against people of color.

It is also important for you to realize that overcoming your racism is paved with many obstacles. It is true that persons of color are often the victims of racism, but you, as a White person, are also victimized without your informed consent. Your journey to enlightenment is different than that of persons of color. It is likely to be filled with unpleasant insights about yourself as a racial being and the realization that you share responsibility for the pain and suffering caused to others. What, however, must you do to overcome your racism?

- First, you must be willing to tolerate the unpleasantness associated with an honest appraisal of your biases and prejudices.

- Second, you must begin to challenge your own racial reality. You must begin to understand yourself as a racial/cultural being and how that potentially distorts your view of race and racism.

- Third, you cannot continue to view racial/ethnic minority groups as disloyal aliens in their own country. You must begin to understand our worldview through experiential reality rather than through the images fed to you by the mass media and the educational system.

- Last, you must take action to combat your own personal racism, that of others, and the unfair practices of our society. You must work to uphold our nation's values of inclusion, respect, and fairness and be guided by the principles of social justice.

Yes, I know, it can seem overwhelming. How can you, a single individual, possibly make any difference? I wrote this book specifically to help you see beyond the anxiety and painful realization of your role in racism. I give specific suggestions about what you can do to overcome your personal racism. And I hope the promise of liberation will motivate you to read this book.

Although the process of overcoming your racism may occasionally be unpleasant, the potential benefits are many. White colleagues and students who have undertaken the journey often remark that they have personally benefited. They have

- Experienced a broadening of their horizons

- Increased their appreciation of people (all colors and cultures)

- Become less afraid and intimidated by differences

- Been able to communicate more openly and clearly with their family, friends, and coworkers

- Experienced a greater spiritual connectedness with all groups

Their effectiveness in relating to others has improved their own personal lives and their functioning in a pluralistic society. More important, they have become valued and respected White allies in the battle against racism. So can you!

What you must keep in mind is the ancient Chinese saying that "a journey of a thousand miles begins with but a single step." You have already taken the first step by picking up this book. But are you willing to take another, and another? Are you up to the challenge? If your answer is yes, read on!

ACKNOWLEDGMENTS

I have written many books before, but *Overcoming Our Racism* has proven to be a labor of love. I wish to thank the many brothers and sisters of color and White allies who have helped me survive—and thrive—despite the negative forces of racism. Knowing them has served to nurture my ideas and has given me strength to continue my multicultural journey. Especially important are my multicultural family: Patricia Arredondo, Judy Daniels, Michael D'Andrea, Allen Ivey, Mary Ivey, Don Locke, and Thomas Parham.

I wish to express gratitude to my editor, Alan Rinzler, whose enthusiasm for this project inspired me to complete it in record time.

More important have been his critical eye and his excellent suggestions regarding the need to speak to readers directly and honestly.

Finally, but even more important, has been the continuing support of my wife, Paulina, son, Derald Paul, and daughter, Marissa. As a family of color in the United States, we have collectively and individually encountered prejudice and discrimination in many forms. These experiences have, at times, been very painful. Despite the negative consequences associated with discrimination, our struggle as a family has made us stronger and more committed to helping others understand and overcome the insidious effects of racism. Without the support of my family, this book would not have been possible.

Derald Wing Sue
Teachers College, Columbia University

Overcoming
Our Racism

Part I
The Problem

1

Are You a Racist?

Are you a racist?
I'm sure you're offended already. Sure you see racism in our society, you read and hear about terrible things done by other people, but what about you, dear reader, you yourself? Can you imagine that you too are a racist? Are you willing to look at yourself, to examine your assumptions, your attitudes, your conscious and unconscious behavior, the privileges you have enjoyed as a White person, and the way you have treated people of color, even with the best of intentions? Are you willing to step into another world that exists in the margins of your consciousness? Let's see!

On January 29, 1996, Thien Minh Ly, a twenty-four-year-old Vietnamese former graduate student of UCLA was murdered while roller blading. He was found lying in a pool of blood, maimed by an excessive number of stabbing wounds to various parts of his body, as well as a slashing wound to his throat. Two White men were later arrested and confessed to the murder. In a letter bragging of the killing, one of the men wrote, "Oh I killed a Jap a while ago, I stabbed him to death." The brutal and torturous killing was sickeningly descriptive of the sadistic delight the two men took in the cries of pain as they maimed, stabbed, kicked, and stomped Ly to death. In the home of the two assailants were found White supremacist paraphernalia. On September 30, 1997, one of the assailants was sentenced to death for the racially motivated murder.

On August 9, 1997, Abner Louima, a Haitian immigrant, was arrested by New York City police officers who took him to their Seventieth Precinct station house. Once there, officers are reported to have dragged the handcuffed Louima to the bathroom, where he was brutally sodomized with a toilet plunger. Four officers were arrested and indicted, as a public outcry regarding charges of police brutality and racism was rampant in the media. Accused of a pattern of tolerating police brutality, the New York City Police Department has come under civil rights investigation by the U.S. Justice Department. Black, Hispanic, and Asian communities say that such a racially motivated brand of justice is not uncommon and has increased against minority citizens. In March 2001, New York City and the police union agreed to pay Louima $8.6 million and to institute reforms within the police department. In 2002, over five years since the incident, the legal process ended when the last remaining officer charged with complicity in the crime accepted a plea bargain from the prosecuting attorney.

OTHER PEOPLE'S RACISM AND HATE CRIMES

Frighteningly, these do not represent isolated incidents. It is difficult for any of us to turn on the TV or read a newspaper without seeing or hearing about such atrocities.

- In 1998, James Byrd Jr., an African American resident of Jasper, Texas, was kidnapped, savagely beaten, chained to a pickup truck, and dragged to death until his head was decapitated and his body was practically shredded. Police found racist tattoos on the body of the three assailants and racist literature in their homes. All have received the death penalty.

- In 1998, Matthew Shepard, a gay White student in Wyoming was viciously tortured, beaten, and killed by

two White men. Shepard's two killers, homophobic
youths, were spared the death penalty after Shepard's
parents asked that they be given life sentences instead.

- In 1999, White supremacist Buford Furrow went on
a shooting spree and wounded several Jewish children
and killed Joseph Illeto, a Filipino American postal
worker because "he was non-White and a government
worker."

- In the year 2000, Benjamin Nathaniel Smith went on
a shooting spree over the July 4 weekend, targeting
Jews, Asians, and African Americans. He wounded six
Orthodox Jews and killed Asian American Won-Joon
Yoon and African American Ricky Byrdsong before
shooting himself.

These and countless other examples indicate that racism and
hatred are alive, well, and thriving in the United States. Indeed,
the decade of the 1990s saw a historic rise in the incidents of overt
bigotry throughout the country. More disturbing, such overt acts of
racism seem to be continuing into the twenty-first century. The
Southern Poverty Law Center reports that hate sites on the Internet rose in the year 2000 to 305, an increase from 254 the year earlier.[1] Expressions of hatred have ranged from murder and mayhem
to physical attacks, threats, and racial epithets. A recently released
study by Klanwatch and the Militia Task Force recorded a record
number of hate groups in 1997, a 20 percent increase over the previous year; reports of the burning of Black churches in the mid-
1990s seemed commonplace; and a report by the National Asian
Pacific American Legal Consortium showed a 17 percent increase
in hate crimes directed toward Asian Americans.[2]

Except for White supremacists, very few of you would deny that
these acts are ugly hate crimes; that they qualify as racist, anti-
Semitic, and homophobic; and that the perpetrators should be

severely punished. The near unanimous public outcry against hate groups and the condemnation of these acts are both reassuring and disturbing at the same time. It is reassuring because the vast majority of White Americans would join us in taking action against those who would target and hurt someone on the basis of skin color or other differences. It is disturbing because fair-minded and decent White folks, those that condemn these heinous acts, and readers like you, also perpetrate acts of racism.

AS AN UNINTENTIONAL RACIST, YOU ARE THE REAL THREAT

As a psychologist who has spent nearly my entire professional life studying racism and antiracism, I am also aware that your abhorrence of racist acts may seduce you into the belief that

- "I am not like them!" "Racists are only the skinheads, the Klan, and White supremacists."

- "Except for those sick people, most Americans aren't racist."

- "I don't discriminate. I'm not prejudiced. I believe in equality."

If you focus on racism as only extreme acts of hatred, then you may convince yourself that you are not capable of prejudice, bias, and discrimination. Let us, however, look at a seemingly different set of scenarios.

The White college president and the Black faculty member were leaving a special meeting late that evening. Both decided to hop a cab back to Columbia University. As the president stepped to the curb to hail a taxi, the Black professor stopped him. "Let me show you something," he said. He gently pushed the college president behind a sign. Stepping to the curb, the Black professor held his arm high and waved to several taxis without luck. They all passed him, despite being empty. He returned to the college president and had him step to the curb. "Now, it's your turn," he said. The president raised his arm, and barely several seconds had passed before a taxi stopped to pick them up!

I've experienced many situations where my Chinese American ancestry has affected how people see me. I remember my first week as a freshman in high school. Mr. Knutson, my counselor, called me into his office to counsel me about taking honors courses. He said, "I'm so pleased that you are my student. I have great hopes for you. I'm going to recommend that you take our accelerated PSSC physics class. In four years, mark my words, I think you will win the Bausch & Lomb science award. You know that it is given to the outstanding senior math and science student." Although I expressed reservations about entering a course designed for advanced sophomores (I was a freshman), he would not take no for an answer. "I know you may be anxious, son, but don't worry. You'll do well in the class because *you people are good at that*," he said.

The Euro-American husband and wife had recently moved to Los Angeles. On this hot Sunday afternoon, they were sightseeing and trying to get acquainted with the neighborhood. They had taken a wrong turn and entered the Hispanic section of South Central L.A. As they came to a red stoplight, several Latino youths crossed the street, laughing and pushing one another in a jesting fashion. Without a word spoken between them, both husband and wife simultaneously hit the door lock on their sides of the car. Seeing this, the youths shouted, "Shame! Shame! Shame!"

In your private moments, most of you would admit to having witnessed or experienced similar reactions and fears as those involved in the three examples above. How many of you, dear readers, have clutched your purses or reached for your wallets when a person of color approached? How many of you, White mothers, have felt pangs of apprehension when you noticed your son or daughter playing with a Black youngster on the playground but not when the youngster was White? How many store personnel tend to pay more attention to a visible racial/ethnic minority shopper than to a White one? Yet many of you would deny that such reactions or behaviors constitute prejudice, stereotyping, or discrimination. Most of you may tend to rationalize away these behaviors:

"The cabdrivers did not stop for the Black professor because of coincidence. It was not bias! How do you know that the taxi that stopped for the college president wouldn't have also done so for the professor if he had waited longer? Why are you making such a big thing out of it? You minorities are just oversensitive!"

"This is what I don't like about being White. We get accused of racism when we are only trying to help. The counselor was well-intentioned and just trying to help the Asian American student. After all, Asians, as a group, have always done better in the sciences."

"Look, if I were in a strange neighborhood and youngsters crossed in front of my car, I would lock it too! My actions are not based on the race of the youths. I would lock the car doors even if it were a group of White students!"

These explanations, I believe, fail to acknowledge the possibility that the actions of the participants may also be due to deeply ingrained biases and fears. Much of my work in psychology has led me to conclude that people are not necessarily *rational* beings but *rationalizing* ones. Very few of you would entertain the notion that your actions are motivated by racist attitudes and beliefs. It is even more unlikely that you would accept the notion that like the earlier examples of hate crimes, these examples are also evidence of prejudice, discrimination, stereotyping, and unwarranted fears.

Although it may be extremely difficult to believe, it is my contention that all of these examples share a common thread: they are manifestations of racism. One form, however, is more harmful than the other. Hate crimes are often perpetrated by avowed racists, whose intent is to consciously and deliberately intimidate and to cause serious injury or death to their victims, but I believe that the more subtle forms of racism expressed by well-intentioned folks, like you, do the greatest overall harm to persons of color.

Even as I write these words, I can sense the incredulousness coming from you, dear reader: *More harmful than overt expressions of racial hatred?* Further, it may shock you to know that I am less concerned with the Klan, the skinheads, or the White supremacists than with the well-intentioned readers of this text. Would it surprise you, for example, to know that the greatest threat to racial minorities in the United States comes from good and decent White folks, lovers of justice and democracy, and moral church-going people?

It is clear to me that the overt bigots of the world are not the culprits who have created the inequalities in our society. To illustrate this assertion, let me ask you the following question: What is wrong with this picture? Even though White Euro-American males constitute only 33 percent of the population, they occupy approximately

- 80 percent of tenured positions in higher education

- 80 percent of the House of Representatives

- 84 percent of the U.S. Senate

- 92 percent of Forbes 400 executive CEO-level positions

- 90 percent of public school superintendents

- 99.9 percent of athletic team owners

- 100 percent of U.S. presidents

What is glaring about this picture can be pinpointed by asking two simple questions: Where are the persons of color? Where are the women?

It isn't White supremacists who create and control the tools that result in such unjust and damaging disparities. It is people you elect to office, teachers who educate your children, business leaders who carry out the policies and practices of their corporations, government leaders, law enforcement officers, physicians, dentists, construction workers, your family, friends, and neighbors. It is you and I!

WHY I WROTE THIS BOOK

Colleagues and friends have warned me that *Overcoming Our Racism* is painful and unpleasant reading, that it will evoke defensiveness in White readers, that it is not for the faint of heart, that most people prefer to avoid the topic, and that many will become angry at having racism pushed into their consciousness. Why, they ask, would I choose to leave the security of academia, depart from the haven of addressing other social scientists, and write a book for ordinary citizens about racism? There are several reasons why I have chosen this path.

First, I believe that racism is tearing this country apart and that racial strife and disharmony will increase as visible racial/ethnic minorities move toward becoming a numerical majority in the next few decades. In 1990, White Americans constituted 76 percent of the population; Census 2000 figures place them now at only 69 percent of the population.[3] In other words, the U.S. population is undergoing a radical demographic transformation that is often referred to as the "diversification of America" or literally the "changing complexion of society." People of color now constitute over one-third of the population, with 45 percent in our public schools. Demographers predict that sometime between the years 2030 and 2050, racial/ethnic minorities will become a numerical majority.

To get some idea of the explosive increase in racial minorities, one has only to look at the following growth factors. During the 1990s, the White population increased less than 7 percent, whereas the Hispanic population grew 58 percent, the Asian American population 50 to 72 percent, the African American population 16 to

21 percent, and the American Indians, Eskimos, and Aleuts 14 percent. These large increases are due to higher birthrates among minorities and heavy immigration from Latin American and Asian countries (over 70 percent of immigrants are people of color).

The demographic shift throughout our nation is revealed in the following figures:

- 50 percent of Californians are people of color.

- 30 percent of New York City residents are internationally born.

- 70 percent of the District of Columbia is Black.

- 66 percent of Miami is Hispanic.

- 37 percent of San Francisco is Asian.

- 67 percent of Detroit is Black.

- Over ten thousand Laotian Hmongs have immigrated to the Minneapolis-St. Paul area.

- The top localities in minority representation by the year 2020 will be in the following order:

District of Columbia	72.6 percent
New Mexico	67.8 percent
Hawaii	64.6 percent
California	62.3 percent
Texas	53.9 percent
Maryland	44.9 percent
Arizona	44.0 percent
New York	43.5 percent
Nevada	42.5 percent
New Jersey	42.0 percent

Increasingly, you as a citizen, educator, or worker will come into contact with culturally different citizens who may not share your worldview, who operate from a reality different from yours.[4] The results may be increased misunderstandings, disagreements, conflicts, and potentially explosive racial situations. This means that each and every one of you must work harder to become culturally sensitive, aware, and skilled in functioning in a pluralistic society. You will need to reach out. You will need not only to acquire new understandings but also to develop new culturally effective communications skills. Strangely, even though we are becoming more diverse, we are not becoming a more integrated nation. Segregation continues in housing, education, and employment.

As different worldviews and lifestyles collide, the inevitable demand for change in every facet of American life will increase. Our traditional ways of doing things will no longer be adequate to deal with the diversity of the country. With the pressure to change will come clashes between competing groups as to which will have the power to make decisions that will affect how you live in this society. The nature of education, how the criminal justice system operates, how business is conducted, and every facet of American life will be challenged. Unless we can resolve these differences peacefully through shared collaboration and allow for equal access and opportunity for all groups in society, our nation will not survive the inevitable turmoil.

Second, I am well aware that the title of this book may be inflammatory and will arouse intense feelings of defensiveness, denial, resentment, and fear among many. Some of you may even accuse *me* of being racist, but of a different color, because I "hate White people." When I testified before President Clinton's Race Advisory Board in 1997, this was precisely the reaction from some citizens watching the testimony on C-Span.[5] I received letters and even e-mail messages stating that the problems of race relations were "due to people like you." I was, they suggested, another Farrakhan fomenting the seeds of hate and blaming White folks for all the wrongs of our society. My testimony was limited to a half hour, making it very difficult to convey my thoughts in an in-depth manner. The brevity of the presentation led me to realize that I needed to communicate more at length with the American public. As a result, I have decided to make my case to the public via a book on racism.

Let me state at the outset that I do not hate White folks. I consider many of my White colleagues, neighbors, and friends to be valuable allies in the battle against racism. However, I also realize that regardless of skin color, every one of us harbors biases and prejudices and has discriminated or continues to discriminate against others. The research on racism and my own personal experiences lead me to this conclusion. And I readily admit that I am not immune either. It is hard for me to believe, for example, that I was born and raised and have lived in the United States for some sixty years without inheriting the racial biases of my forebears. Such a false belief, I am certain, would be the height of naïveté or would indicate a lack of contact with social reality. The title of my book therefore reflects social-psychological reality. We cannot and must not mute this reality.

Third, I have spent over thirty years studying the causes of racism and the need to combat it on individual, institutional, and societal levels, and I have written extensively about society's need to overcome bias, discrimination, and prejudice. Yet, as my wife has frequently reminded me, my work is often insulated in academia, where it is "objectively" discussed as an academic subject, seldom reaches the layperson, and artificially restricts the necessary but intense feelings that flow from the topic.

In the halls of the ivory tower, the topic of racism often becomes a sterile academic exercise, following the mantra "emotions are antagonistic to reason." Yet any honest discussion of race and racism is bound to evoke strong emotional reactions in many of you. These feelings may deal with anger ("Don't you dare accuse me of being racist!"), contrition ("I feel guilty, I should have done something"), defensiveness ("I already do enough for minorities, what more do you want from me?"), helplessness ("The problem is too big . . . what can I do?"), shame ("I can't face my minority friends after what I said"), being turned off ("I have other priorities in life"), and fear ("Look, as a White man I can't find a job anymore").

These reactions are unpleasant and produce discomfort in most of us. No wonder it is easier for you to avoid talking or thinking about race and racism than to enter into a searching dialogue about the topic. The academic protocol and—to some extent—the politeness protocol serve as barriers to open and honest dialogue about the pain of discrimination and how each and every one of you perpetuates bias through your silence or obliviousness. Indeed, choosing not to do anything about racial injustice is as bad as the direct actions of those who discriminate.

Albert Einstein once wrote, "The world is too dangerous to live in—not because of the people who do evil, but because of the people who sit and let it happen."

Fourth, as a youngster, the many experiences of prejudice and discrimination made me keenly aware of the great psychological toll that racism takes on persons of color. I have been frequently reminded by personal experiences that my racial and cultural heritage is quite different from many in this society. Some of these reminders have been pleasant and validating; many, however, serve to invalidate, diminish, and strike at the core of my racial identity and self-esteem. The well-intentioned high school counselor who tracked me into math and science courses because "you people are good at that," classmates who teased me by making fun of my "slanted eyes," or the taxi driver who complimented me for "speaking good English" are constant reminders of my minority status in this society.

At a very young age, I became aware of widespread stereotypes about Asian Americans, how physical differences could be objects of scorn, and how minorities are often perceived as aliens in their own country. Even though these incidents often come from well-intentioned individuals, they are nevertheless painful to bear. Most racial/ethnic minority groups have been exposed to many forms of prejudice, stereotyping, and discrimination; some are quite overt, intentional, and hurtful, but most are what psychologists now call *micro assaults*. I now realize that understanding the harm inflicted on people of color must begin with reaching our families, friends, and neighbors. But most of all, reaching you, my dear readers, is very important. Through all my work in the field, I have come to realize that if you can truly understand the pain of racism and the psychological toll it takes on both the victim and the perpetrator, you will be motivated to change.

Fifth, I also became very aware of how you, the average White Euro-American, seem oblivious to issues of race, how you often minimize the impact of racism, and how you often deny being racist but will tell or laugh at racist jokes, avoid persons of color in your social circles, and engage in practices that discriminate against minorities. I often wondered what were the causes of racism, why some people were so intolerant, why good and decent White folks often seemed oblivious to their own biases, and what people could do to combat bigotry and discrimination?

Yet when I have attempted to dialogue with you about race and racism, you have often told me that race is unimportant, that people are people, and that we should treat everyone the same. After years of work in the field of diversity and multiculturalism, I now recognize the many hot buttons that are pushed. You, my dear reader, are disinclined to discuss race because you are fearful that whatever you say or do might label you a racist. In actuality, however, I believe the barrier is much deeper. What you really fear is related not only to being perceived as being racist but also to the dreaded realization that it may be true! It is painful for you to realize that you, as a White person, are racist, that your actions and beliefs hurt and oppress others, and that your self-image of being good, moral, and a decent human being conflict with this self-insight.

In general, coping with racism not only has helped shape my personal identity but also has played a large role in my desire to study the causes, effects, and conditions we need to create to overcome overt and covert forms of racism. When I was invited to testify before President Clinton's Race Advisory Board, I shared with them the results of my research and work on race relations. Among the many points I made were the following:

- Bigotry and racism continue to be two of the most divisive forces in our society.

- The need to address issues of race, culture, and ethnicity has never been more urgent.

- Most citizens of this nation seem ill equipped to deal with these topics.

- Racial legacies of the past continue to affect current policies and practices, creating unfair disparities between racial/ethnic minority and Euro-American groups.

- Such inequities are often so deeply ingrained in American society that they are nearly invisible.

- The greatest challenge this nation faces is how we can become a multicultural society that values equal access and opportunity.

- Our greatest hope toward solving the problems of prejudice and discrimination lies in an honest examination of ourselves as racial/cultural beings.

Overcoming Our Racism leaves no wiggle room for avoidance and ambiguity. It reflects my personal belief that it is impossible for any of us, those born and raised in the United States and those who have been exposed for some time to our culture, not to inherit the biases, stereotypes, fears, and "isms" of our society. So I again ask you the question, "Are you a racist?"

Please don't be afraid to answer honestly. If your answer is yes, don't let the negative feelings overwhelm or paralyze you. Rather than feeling guilty or ashamed, you should feel proud about the strength and courage it took to confront your own biases. You have taken the second, but perhaps the most difficult and biggest, step toward liberation and ultimately to becoming a valuable ally in combating racism. I congratulate you and look forward to our journey together.

If you still, however, have difficulty dealing with my question and its assertions, that's OK. At least you have been courageous enough to entertain such a notion. So stick with me. Don't give up now! Regardless of whether your answer is yes or no, I want you to continue asking this question throughout the book.

What You Can Do to Overcome Racism

In this section are questions, exercises, and a brief inventory that may aid you in further self-exploration of topics related to race and racism.

Exercise Number 1

Overcoming your racism means paying attention to the racist thoughts, fears, and feelings that you possess. Earlier in this chapter, we posed three examples of unintentional and unconscious racial biases and fears that affect human behavior: differential outcomes when a White or Black man hails a cab, a well-intentioned counselor attempting to help a Chinese American student, and the White couple's locking of their car door in the presence of Latino youths. These are not atypical reactions by White folks in similar situations.

- If at all possible, it would be beneficial for you to discuss these situations with others (classmates, members of your book-reading club, partner, close coworker, colleague, and so forth).

- More valuable might be to initiate a discussion with people of color (racially mixed group or friend).

- As you reflect back over interactions with people of color and those with race-related implications, can you identify your own thoughts, reactions, and feelings? What implications do you draw from them?

Address the following questions related to the three examples and others you may have experienced:

1. What explanations do you have for these incidents?

2. In what ways may they be manifestations of racial fears, apprehensions, and stereotypes?

   - In the taxi-hailing incident, was the result coincidence or fears by White cabdrivers that Blacks are inherently dangerous and not to be trusted?
   - Did the White counselor harbor a stereotype that Asian Americans are good in math and science? Even though the counselor was well-intentioned and might have been operating from a positive stereotype, how might it still hurt the minority student?
   - Did the White couple fear that the Latino youths crossing in front of their car would engage in some form of mischief or criminal behavior?

3. Have you ever experienced similar reactions in other race-related situations? If so, think about them carefully and if possible discuss them with others. What do they mean to you?

Exercise Number 2

Think about the following groups and give your immediate overall emotional reactions. Are your feelings positive or negative? Good or bad?

1. African Americans
2. Asian/Pacific Americans
3. Latino/Hispanic Americans
4. Native Americans
5. White Americans

Discuss or consider what these reactions mean for you. Do they indicate bias? Do they indicate stereotypes? Do they indicate prejudice?

Exercise Number 3

Feelings of apprehension, anxiety, or outright fear in interracial situations are often indicative of racial stereotypes, biases, and prejudices. Oftentimes you may be unable to identify the specific feelings or reasons for your fears. You tend to deny them or make excuses for your feelings and behaviors. That is one of the primary reasons you may have difficulty confronting your racism. The first step is to be honest about your feelings. Take the short test on the following page.

On a scale from 1 to 5, rate the degree of discomfort you are likely to experience in the following situations. *Discomfort* is defined as the degree of anxiety or apprehension you experience. Use the following scale: 1 = no discomfort; 2 = minimal discomfort; 3 = mild discomfort; 4 = high discomfort; 5 = overwhelming discomfort. Write in the number that best describes your feelings.

Racial Discomfort Scale

1. Entering an elevator in a deserted hotel where there are three Black men already inside   _____

2. Becoming aware that your son or daughter is romantically involved with a person of color   _____

3. Realizing that you are the only White person in a Latino neighborhood   _____

4. Seeing that your five-year-old son or daughter has paired off with another youngster of color on the school playground   _____

5. Going into a Chinese restaurant where all the patrons and employees are Asian   _____

6. Having to take a stand on affirmative action in racially mixed company   _____

7. Having a Black person be your personal physician   _____

8. Voting for a person of color for president of the United States   _____

9. Having a person of color ask you out on a date   _____

10. Telling Latino colleagues that you employ a Mexican American maid   _____

Scoring Key: 0–10 = continuing denial of or minimal unconscious/conscious racist attitudes and feelings; 11–30 = mild to moderate levels of unconscious/conscious racist attitudes and feelings; 31–40 = moderate to high levels of unconscious/conscious racist attitudes and feelings; 41–50 = strong and overwhelming unconscious/conscious racist attitudes and feelings.

This is certainly not a scientific test but rather a subjective one that can be used to stimulate exploration and discussion of feelings. Some questions that you can ask yourself are these:

1. Why do I feel uncomfortable in these situations? Would I feel equally uncomfortable if I were to change the race of the person(s) in the situation? For example, if the person(s) were White, would it affect my comfort level? Why?

2. What specific feelings am I experiencing? Fear? Guilt? Threat? Revulsion? Where are the feelings coming from?

3. What are the reasons for these feelings? For example, question number 1, in which you enter an elevator with three Black men, might evoke fears of being assaulted or robbed. Is it due to stereotypes that Black men are likely to be angry, hostile, and prone to violence and crime? In question number 2, does your discomfort have anything to do with a belief in the inferiority of persons of color and that your son and daughter deserve better?

2

What Is Racism?

You may be asking yourselves some questions at this point: "What is racism? How is it different from prejudice, discrimination, bias, and bigotry? You have used the terms *anti-Semitism* and *homophobia* as well. Are they not forms of prejudice? When you talk about race, what do you mean? Aren't you overgeneralizing when you use group references like African Americans, Asian Americans, or even White Americans? All of these terms are confusing. It seems like people use them differently. Why can't we just talk about 'people' and not get hung up with racial labels?"

First, it may surprise you to know that academicians are often equally imprecise and inconsistent in their use of such terminology. Part of the problem resides in the hot-button nature of the terms. First, the word *racism* often evokes intense and passionate feelings and beliefs that cloud a person's ability to communicate clearly and to influence others via sensitivity and logic. Think about it. If I were to say the word racism, what would be your first reaction? What images come to mind and what feelings do you experience? The hot rhetoric and confrontations that arise are disturbing to groups and individuals and elicit associations with affirmative action, quotas, political correctness, and other emotionally laden terms.

Second, defining concepts is difficult because people often use the same terms for different things or different terms to mean the same thing. So it is very important for you to have a common referent when you begin your journey to understand the meaning and insidious nature of racism. Benjamin Whorf, a well-known linguist, has revealed how language shapes thoughts and influences the perception of reality.[1] Let's, therefore, take a stab at clarifying what we are talking about.

WHAT IS PREJUDICE AND WHAT ARE STEREOTYPES?

The most commonly accepted definition of *prejudice* is that used by social psychologist Gordon Allport.[2] Simply put, prejudice is bias expressed through negative or positive opinions, beliefs, or feelings toward individuals who belong to a certain group or fit a certain category. It is different from a *preference* for someone or something: I prefer eating rice and noodles over breads or potatoes, summers over winters, and dark suits over light ones. In all three cases, my preferences were developed over an extended period of time through direct, extended, and broad experiences.

The unfavorable or favorable dimension of prejudice, however, is an overgeneralization not based on reason or actual experience. For example, you may possess unfavorable reactions or beliefs toward Black people but have limited or no contact with members of the group. Your racial prejudice is composed of an *attitude* component (negative or positive) and a *belief* component that is overgeneralized or erroneous. Despite contradictory information in the face of a negative belief or attitude, you continue to hold on to your prejudices. For example

1. Many of you may hold negative attitudes toward African Americans in the form of dislike, disgust, apprehension, or discomfort, based on unwarranted beliefs that they are less intelligent, prone to crime, dangerous, unclean, and untrustworthy.

2. A dislike of Asian Americans is often paired with a belief that they represent a threat to the American economy and are taking jobs away from "true Americans."

3. An antipathy toward Latinos is paired with the belief that most are lazy illegal immigrants filling up our welfare rolls and exploiting the goodwill of the country.

4. Avoidance of Native Americans is based on a feeling that they are uncivilized drunkards and primitive heathens who tend to be unsanitary.

In summary, racial prejudice has three major components: it is negative in nature (hatred, fear, or dislike), based on faulty or unsubstantiated data, and rooted in an inflexible generalization. This last quality of racial prejudice is a central characteristic of stereotypes. *Stereotypes* may be defined as rigid and inaccurate preconceived notions that you hold about all people who are members of a particular group, whether it be defined along racial, religious, sexual, or other lines.

The belief that a group (Native American, Latino American, and so forth) has specific traits is applied to all members without regard for individual variations. Although stereotypes can be either positive or negative (Asian Americans are very intelligent, hardworking, and law-abiding versus Asian American men are unassertive, passive, and sexually unattractive; or African Americans are good athletes and musically inclined versus African Americans make poor scholars), they share a common characteristic: they are inaccurate portrayals and are usually evaluated from some group perspective.

The danger of stereotypes is that they are impervious to logic or experience. All incoming information is distorted to fit your biased belief system. For example, people who are strongly anti-Semitic will accuse Jews of being stingy and miserly and then in the same breath accuse them of flaunting their wealth by conspicuous spending.

Or a person who believes that African Americans are intellectually inferior and meets a highly intelligent Black person may rationalize away the contradiction by thinking that he or she is an exception.

These examples raise a number of questions: Why would you hold on to stereotypes in the face of contradictory information or experience? Wouldn't your belief system change when confronted with facts? Answers to these questions become very complex because they strike at the very core of how human beings categorize and process information (cognitive processes). According to social psychologists, the process of categorization and the tendency to distinguish between differences are natural phenomena used by people to make distinctions between groups, objects, situations, and events. Further, as I have stated in Chapter One, people are not necessarily rational beings but rationalizing ones. And this happens to be one of the primary reasons why stereotypes are so unchangeable: they are rooted in normal psychological processes. Let us briefly explore the ramifications of this statement.

Categorization is the process of identifying differences between groups and bundling those characteristics into separate meaningful units. Your brain is very good at categorizing information and experiences into discernible categories: friend-foe, good-bad, safe-dangerous, and so forth. It appears that this process is the brain's attempt to make sense out of the world by simplifying the overwhelming amount of data that you encounter in your daily life. This process is a necessity for both survival and quick decision making. Discerning differences can occur on a conscious or unconscious level. Social scientists now recognize that much of the brain's categorization occurs automatically, outside the level of your awareness.

Most of you have learned or have been conditioned to believe that not all differences are equal in meaning, importance, and salience. Hair color, height, and weight are often less important than skin color, which is extremely salient in our society. In the case of stereotypes, it has been found that you tend to group differences that relate most to cherished values that you hold. If you value intelligence, you may be quick to judge another group as less intelligent or stupid. Believing that your own group is more intelligent results in feelings of superiority and enhances self-pride. If you value hard work and perseverance, you may perceive other groups as lazy or as quitters.

Stereotypes, therefore, often serve the function of making you feel better about yourself or about members of your group. Believing that the United States is the most technologically advanced nation in the world and that science and rationality are the cornerstones of the society may lead you to believe that other groups or societies are undeveloped, primitive, and uncivilized. Despite the fact that anthropologists warn us that judgments of cultural evolution are value laden, many people continue to view American Indians or African society as primitive, uncouth, and uncivilized; therefore its members are also "savages." Part of the mechanism used to feel good about yourself includes believing that you are unique and then exaggerating your "good features," while minimizing these desirable traits in other groups.

Herein lies one of the biggest challenges to combating stereotypes: your self-image and self-esteem are often formed from the fabric of the stereotypes you hold! If your belief in the intellectual superiority of your group (and by extension you) is partially or wholly based on viewing another group as less intelligent, or if your belief that your achievements in life are due to hard work and perseverance is based on perceiving another group as lazy and lacking motivation, then these different sides of the same coin become intertwined in a symbiotic relationship. Directly challenging a stereotype results in discomfort and a potential loss of self-esteem, a threat to the positive image you hold of yourself.

Because stereotypes make you feel better and have become a part of your positive identity, challenging them is likely to make you defensive. You will either avoid situations or events that challenge your stereotypes or engage in psychological maneuvers to protect your worldview. Leon Festinger, a well-known psychologist, formulated what has come to be known as *cognitive dissonance theory*.[3] Simply stated, the theory asserts that when you encounter information or experiences inconsistent with a strongly held belief or opinion, a state of dissonance is induced. The existence of dissonance produces discomfort, and you will seek to reduce or eliminate it.

Research has shown that people may use several defensive maneuvers to accomplish this task: (1) you may compartmentalize the discrepant information by judging it to be irrelevant to your belief system, (2) you may selectively seek information that serves to support your original belief while avoiding information that invalidates it, or (3) you may derogate or discredit the source of the contradictory information. Interestingly, when stereotypes are involved, option (4), changing your opinion or belief in the face of contradictory information, is one of the least likely cognitive maneuvers to be employed.

A common stereotype of Asian Americans, for example, is that they make poor leaders because they are unassertive, poor in people relationships, and inarticulate. How you may use the three defensive maneuvers to hold on to your stereotypes when confronted by contradictory information is illustrated by the following:

1. If, as an employee, you harbor the just-cited stereotype and encounter an Asian American manager who is forceful, decisive, and skilled in working with people, this belief becomes challenged and produces dissonance. Rather than questioning your beliefs about Asian Americans, you may simply avoid thinking about the implication of the discrepant facts by refusing to connect the two or conclude that the manager is an exception (*compartmentalization*).

2. Suppose you are a White student attending a class taught by a professor on the social psychology of race. When your image of Asian Americans is challenged in the course, you actively search for information supporting your contention that Asians make poor leaders. The information you present is based on studies indicating that they are underrepresented at managerial and supervisory lev-

els. You fail, however, to examine data indicating that Asian Americans often encounter bias and discrimination in their quest for promotion and advancement in the organization (*glass ceiling*).

3. A female diversity trainer presents numerous examples and facts to an audience that challenge their stereotypes about Asian Americans. Afterwards several of the participants have only negative things to say about the trainer: "she's a bleeding-heart liberal," "she's an academician who has never worked in industry before," "her training is in English literature and not science," or "she's an opinionated person who's lost her sense of objectivity." By discrediting the communicator, the information and assertions made by the trainer are invalidated.

All three defensive maneuvers share the common purpose of preserving your view of the world and reducing dissonance. Social scientists have found that changing stereotypes is extremely difficult. In a future chapter, we will present strategies that can be employed to overcome stereotypes.

WHAT IS DISCRIMINATION AND RACISM?

Although it is unpleasant for persons of color to be around people who are prejudiced or hold stereotypes, the prevailing belief is that their presence does little direct harm as long as their prejudices are not acted on. (New research now challenges this belief, but I will discuss this matter later.) In other words, as long as it remains only an internal attitude or belief, most people of color can tolerate such situations. When, however, you express or act on your prejudices, it becomes *racial discrimination*. Racial discrimination is any action that differentially treats individuals or groups of color based on prejudice.

Although the term *discrimination* has acquired a negative connotation, it is important to note that in itself it is not necessarily undesirable. Again, it appears that discrimination is rooted in normal psychological processes. This is especially true when we use valid criteria to differentially discriminate and select individuals for colleges, graduate schools, professions, and our friends or life partners. For example, no one would find fault with a person who must undergo surgery and chooses a physician who is more experienced than a less experienced one. Likewise, when teachers differentially grade their students' performances and assign them A's, B's, C's, D's, and F's, few of you would find fault with the practice. Discrimination based on prejudice, however, is another matter. In most cases, racial discrimination is considered illegal and immoral. It is important to note that like prejudice and stereotyping, racial discrimination can occur between and among any group combination: between Asian American and African American, Euro-American and Latino or Hispanic American, and so forth. Asian Americans can be prejudiced against African Americans; African Americans against EuroAmericans; Latino Americans against Native Americans.

Only Whites Can Be Racist

The definition of racism, however, has traditionally been confined primarily to White Americans. Two underlying assumptions are often made: all White Euro-Americans are racist, and only White people can be racist. Spike Lee, the well-known Black filmmaker and producer of films such as *Do the Right Thing*, *Jungle Fever*, *Malcolm X*, and *Bamboozled*, has created quite a fervor with his remark that "all Whites are racist."[4] I am sure that you have heard this statement before, and like other Whites, you've probably experienced denial, anger, defensiveness, guilt, or feelings of helplessness. When my graduate students ask whether I believe that Whites are racist, I usually respond with a qualified yes.

I try to explain to them that although racism shares many of the features associated with racial discrimination, they are not the same. Both are composed of an attitudinal component (racial prejudice) and a behavioral component (discrimination). Racism, however, is different from racial discrimination because it is a pervasive and systemic exercise of real power to deny minorities equal access and opportunity, while maintaining the benefits and advantages of White Americans. In the United States, it is White folks who dominate and control the institutions and social policies that create and enforce "American" cultural values and norms. Relative to White people, persons of color are relatively powerless on a societal level. On the basis of that fact alone, racism in the United States can only be attributed to White Americans and not to persons of color!

Now I know that these statements have probably pushed buttons in many readers. Why, you may ask, am I attributing racism only to White people? Can't people of color be racist as well? Haven't I already acknowledged that racial prejudice and discrimination are also directed at White folks? Before I address your reactions and questions, stay with me for the moment. Know also that my answer is not tinged with anger, bitterness, blame, or negativism. I believe it to be an honest one, and I hope you will allow me the opportunity to explain my assertions before you make a decision regarding their validity.

Definition of Racism

Racism is any attitude, action, or institutional structure or any social policy that subordinates persons or groups because of their color. It is different from racial prejudice, hatred, or discrimination because it involves the *power* to carry out systematic discriminatory practices in a broad and continuing manner. The subordination of persons of color in the United States occurs not just on an individual level but also in the activities and procedures of our institutions, corporations, and social systems.

For example, studies continue to demonstrate that minorities consistently receive inferior housing, education, and health services. In general, the social structures and policies in our society have two corresponding but complementary outcomes: they discriminate against people of color, and they maintain advantages and benefits to White Americans. Because it is White Americans who control these systemic forces in the society and who enforce cultural norms and values, they are the only ones capable of systemic discrimination. Because people of color do not possess the power to enforce their prejudices on a large systemic scale, minorities, by definition, cannot be racist!

My experience tells me that many White readers, such as you, will either be angered or turned off by this assertion, so let me try to clarify its meaning. First, minorities can be biased, can be discriminating, and can hold stereotypes as well. On an individual basis, people of color are no less prone to being prejudiced. As I mentioned earlier, being born and raised as a Chinese American in this society for some sixty years means that I have also inherited detrimental attitudes, beliefs, and feelings toward other groups. Many White patrons to small Chinatown restaurants in San Francisco or New York are not aware that there is often both a Chinese and an English menu, with prices much less for Chinese American patrons. It's not uncommon in an ethnic minority neighborhood for persons of color to discriminate against White Americans.

Prejudice and discrimination are not confined to any one group. But a prejudiced Black CEO, for example, is less likely to do harm to White employees than a prejudiced White CEO to employees of color. For one thing, the Black CEO is likely to be accountable to a corporate board, to stockholders, and to officers and employees of the organization who are overwhelmingly White! Further, the policies, practices, and structures of the organization continue to be ethnocentric and monocultural. They come from a White perspective and are stacked to favor White folks. In general, minorities do not possess a share of economic, social, and political power equal to that of Whites in our society; they are by definition unable to be racist. I realize, however, that discrimination, stereotyping, and oppression hurt and injure, regardless of whether or not we define it as racism.

Second, even though my assertion may arouse defensiveness in White readers, I hope that understanding my reasoning will be sufficient to view the issue from another perspective. It is not an issue of blame nor of saying that one group is better than the other. As we will see in a later chapter, it is White supremacy, *not you*, at which my grievances are directed.

Having made these points, I will try to be more specific in describing the dynamics and characteristics of racism. A well-known social psychologist, James Jones, has described three increasingly complex manifestations of racism.[5]

1. *Individual racism* is perhaps that which is most known by the American public. Though it is often associated with the overt acts of racial hatred and bigotry committed on an individual level, it is far more insidious and all-encompassing than the commission of hate crimes. Individual racism is any attitude or action, whether intentional or unintentional, conscious or unconscious, that subordinates persons or groups because of their color. It can be manifested in overt, intentional, and conscious efforts to harm (the White supremacist), or it can be subtle, unintentional, and unconscious (well-intentioned persons). An example of the latter may be addressing an elderly Black man by his first name while calling an older White man by the formal last name, "Mr. Jones."

2. *Institutional racism* is any institutional policy, practice, or structure in governments, businesses, unions, schools, churches, courts, and law enforcement entities by which decisions are made as to unfairly subordinate persons of color while allowing other groups to profit from such actions. Examples include housing patterns, segregated schools, discriminatory employment and promotion policies, racial profiling, and inequities in health care, segregated churches, and educational curricula that ignore or distort the history of minorities.

3. *Cultural racism* is the individual and institutional expression of the superiority of one group's cultural heritage over another group's (arts, crafts, language, traditions, beliefs, and values) and its imposition on racial/ethnic minority groups. When, for example,

White Euro-Americans use power to perpetuate their cultural heritage and impose it on people of color while diminishing the importance of or destroying another group's way of life (cultural genocide), it represents racism of the extreme kind. History is replete with governmental actions used by the United States to stamp out the language and religious practices of Native Americans. In cultural racism's contemporary form, some teachers forbid the use of a second language in their classrooms.

In the next chapter, I will discuss the oppressive implications of these three forms of racism, but let us now briefly turn to some terms we have used and will use in reference to racial groups.

WHAT'S IN A NAME? RACE AND RACIAL/ETHNIC GROUP TERMS

I'm sure that you have heard these terms used: African American/ Black, American Indian/Native American, Asian American/Pacific Islander, and Latino/Hispanic American. They have emerged as commonly used terms to refer to four recognized racial/ethnic minority groups in the United States. These terms, however, are by no means without controversy, nor do those who are classified as belonging to the group universally accept them. Because I will be making reference to racial/ethnic groups throughout the book, it is important to clarify some problematic issues lest they continue to create confusion.

The terms I use to describe various racial/ethnic groups are intermixed with scientific, political, and popular meanings. Most scientists, however, use the term *race* to refer to a biological classification system determined by physical characteristics of genetic origin. These physical differences include but are not limited to skin pigmentation, head form, stature, color and texture of body hair, nasal index, lip form, and so forth. The clustering of these traits is used to distinguish subgroups of humankind from one another. Many difficulties exist, however, in using race as a descriptor.

The Biracial or Multiracial Issue

Several years ago, a good friend of mine made a very provoca-tive statement. In discussing the issue of racism, he said that we were wasting our time trying to overcome racism because it would eventually occur on its own. When I pressed him further, he said the only solution to the elimination of racism was "to breed it out." He stated that his daughter (White) had married an Asian Ameri-can man and that his youngest son was dating a Latina. Further, he announced, he knew that many of his White friends had children who were involved in interracial relationships.

If you think seriously about this statement, it seems to make much sense. After all, isn't President Bush's nephew a Latino, who even campaigned in Hispanic communities for him? And isn't the Bush family known for being very conservative? Aren't they also modeling what is happening in this nation by their acceptance of an interethnic marriage? Doesn't this mean that racism will eventually die because our future offspring will all be biracial or multiracial?

An increasing number of people have mixed ancestry, and many of them prefer not to be identified with one specific racial/ethnic group. For the first time in history, the number of biracial babies is increasing at a faster rate than the number of monoracial babies. The numbers of children, for example, who have one White parent and the other Black, Asian, or American Indian tripled from 1970 to 1990.

These individuals may prefer the terms *biracial, biethnic, bicultural, multiethnic,* and the like. A whole new vocabulary associated with this phenomenon is increasingly finding its way into the social sci-ence literature (for example, *Afroasian*—people of African and Asian heritage, *Eurasian*—people of mixed White European and Asian an-cestry, and *Mestiza*—people of Indian and Spanish ancestry). Indeed, in recognition of the increasing number of mixed-racial-heritage per-sons, the 2000 U.S. Census allowed individuals to mark off more than one racial/ethnic descriptor.[6]

Although it may seem to make sense to you that eventually everyone will be multiracial, the elimination of racism is questionable. Even though the 2000 Census allowed people to check more than one box to represent their race, only 2.4 percent of the respondents (6.8 million) did so. It is estimated that this is a gross underestimation. In other words, biracial or multiracial persons, for one reason or another, continue to self-identify with only one race. There is considerable speculation that the rule of *hypodescent* exists strongly in our society: the practice that assigns the person of mixed racial heritage to the least desirable social status. Further, a racial hierarchy seems to exist, where African Americans seem to occupy the lowest rungs of the status hierarchy. Although it is possible that interracial marriages and their multiracial offspring may eventually challenge racism, the belief may remain a false hope.

The Elusive Nature of Race Classification

Generally, three broad racial types have historically been identified: *Caucasoid* (White Americans), *Mongoloid* (Asian/Pacific Islander, and Native Americans), and *Negroid* (Black Americans). Attempting to classify people according to these three schemes is fraught with inaccuracies and difficulties.

First, there are many more similarities between groups than differences. Human beings are members of the same species. Indeed, recent DNA comparisons strongly support the out-of-Africa theory: modern man first evolved in Africa and scattered to populate Europe, Asia, and other parts of the world. Interestingly enough, there are many more differences within racial groups than between them.

Second, biological definitions assume inbreeding within geographically isolated groups, which leads to and perpetuates distinct physical traits. Frequent migrations, historical invasions, and explorations make this assumption dubious.

Third, biologists are in disagreement among themselves as to how many races exist in the world, with estimates ranging from three to two hundred! Census 2000 allows for sixty-three possible racial categories. In essence, little agreement exists about the biological criteria that define race. Why then do we use it at all? Why don't we do away with it and spare our nation from the misuse and antagonistic machinations that it creates?

I don't believe we will ever be able to eliminate the use of race as a categorical entity. Ever since it entered the English language some three hundred years ago, its social consequences have been felt in every facet of our lives. Regardless of its biological validity, race and its social meanings affect how each of you views other racial groups and yourselves.

For example, one 1995 study found that White Americans still hold similar stereotypes to those held back in the days of slavery: 20 percent of the public believe that Blacks are intellectually inferior, 19 percent believe that they have thicker craniums, and nearly 24 percent believe that they have longer arms. These are not unlike the views expressed by golfer Jack Nicklaus (that African Americans are born with the wrong muscles to play golf) and by Al Campanis, a former Dodger executive, and former sportscaster Jimmy "The Greek" Snyder (that Blacks are great athletes but poor scholars).

Despite these weaknesses and pitfalls, race has important social meanings, and I will use the following terms throughout the book. As we use these racial/ethnic designations, please keep in mind the following:

1. Some racial/ethnic terms may be accepted in some regions but not in others, and some generations prefer one to the other. For example, we use the term *Hispanic* to refer to individuals with ancestry from Mexico, Puerto Rico, Cuba, El Salvador, the Dominican Republic, and other Latin American countries. Some individuals, however, prefer the term *Latinos* or *La Raza* (the race). Some younger ethnically conscious Hispanics with roots from Mexico may refer to themselves as *Chicanos*, to indicate racial pride and consciousness.

Many older Mexican Americans, however, consider it an insulting reference, associated with the uneducated and exploited farmhands of the Southwest.

It is also important to note that people who identify their origin as Spanish, Hispanic, or Latino may be of any race. In other words, the categories Hispanic and Latino are not racial designators but ethnic ones.

Those individuals who trace their ancestry to Africa may prefer the term *Black* to *African American*. The latter term links identification to country of origin, whereas the former term is a much more political statement of identity arising from the late 1960s. Likewise, many older individuals of Asian ancestry prefer the term *Oriental*, whereas the younger members prefer *Asian American* because it reflects a self-identification process rather than an imposed identity by the larger society.

2. Second, racial/ethnic references may be problematic because they potentially fail to acknowledge ethnic and cultural differences within the group; these terms often submerge many groups under one label. The term Asian American technically encompasses some twenty-nine to thirty-two distinct identifiable Asian subgroups, with their own culture, language, customs, and traditions (Chinese, Japanese, Korean, Filipino, Vietnamese, Asian Indian, Laotian, Cambodian, and so forth). The same can be said of the label Hispanic American (Mexican American, Puerto Rican American, Cuban American, and so forth).

In the 1980 and 1990 counts, people could pick from only five racial categories: White, Black, Asian/Pacific Islander, American Indian/Alaskan native, or other. Because being Hispanic is considered an ethnic trait and not a race, ten possible categories emerged. In the 2000 Census, however, individuals could select from sixty-three racial categories (for example, Native Hawaiians and other Pacific Islanders are being counted for the first time). Adding the choice of Hispanic or non-Hispanic creates 126 possibilities! Although only 2.4 percent, or 6.8 million people, selected more than one racial category, many individuals are uncertain of the implications. Because racial counts are used to determine antidiscrimination laws, voting districts, and funding for minority constituents, many organizations have expressed concern as to how multiracial people will be counted.

3. References to *European American, White, Caucasian American,* and *Anglo* are also filled with controversy. Anglo is perhaps least appropriate because it technically refers to people of English descent (or more distantly, of Germanic descent). People who trace their ancestry to Italy, France, and the Iberian Peninsula may object to being called Anglo-American. My experience has been that many Whites in our society also react quite negatively to that term; they prefer to refer to themselves as Irish American, Jewish American, Italian American, and the like. The terms White and European American, however, are beginning to gain wider usage; this is especially true of the latter because of the emerging trend of identifying the region or country of ancestry for the various groups.

Although the U.S. Census Bureau now recognizes many racial categories, for purposes of simplicity, I will continue to make reference primarily to the four traditional racial/ethnic minority groups for several reasons. First, they are labels created and used by government reporting agencies such as the U.S. Office of Management and Budget and the U.S. Census Bureau. Second, for purposes of discussing group differences and organizing our discussion around multicultural and diversity variables, such terms are a necessity. Third, it is important to note that reference to any group is necessarily fraught with hazards involving overgeneralization.

I am aware that such groupings are oversimplifications and apologize to readers who find any of them offensive. Generalizations are necessary for us to use, especially when they are based on studies revealing intra- and intergroup differences; without them, we would have great difficulty communicating with one another. They serve as guidelines for understanding others and must be tentatively

applied; the important point is that we must be flexible in changing our impressions based on realistic information.

👉 What You Can Do to Overcome Racism

What stereotypes do you hold of different racial/ethnic minority
groups? This is a difficult question to answer for several reasons.
First, most Whites, such as you, possess limited accurate information about various racial/ethnic minority groups. Your world
consists primarily of relations with other White folks, you are surrounded by a White educational system and a media run by White
folks, and you probably have lived most of your life in White neighborhoods.

Second, many of the images and stereotypes you possess about
people of color are deeply embedded in your unconscious and are
outside your level of awareness. They have been historically conditioned from the negative or fearful reactions of family members,
friends, associates, the media, and our educational system. The lack
of knowledge about other racial groups and the misinformation you
are fed from biased sources feed into stereotypes. Try these three
exercises.

Exercise Number 1

Let us take an assessment of the extent of your knowledge concerning various racial groups.

To test your knowledge of terms and concepts related to the
belief systems, life experiences, and historical events of different
racial groups, see how you do on this self-test.

Racial Knowledge Inventory

1. What is a *Curandero*?

2. What does the term *Nisei* mean?

3. What does the *one drop rule* mean?

4. What does *chi* mean?

5. The acronym NAACP stands for what?

6. What is meant by the term *La Raza*?

7. Among Native Americans, what does the expression *noninterference* mean?

8. Name the native language of the majority of Sikh immigrants.

9. What is the *Tuskegee experiment*?

10. What does *yin and yang* mean?

Answers to these questions are very basic and generally well-known by the particular racial/ethnic minority group from which they are derived. If you were able to answer even three of these correctly, you have done far better than the majority of White folks. The level of knowledge and understanding by White Americans of racial groups in our society is so minimal that misinformation, false beliefs, and stereotypes take their place. Check your answers to the following key. Please keep in mind that answers to these questions are much more complex than given here.

Answers: 1 = an indigenous healer in some Latino communities; 2 = a first-generation Japanese American; 3 = even one drop of Black blood making the person Black (practice of hypodescent); 4 = the energy source of body or person; 5 = the National Association for the Advancement of Colored People; 6 = the race or lineage; 7 = not to interfere with others and to observe rather than react; 8 = Punjabi; 9 = an immoral and unethical medical experiment using African Americans as guinea pigs; 10 = the balance of two opposing forces (good-bad, hot-cold, and so forth).

Exercise Number 2

If indeed you lack accurate knowledge and information about the history, cultural values, and life experiences of people of color, then I would ask, What are the preconceived notions and stereotypes that have taken their place? If you are to rid yourself of stereotypes, it's important to make the unconscious thoughts, fears, and biases conscious. Try this activity. Ask yourself this question: When I think of (African Americans, Asian Americans, Latino/Hispanic Americans, or Native Americans), (1) the images that come to mind are . . . and (2) the feelings I experience are . . . Freely associate and write down the first descriptors, thoughts, and feelings that flood over you.

Racial/Ethnic Group	Images	Feelings
African Americans/ Blacks	_____	_____
Asian Americans	_____	_____
Latino/Hispanic Americans	_____	_____
Native Americans	_____	_____

1. In looking at the thoughts and feelings that you've put down, can you see any themes that characterize your responses? For example, do the stereotypes and images for the various groups fall into positive or negative descriptions?

2. If you have been unable to identify or write down thoughts and feelings associated with the group, what meaning do you make of that? Are you fearful of being labeled a racist? Are you suffering from racial amnesia? Are you fearful that uncovering these images will unearth things you don't want to know about yourself?

3. Where do you think you received these images? Are they accurate? How have they affected your behavior toward people of color?

4. If you are unable to unearth these racial stereotypes, thoughts, and feelings, look at the following common stereotypes found to be most associated with people of color and their particular group. Use these to help you explore your innermost thoughts and feelings.

African American Stereotypes: hostile, angry, impulsive, musically inclined, good athletes, large sex organs, criminals, insatiable sexual appetites, unintelligent, lack abstract thinking, superstitious, concrete, can't swim, dense craniums, animalistic, undesirable, drug dealers, smelly, mentally retarded, mentally ill, addicts, abnormal, pimps, prostitutes

Asian American Stereotypes: passive, lack leadership skills, poor drivers, inarticulate, bright, hardworking, studious, quiet, women are domestic and exotic, men are unassertive, unmasculine and sexually unattractive, good in science and technology, family oriented, stingy, disloyal, poor English, funny slanted eyes, subhuman, spies, wealthy, sneaky, back stabbers, model minority

Latino/Hispanic American Stereotypes: carefree, irresponsible, greasy, lazy, poor, welfare recipients, illegal aliens, criminals, dangerous, uneducated, poor English, religious, untrustworthy, liars, drug dealers, farmworkers

Native American/American Indian Stereotypes: savages, primitive, bloodthirsty, uncivilized, animalistic, passive, uneducated, uneducable, superstitious, poor, drunkards, impulsive, noncompetitive, subhuman

5. Now, what feelings do you associate with each of these groups? Do you feel revulsion, anger, sadness, disgust, fear, anxiety, positiveness, negativity, avoidance, contamination, nothing, or what? Where do you think these feelings come from? Do they come from the influence of family, friends, peers, and so forth?

Exercise Number 3

Because we have little actual experience with racial/ethnic minority groups and acquire misinformation from secondhand sources, the dispelling of stereotypes requires several conditions:

- Examining already existing misinformation we possess

- Dredging up the embedded irrational fears and emotions attached to these images

- Replacing stereotypes with realistic facts and information and letting go of irrational fears and negative feelings

Both exercises number 1 and number 2 are aimed at the first two conditions. Acquiring new and realistic information about other groups means being exposed to materials or experiential situations that challenge preconceived notions. Try some of the following suggestions in your daily lives. These will be elaborated in later chapters.

- Widen your circle of friends and acquaintances to include people of color.

- Attend racial/ethnic minority community events.

- Read literature by minority authors about their history, values, hopes, aspirations, and lifestyles.

- Pay attention to Public Broadcasting System (PBS) programs that deal with issues of race.

- Make a special effort to acquire books and reading materials produced by minority organizations.

- Take a formal course at a local college on racial/ethnic minority groups.

- Visit an ethnic studies department at a local college and make a concerted effort to note the many resources about the diverse groups in our society.

3

Do You Oppress?

Racial oppression is the unjust persecution and subjugation of groups and individuals based on their visible phenotypical characteristics. In our society, the color of your skin or certain distinguishing physical features may become the primary markers by which discrimination is carried out. Racial oppression is a defining feature of our nation's history. It is often difficult for those of you who live in a "democratic nation" to realize or acknowledge the full extent of your own government's role in the racial oppression of its own citizens. Harder to admit is your own complicity in being either an active or passive participant in the oppression of others. Yet if you are to combat the injustices of racism, you must be honest with yourself and entertain the notion that you have oppressed others whether knowingly or unknowingly.

INDIVIDUAL RACIAL OPPRESSION

An important question I would pose to you, dear reader, is this: Do you oppress? I would suspect that you would not feel comfortable with answering such a question. At one level, many of you would be inclined to answer no, but at the same time, you find the question accusatory, annoying, and tinged with guilt. These reactions, I submit, arise from some awareness that the actual answer may be a qualified or rationalized yes. To understand the many facets of racial oppression and its consequences, let's look at their manifestations.

The Conscious-Deliberate Racial Oppressor

I daresay few of you fall into this category.

Racial oppression can occur on a *conscious* (intentional) level or an *unconscious* (unintentional) one. Most of you are very aware of the conscious and intentional acts of cruelty perpetrated against people of color. These are actions of conscious and deliberate racists, the White supremacists, who believe in the superiority of Whites and the inferiority of persons of color. The assassination of Martin Luther King, the lynching of Black and Asian people, the incarceration of Japanese Americans, the spreading of smallpox among the Native American population, refusal to integrate schools, using persons of color as guinea pigs in medical experiments, and countless other examples can be found throughout history up to the current time. More commonplace everyday examples of individual acts include making racial slurs or name-calling, telling racist jokes, giving racial/ethnic minority employees low ratings at work, or refusing to sell a home or move next door to a person of color.

Most individuals who consciously oppress are well aware of their beliefs in White supremacy and the inferiority of persons of color. These are individuals who may vary from being the extreme White supremacists to those who might be prejudiced but subtler in their actions. The latter are not likely to act out their hostility in direct and obvious ways. They are the ones who will simply discourage their sons and daughters from associating with persons of color, move to all-White neighborhoods, and in the privacy of the voting booth endorse candidates and legislation that oppress racial minorities. In all of these cases, however, their conscious racist thoughts and feelings show up in both attitudes and behaviors.

The Unconscious-Unintentional Racial Oppressor

In all probability, you fall into this category. Please don't let your negative reaction to my assertion turn you off from reading further.

Racial oppression of an unconscious or unintentional nature is more difficult to identify than that expressed by the conscious and deliberate racist. Its unconscious nature allows you to maintain the illusion that you do not engage in racial oppression. In keeping with my assertion that no one is immune from inheriting the biases of our ancestors, it would appear that the majority of you fall into this category.

Thomas Pettigrew, a social science researcher found that approximately 15 percent of White Americans could be described as extremely racist—conscious and deliberate racists; another 60 percent conformed to the racist ideology of the society, and another 25 percent are active in combating racism if they recognize it.[1] As we shall shortly see, however, even those of you who fall into this latter group, in some ways, may engage in unintentional racial oppression. To me, these latter two groups qualify as unconscious and unintentional racists. These are individuals, such as you, who consciously endorse egalitarian principles, profess to be fair-minded, deny that you possess biases against people of color, and would never deliberately discriminate.

Social psychologist, John Dovidio, in testimony with me before President Clinton's Race Advisory Board in 1997, stated that as we have become a more sophisticated nation, the face of racism has changed significantly.[2] The "old-fashioned" form was generally overt, direct, and oftentimes intentional, usually carried out by the conscious-deliberate racist. It strongly stressed the inferiority of most racial/ethnic minority groups and continues to be highly visible in the form of hate crimes.

Although these overt acts of racism injure, frighten, and kill innocent people, they are perhaps less damaging to people of color than what psychologists label *modern* or *contemporary racism*. According to Dovidio, modern racism is unconscious, indirect, subtle, and unintentional; more likely expressed in a failure to help (unconscious-unintentional racist) than in a conscious desire to hurt (conscious-deliberate racist); and more likely to emerge not when a behavior would appear prejudiced but when other excuses can be offered for the biased behavior.

I believe that this contemporary form of racism is many times over more problematic, damaging, and injurious to persons of color than overt racist acts. Indeed, the extreme acts by conscious-deliberate racists represent very minimal threat to the overall quality of life of most racial/ethnic minorities. Space does not permit me to mention the voluminous amount of research that supports these contentions, but let me summarize a few of them.

Laboratory studies confirm the fact that even those of you who consciously believe in egalitarianism and stand against prejudice and discrimination can possess dual but opposing attitudes. On the conscious level you are nonbiased, but on an unconscious one you tend to associate negative beliefs and attitudes toward persons of color. Let us assume, for example, that you are a subject in a study being conducted by Dovidio. As a consciously nonbiased subject, you are exposed to subliminal pictures of a White or Black face. These pictures are presented at such a high rate of speed that you are unaware of seeing them. As a White person, when flashed pictures of a Black face, you are quicker to associate negative traits than when shown a White face. You are also more likely to behave in a more hostile manner in response to frustrating situations if you have been "primed" by a subliminally presented picture of an African American face, as opposed to the presentation of a White face. Your reactions are precisely the same as most of the White subjects in Dovidio's experiments (unconscious-unintentional racists)!

In other studies, it was also found that as a White person you will react physiologically when touched by an African American experimenter but not when touched by a White experimenter, and you are quicker to link the word *white* with positive words such as *smart*, *ambitious*, and *clean* and the word *black* with negative words such as *lazy*, *stupid*, and *welfare*. The conclusion is that due to social conditioning, it is impossible for any of you not to inherit the negative associations of people of color with inferiority and pathology. These associations are so deeply ingrained that they are outside your conscious awareness and occur almost automatically when race-related situations or materials are encountered.

Yet you could argue that these attitudes and stereotypes are not necessarily harmful, especially if they do not affect your behavior toward people of color. Although true to a certain extent, it is difficult if not impossible for such attitudes not to affect behavior. Unconscious biases may ultimately influence behaviors when people are placed in interracial situations. Some time back, a highly popular TV program called *Candid Camera* captured unsuspecting civilians in baffling, embarrassing, or illogical situations created by the producers. The program was an immediate hit because viewers were in on the joke and found the reactions of naïve citizens hilarious.

In one particular study using the *Candid Camera* format, naïve housewives were interviewed as to their attitudes and beliefs toward minority youths. As would be expected, nearly all indicated that they harbored no prejudice against Black or Latino youngsters. The experimenters selected only those who met rigorous criteria related to sincerity and honesty. If there was even the slightest doubt that a subject answered honestly due to social desirability or political correctness, they were eliminated from the study. Unbeknownst to the women who were selected, they were videotaped while shopping at the neighborhood grocery store. On their journey, they passed male confederates (young teenagers in league with the experimenter) who were instructed to always pass the woman on the purse side of her arm. The confederates were dressed identically; the only difference was their race/ethnicity (White, Black, or Latino).

Interestingly, a large proportion of White housewives changed the purse from one arm to the other (away from the minority youngster) whenever they passed. These actions seldom occurred if the youngster passing was White! In most cases, I would suggest that the housewives harbored unconscious fears of potential criminal behavior on the part of minority youngsters. When confronted with their actions and shown videos of their purse passing, however, the majority continued to deny that it had anything to do with the race/ ethnicity of the youngster. More important, they appeared sincere in their denials, leading experimenters to conclude that their stereotypes and fears were outside their awareness.

Rationalizing Away a Failure to Help

Even if the unwarranted fears and biases of the housewives caused them to protect their purses by switching it away from the youngsters of color, you might argue that no harm has been done. Indeed, many social scientists do make a distinction between prejudiced attitudes and harmful behavior. Being prejudiced, the argument goes, does not hurt or harm unless it is manifested in behavior. Even in the just-cited case, it is difficult to argue that the behavior resulted in harm or oppression. I will return to this issue shortly, but evidence now exists that negative attitudes or stereotypes that exist in our society, even if not behaviorally expressed, may have negative consequences to minorities.

Let us look at another study conducted by social psychologist Dovidio and his colleagues.[3] Reasoning that unintentional racists would not consciously discriminate against persons of color when appropriate behaviors are clearly defined, the experimenters created emergency situations in which the victims were either White or Black. Two experimental conditions were created: witnessing the emergency alone or witnessing the emergency with other people. In what they called "the clearly defined situation," subjects were led to believe that they were the only ones witnessing the emergency (for example, an injured White or Black motorist in a disabled car). In this condition, White bystanders offered help at a high rate (over 80 percent of the time) whether the victim was White or Black. However, when the White bystanders were led to believe that others also witnessed the event, the Black victim was helped half as often as the White victim (38 percent versus 75 percent)!

How do we make sense of the findings? First, people with unconscious biases are less likely to be affected in situations where appropriate behaviors are clear. If they are the only people watching an emergency situation, they are *aware* that others, but more important they themselves, can interpret that "a failure to help" constitutes racial bias. When they believe others are also witnessing the emergency, the situation becomes less clearly defined because it allows White bystanders to justify their lack of involvement with other excuses. For example, "I thought someone else would surely help." If this were true, however, why did they continue to help the White victims at such a high rate (75 percent of the time)? Findings such as these have led social psychologists to discern three additional principles of modern racism.

- First, the modern form of racism is most likely to be revealed through your failure to help rather in a conscious desire to hurt. To directly harm others on the basis of skin color is racial oppression in the most blatant form. Inaction on your part, however, is more difficult to label as racial bias.
- Second, modern expressions of racism are more likely to emerge when other rationales or excuses can be given for a biased action or decision. In other words, as an unconscious-unintentional oppressor, you find other apparently legitimate reasons to justify your biased behaviors and maintain the illusion that you are unbiased. It appears that the more ambiguous the situation, the more likely that bias will make its appearance.
- Third, unintentional bias can result in significant harm. For example, if the situation regarding the Black and White motorists were of a life-threatening nature, the Black motorist would be likely to die twice as often as the White counterpart when your unintentional bias operates!

INSTITUTIONAL RACIAL OPPRESSION

Institutional policies and practices that deny rights and opportunities to groups of color can be legitimately considered racially oppressive. In this case, biased but accepted institutional practices based on customs and laws can have devastating results for racial/ethic minorities. Whether intentional or unintentional, direct or indirect, the consequences are manifested in harm for groups of color while protecting and advantaging White folks. Believe it or not, you probably unknowingly support institutionally sanctioned policies and practices that oppress persons of color.

The adverse impact of institutional racial oppression is found in education, economics, health services, politics, and housing. Individual racial oppression harms on an individual basis, but institutional racial oppression is widespread, systemic, and affects persons of color on a massive scale. Institutional racial oppression can be blamed for

- Pathologizing the lifestyles and cultural differences of minority groups through media portrayals and biased educational curricula

- Creating poverty rates for African Americans that are three times that of White Americans, providing inferior health care that results in the highest infant mortality of any ethnic/racial group, and perpetuating an inferior standard of living that results in a life expectancy that is five to seven years shorter than their White counterparts

- Decimating the Native American population through wars and diseases that resulted from contact with Europeans, justifying oppressive acts through good intentions to "civilize the Indians," which resulted in their loss of languages and disruption of their cultural traditions, and forcing them from their homes onto reservations

- Discriminating against Latino Americans so that they are overrepresented among the poor and have higher

unemployment rates and substandard housing, and
creating living conditions that result in their suffering
more health problems and receiving inferior health care

- Passing biased exclusionary laws against Asian Americans (Chinese Exclusion Act of 1882) because they
were blamed for causing race problems, interning loyal
Japanese Americans during World War II because they
posed a threat to national security (but not White
ethnics like the Italian and German Americans), and
using biased promotion criteria to prevent Asian
American workers from getting upper management
and executive level positions

Overt and Deliberate Institutional Racial Oppression

Institutional racial oppression, like its individual counterpart,
can have a conscious-deliberate component or an unconscious-
unintentional one. For example, laws in our nation deliberately justified the system of slavery: Blacks were defined in the constitution
as three-fifths of a man; the *separate but equal doctrine* of education
resulted in inferior education for minorities; measures were imposed
on Native Americans to prevent births within the group (three
thousand hysterectomies in the 1970s for no medical reasons); lands
were seized from the indigenous people of this country; and laws
were passed against Asian Americans that prevented ownership of
land and denied them the rights of citizenship. It is often said that
Hitler praised the efficiency of how the English colonists extermi-
nated Native Americans and got the idea for concentration camps
and the efficiency of starvation by looking at U.S. history!

Deliberate use of institutional racism continues to occur in our
society. Many private clubs and organizations continue to use criteria (astronomical membership fees, coming from the "right family," or other select attributes) to exclude "undesirable elements"
(persons of color) from becoming members. Real estate associations

continue to discriminate against Black and Latino home buyers to prevent lowering of housing values and panic selling by Whites. Discriminatory lending practices by banks and racial profiling by law enforcement agencies continue to abound in our society. Most of us would agree that intentional racist policies that are purposely meant to adversely affect one group while advantaging another are not only immoral but also illegal. Although these obviously overt racist policies and customs have declined, more subtle and disguised forms of institutional discrimination have replaced them.

Covert and Unintentional Institutional Racial Oppression

Perhaps more insidious are the unintentional forms of institutional racism. These are the institutional policies, practices, customs, and norms by which organizations function. They are often referred to as *standard operating procedures* (SOPs), and they underlie education, economics, health services, politics, and housing. On the surface, they appear to be bias-free policies that are applied equally to everyone regardless of race, creed, or color. The argument is that treating everyone the same preempts the possibility of discrimination. Policies, after all, cannot distinguish whether an employee who is being considered for promotion is Black, White, Yellow, Brown, or Red.

Yet what happens when these procedures or the criteria used, although universally applied, result in significant differential and adverse impact for certain groups? What happens if they result in greater capital punishment, inferior education, high rates of poverty, lack of adequate medical care, higher unemployment rates, and greater rates of physical and mental illness for persons of color? Wouldn't these SOPs, on the basis of outcome, be considered forms of institutional racial oppression? One glaring example of disparities resides in bank lending policies and practices for White versus Black home owners. We know, for a fact, that Blacks and Latinos are more likely to be denied mortgages, and when they qualify, they pay a significantly higher interest rate than their White counter-parts. Bank representatives argue, however, that they do not dis-criminate against minority home owners. Rather, they use sound business practices based on credit history, income, location, and pro-jected real estate appreciation to determine creditworthiness of applicants. These are fairly applied to all applicants. Race, they con-tend, is not a factor in their "color-blind" approach. Lenders also point to how their banks possess a consistently good record in serv-ing the community in which they are located. The hidden bias, however, can only be unmasked by deconstructing basic assump-tions in the "sound business practices."

First, a recent study in 2002 by the Center for Community Change found that the practice of using income and credit history was seriously flawed.[4] One would expect, for example, that Blacks and Latinos with identical income to their White counterparts would pay approximately equal mortgage rates. Astonishingly, what they found was that a far greater number of Latino and Black home owners paid higher rates when their incomes rose! In other words, the lender's policy of using wage and credit history did not prevent disparities in lending rates.

Second, banks often counter that one of the reasons is that the neighborhoods in which minorities own homes are riskier in that they do not appreciate well. This risk is taken into consideration when determining the viability of an application. Naturally, risk translates into increased denials and higher interest rates. The prob-lem is that most minority home owners live in neighborhoods that are often considered "less desirable" than White ones so that appre-ciation is naturally slower. In other words, structural segregation in real estate unfairly penalizes minority home owners, and policy based on location only reinforces discrimination on an institutional level.

Third, banks often point to the fact that sound business princi-ples guide their decisions and that they do serve neighborhoods where they have branches. They point to their good loan record in serving the communities in which they are located. The problem with this argument is that it fails to recognize the fact that banks and savings and loan institutions are predominantly located in White neighborhoods, with few in minority ones! In other words, SOPs or business as usual can dramatically affect the quality of life of our minority citizens.

Likewise, a recent study found that African Americans and Hispanics who are suffering from AIDS were seriously underrepresented in clinical trials when compared with their White counterparts.[5] Although they are more likely to suffer from HIV infection, they are half as likely as Whites to participate in treatment trials and half as likely to receive newer experimental medicines. Even when socioeconomic status and insurance were equated, the disparity did not disappear. Medical researchers often select their subjects on the basis of proximity to their research centers and the likelihood of patients' staying for the completion of the study. Researchers avoid recruiting minorities, drug users, and the homeless because they are believed to be unreliable and to comply poorly with directions. Further, most major study centers are located in predominantly affluent White urban areas, removed from minority neighborhoods.

CULTURAL RACIAL OPPRESSION

Culture is an integrated matrix of human thoughts, actions, customs, values, beliefs, and assumptions that helps define reality, provides a pattern for living, is transmitted through a socialization process, and is passed down from one generation to the next within a group of people. Although culture is dynamic and evolving, its core values and characteristics remain remarkably stable over extended periods of time. Who we are as a people, group, and nation is defined by the cultural context into which we are born. Personality may define the individual, but on a larger scale culture defines a society. Culture is found in our standards, norms, values, music, religion, language, and aesthetics.[6]

The components of White Euro-American culture, for example, can be characterized by a series of values and beliefs: rugged individualism in which the psychosocial unit of our society is the individual; a competitive spirit that emphasizes winning and external achievement as measures of worth and success; use of standard English; religion based on a single god (that of Christianity); Protestant work ethic; objective, rational, and linear thinking; the nuclear family as the ideal social unit; aesthetics—music and art—based on European culture; and ideal physical attributes of attractiveness—fair skinned, blond, blue-eyed, thin, and youthful. This last category, in combination with other Euro-American standards, can be detrimentally imposed on persons of color who possess dark skin, black hair, and different physical features.

Racialization, or how we as a people and nation think about race, is passed on within Euro-American culture. Time and space do not permit me to trace or try to explain in detail the beginning manifestations of racism and racist ideology. But studying our cultural history indicates an implicit and explicit equation between people of color and pathology.

Influential medical journals, scientific papers, and many subsequent laws were based on the racialized notion that the anatomical, neurological, endocrinological, psychological, and lifestyle aspects of Blacks, Indians, and Asians were inferior to that of Whites; these groups represented adolescent races in a stage of incomplete development. African Americans, for example, were believed to have smaller brains but thicker craniums, and early intelligence test developers believed that Mexican Americans and Spanish Indian families were uneducable.

Centuries of slavery, constitutional statements that considered Blacks and Indians less than human, and a policy that forbid Native Americans from practicing their "subversive" religious ceremonies until the 1974 Indian Freedom of Religion Act speak to the history of cultural racism. Even though a strong case can be made that these past practices have been largely eliminated, the dynamics of racial cultural oppression continues to manifest itself in ethnocentric monoculturalism. The next chapter will address this social-psychological concept more fully.

Suffice it to say that a strong component of cultural oppression is *ethnocentrism*, a tendency to perceive other cultures and lifestyles negatively while perceiving one's own group as possessing a more desirable or superior way of life. Although ethnocentrism is not confined to any one group, in the United States Whites control the tools of power and can impose their culture on other groups (persons of color), thereby engaging in cultural oppression. Cultural racial oppression imposes and encourages assimilation (becoming an "American") on minority groups but is based on a false no-win premise. The myth of the melting pot is certainly an example, because the hidden assumption is that all groups will be accepted and given full status and privilege once assimilation is complete. Though this is true for White European immigrants, persons of color are excluded. Despite how acculturated persons of color may become, they continue to be seen as second-class citizens and foreigners. The following statement was made by a second-generation Chinese American:

> The truth is, no matter how American you think you are or try to be, you do not look "American." If you have almond-shaped eyes, straight black hair, and a yellow complexion, you are a foreigner by default. People will ask where you come from but won't be satisfied until they hear you name a foreign country. And they will naturally compliment your perfect English.[7]

A study conducted in 2001 in which 1,216 adults were polled reveals the mind-set that White Americans have toward their fellow Asian American citizens. Nearly one-third indicated that Chinese Americans, for example, would be more loyal to China than the United States, and one-half believed that Chinese Americans would pass secrets to China. It appears that Asian Americans continue to be viewed as foreigners and potentially disloyal. In his book, *My Country Versus Me*, Wen Ho Lee, a patriotic Los Alamos National Laboratory scientist, recounts how he was falsely accused of espionage and of passing top-secret nuclear information to China and how he was persecuted by the U.S. government and imprisoned because of his racial heritage.[8] To many Asian Americans, the incident brought back painful memories of the incarceration of Japanese Americans during World War II. After several years of investigation and 278 days of solitary confinement, the government's case fell apart. Just before Lee's release, Judge James Parker, the federal judge, issued an unprecedented apology to Lee:

> I believe you were terribly wronged by being held in custody pretrial in the Santa Fe County Detention Center under demeaning, unnecessarily punitive conditions. I am truly sorry that I was led by our executive branch of government to order your detention last December.
>
> Dr. Lee, I tell you with great sadness that I feel I was led astray last December by the executive branch of our government through its Department of Justice, by its Federal Bureau of Investigation, and by its United States attorney for the district of New Mexico, who held the office at that time.
>
> The top decision makers in the executive branch, especially the Department of Justice and the Department of Energy and locally . . . have caused embarrassment by the way this case began and was handled. They did not embarrass me alone. They have embarrassed our entire nation and each of us who is a citizen of it.
>
> I sincerely apologize to you, Dr. Lee, for the unfair manner you were held in custody by the executive branch.[9]

THE MANY FORMS OF
RACIAL OPPRESSION

According to the 2001 edition of *Webster's II New College Dictionary*, *oppression* is the persecution or subjugation of individuals or groups by unjust use of force or authority. Oppression is a fact of life in human existence. History is rife with examples of whole governments and dictatorships exercising cruel and unjust power over individuals, groups, and whole nations. Historic figures such as Genghis Khan, Napoleon Bonaparte, and Adolf Hitler led their followers in a concerted effort to conquer the world and to impose their will on those who stood in their paths. During their reigns of oppression and terror, they engaged in genocide, mistreatment, abuse, and cruelty toward whole groups of people.

Many of you can easily see the tools and the results of political oppression. Oppression by means of force or authority has an intimidating component: the use or threat of punishment and physical harm. In the extreme case, it can be inflicting bodily pain on individuals through beatings, torture, and imprisonment, or it can be causing the death of those who are the victims. It may involve imposing unwanted living conditions on persons by lowering their standard of living (scarce supplies of food and water, inadequate shelter, and exposure to harsh and unpleasant climactic conditions), taking away their property, or enforcing hard labor without adequate compensation. The consequence of oppression may be death, physical debilitation, and emotional suffering (anxiety, fear, depression, anger, frustration, and feelings of helplessness and hopelessness). In many cases, it results in blocked and restricted opportunities and a significant loss of freedom.

Oppression is not limited to wars against nations. It can be carried out in the form of persecution against its own citizens as well. In the case of Hitler, he directed his wrath against not only the rest of the world but also his own citizens (Jews, gays and lesbians,

Gypsies, the physically disabled, and the mentally ill). The Cultural Revolution in China, the 1995 Rwanda genocide, and the rule of the Taliban in Afghanistan not only speak to historical and contemporary examples of political oppression but also to the continuing existence of the cruel and unjust exercise of power and control over others.

Oppression can occur against groups based on religion, social class, ethnicity, and many other group markers. Women, persons with disabilities, the elderly, gays, lesbians, and bisexual persons can all be victims. In our nation and throughout the world, racial differences have been a common source of oppression. Racism uses oppression to denigrate, control, intimidate, and restrict equal access and opportunities for persons of color.

In light of our previous analysis of individual, institutional, and cultural racial oppression, it might be helpful to see how they have operated and continue to operate with respect to persons of color. In essence, racial oppression has the dual effect of depriving one group (persons of color) of power, wealth, and status while consolidating it for another (Whites). In the past, dominance was maintained using physical force and violence, but it is more covert today. Nevertheless its manifestations continue to exist in one form or another: *individual level*—beatings, castration, torture, cattle prods, rape, hard labor, degrading job roles, imprisonment, racial epithets, ridicule, negative media images, and so on; *institutional level*—medical experiments (Tuskegee), restrictive laws, institution of slavery, tracking of minority children, destruction of minority housing through urban renewal, poor access to health care, tokenism, housing restrictions, biased justice system, and so on; and *cultural level*—ethnocentric monoculturalism, equating racial/cultural differences with pathology and deviance, perpetuation of stereotypes, miseducation, and so forth.

Earlier in this book, I made two major points: First, it is impossible for any of you born into this world not to inherit the biases and stereotypes of your forebears. Second, even when you do not act out prejudices, you can create a climate detrimental to persons of color. In a strange sort of way, your attitudes may oppress by creating a hostile, invalidating, and toxic environment. This assertion of mine has consistently run counter to many other social scientists, who echo the following phrase about the operation of racism: "Sticks and stones may break my bones (discrimination), but words will never hurt me (prejudice)."

First, words can hurt. Hurt you a lot. Name-calling, especially racial slurs, is often born from ignorance (children who strike out in anger or defense but do not know the meaning of the terms) or prejudice (adults who do it to derogate an entire racial/ethnic group). It hurts people, especially children, to be put down in such a cruel fashion, to be told you and your group are undesirable, and to be held in disdain.

Second, studies on racial identity development have documented how the overall stereotypes, expectations, and beliefs of minority inferiority may result in people of color coming to believe in their own inferiority. They may, as a result, suffer from low self-esteem and come to doubt themselves and their ability to succeed in this society.

Third, it has been demonstrated that teacher attitudes can undermine the performance of students of color through what is called a self-fulfilling prophecy. If White teachers expect their young students of color to do poorly, the students may fulfill those expectations.

Finally, psychologist Claude Steele at Stanford University has identified a process that he labels *stereotype threat*.[10] In our society, students of color, particularly Blacks and Latinos, labor under a stigma that they are intellectually inferior and will do poorly in school. Their school grades and Scholastic Assessment Test scores are significantly below those of their White counterparts. Steele believes that the underperformance of Black students, for example, is not due to biology or lack of preparation but to a perceived stereotype threat (majority group members' belief that Blacks possess lesser ability).

Steele reasoned that stereotype threat is aroused when persons of color believe that their performance is likely to confirm or disconfirm a stereotype about one's group. The threat itself instigates two psychological processes: the first is apprehension that one will be evaluated by the stereotype or confirm it, and the second is protective disidentification, or a tendency to reject the situation, deeming it irrelevant or unimportant. In other words, by telling oneself that one doesn't care about the situation and that it doesn't mean much, the person separates his or her self-esteem from the outcome. Both processes, however, result in lowered performance, because in the first case the anxiety may disrupt concentration and in the latter it unmotivates the person.

Steele tested this hypothesis by selecting outstanding Black and White math students and giving them a test taken from a very difficult section of the Graduate Record Examination. Students were exposed to one of two conditions: a diagnostic condition (high stereotype threat), in which Black and White students were told that the exam was a test of problem solving and verbal abilities, and a nondiagnostic condition (low stereotype threat), in which Black and White students were assured that the exam was not a test of ability or problem solving. The results confirmed Steele's theory of stereotype threat. Whites consistently did better than Blacks in the high-threat condition, but no difference in performance was found in the low-threat condition!

In other words, when the environment is emotionally loaded with negative stereotypes, it can be a powerful force in undermining maximal performance. Even if one does not discriminate on the basis of negative beliefs about minority groups, prejudice, stereotypes, and negative expectations can have devastating consequences on persons of color. In that respect, biased beliefs alone may result in oppression!

YOUR ROLE IN OPPRESSION

The question of your complicity in racial oppression must be faced directly, without defensiveness, and with courage. Think, for example, about your own life situation. Do you avoid persons of color? Do you harbor stereotypes and beliefs about Blacks, Asians, and other minority groups? Are you active in combating racism and bias in the schools and workplace, or are you indifferent? Do you let racism issues fade from your consciousness? Just how do you reap the benefits of the victimization of people of color? Do you live in a predominantly White neighborhood? What does that mean to you? Have you ever used racial slurs? Look in the mirror. Do you like what you see?

When I ask the question, Do you engage in racial oppression? I submit that the only response you can give is yes. The oppression you engage in is not necessarily the overt, intentional, and individual acts of violence perpetrated on our citizens of color. But it is no less damaging, and in many cases it is many times more harmful than its intentional counterpart. Because you have been born and raised in a racialized cultural context, your role in oppression is often unintentional, automatic, habitual, and outside your level of awareness. You have been miseducated about your history of oppression, falsely sold a bill of goods about the superiority of White culture, and given implicit messages about the inferiority of persons of color. You have internalized these beliefs and values and unknowingly act on them to the detriment of minority groups. According to psychologists Hanna, Talley, and Guindon, all of us engage in what they call *secondary oppression*.[11] Although you may not actively oppress through blatant force, most of you are secondary oppressors because you benefit from the historical and continuing oppression of others. As you will see in the next few chapters, racial oppression in our society results in *White privilege* (the unearned benefits of power, wealth, and status) while it disadvantages groups of color.

Perhaps the question you should ask yourselves is not whether you engage in or benefit from racial oppression. The more important question is, Once you become aware of your role in the racial oppression of others, what do you do about it?

What You Can Do to Overcome Racism

Because the conscious-deliberate racial oppressor is unlikely to willingly choose this book to read, the following section is meant for those of you who unknowingly and unintentionally engage in or support the racial oppression of people of color. As I have mentioned in the last chapter, much of the task in overcoming your racism involves making the "invisible" visible. Racial amnesia born from protecting you against the unpleasant realization about your complicity in racial oppression is difficult to overcome. To do so requires an active pursuit of self-truth and the ability to bear the pain and discomfort from looking at your own racism. The following exercises may be helpful in your journey to liberation.

Exercise Number 1

We have identified three forms of racial oppression: individual, institutional, and cultural. These can occur at a conscious-intentional level or an unconscious-unintentional one. Take the following two inventories and see how you do. Afterward, use these statements and apply them to your own beliefs, assumptions, and behaviors.

Rate yourself on the following statements on a continuum from 1 being "disagree strongly" to 5 being "agree strongly." Write in the number that best describes your view.

Conscious Racial Oppression Scale

1. I believe in White supremacy.   _____

2. People of color, especially Blacks, are
   genetically inferior.   _____

3. Native Americans are savages.   _____

4. Integration is bad.   _____

5. I use racial slurs.   _____

6. Mexicans and Blacks should be placed in
   vocational schools.   _____

7. Japs and Chinks cannot be trusted with
   state secrets.   _____

8. Salespersons should pay extra attention to
   Black customers because they are up to no good.   _____

9. Private organizations have a right to prevent
   minorities from becoming members.   _____

10. Minorities are prone to criminal behavior.   _____

Scoring Key: Scores from 21–50 indicate high racial oppression. Most of you, however, are likely to obtain scores that vary from 10–19. As an unconscious-unintentional racial oppressor, you realize that endorsement of these statements is obviously racist. You are therefore likely to deny them vigorously. They are definitely against your own conscious beliefs of equality and fairness. Does this confirm your belief that you do not oppress?

Now I want you to take the following test. Rate yourself on the following statements on a continuum from 1 being "disagree strongly" to 5 being "agree strongly." Write in the number that best describes your view.

Unconscious Racial Oppression Scale

1. I believe in the melting pot. _____

2. When I see a Black person, I don't see color. _____

3. All of us have equal opportunity. _____

4. I don't laugh at racist jokes. _____

5. I don't use the terms *black lie* or *white lie*. _____

6. I don't invest in companies with racist policies and practices. _____

7. I don't benefit from racism. _____

8. Everyone has an equal chance to make it in this society. _____

9. We are all Americans. _____

10. Affirmative action programs are reverse racism. _____

It is difficult to use scores alone on this inventory to ascertain your unconscious biases and behaviors. In the first test, your scores were probably very low. You were probably very aware of their meaning because the items were obviously racist in content. Items on the Unconscious Racial Oppression Scale, however, are more hidden in the guise of democratic principles.

In most cases, the conscious-intentional racist will score extremely high on this scale. But it is also possible that you, the unconscious-unintentional racist, will have elevated scores, although not as high. That is because many of these statements are rooted and hidden in what appears to be democratic beliefs and principles. The only major way to distinguish between you and the conscious-deliberate racist is your conscious belief in the values of equality as applied to people of color.

In later chapters, a fuller explanation will be given as to the biased nature of these broad statements. For purposes of brevity, I provide some brief glimpses of underlying biased assumptions and meanings to the just-cited statements. You may wish to explore their meaning prior to reading the next few chapters.

Biased Assumptions

- *Statement 1*: Applies to White people only. No matter how assimilated people of color become, they are still not allowed the full privileges of the society.

- *Statement 2*: Very difficult to do. Avoiding seeing race may itself be racist.

- *Statement 3*: Untrue. The land of opportunity has historically disempowered minorities.

- *Statement 4*: Almost everyone has laughed at racist jokes.

- *Statement 5*: Unconscious use of language reflects bias: *blackball*, *black sheep*, and *black lie* are all negatives associated with Blackness.

- *Statement 6*: If you are invested in the stock market in any way, purchase goods and services from companies, belong to organizations of any form (Boy Scouts, private clubs, and so forth), you unintentionally support biased organizations.

- *Statement 7*: An inspiring statement, but untrue with respect to race and socioeconomic class.

- *Statement 8*: Not all groups or individuals have an equal chance to succeed.

- *Statement 9*: Although true, it has been generally practiced to refer to Whites only.

- *Statement 10*: Complicated. Affirmative action programs attempt to level the playing field. Indeed, one might say that the current structure and practice of our society has affirmative action for Whites already.

Exercise Number 2

To more thoroughly understand the operation, meaning, and effects of racial oppression, several videos are recommended. The films are especially informative and effective when watched with others and used to help process their meaning. They are *Skin Deep*, *A Class Divided*, and *Blue-Eyed*.

Exercise Number 3

On a sheet of paper, list all the forms of individual, institutional, and cultural racial oppression you can identify. Again, if you can do this as a group exercise it would be more effective. Some examples of types of racial oppression to help you start are the following:

1. Individual racial oppression (conscious versus unconscious)
   - Behaviors
   - Attitudes
   - Socialization
   - Self-interest
2. Institutional racial oppression (conscious versus unconscious)
   - Education
   - Economics
   - Law
   - Health services
   - Housing
   - Politics

3. Cultural racial oppression (conscious versus unconscious)
   - Music
   - Religion
   - Standards, needs, norms
   - Aesthetics

Which of these have you engaged in or profited from?

4

What Is Your Racial Reality and That of White America?

As indicated in Chapter Three, both individual and institutional racism are intimately linked to your culture. Euro-American culture is racialized and enforces its cultural views by defining the reality of its citizens. In fact, I would argue that the ability to define reality is perhaps the most insidious and potent form of power. Trial lawyers, public relations consultants, and politicians are well aware of this fact.

Take, for example, the trial of several police officers who participated in the brutal 1991 beating of Rodney King, an African American. The horror of that incident was captured in a home video that jolted the American public. Indisputable evidence was captured on videotape of the officers' raining blow after blow upon King and repeatedly kicking and taunting him as some thirty officers stood by watching the cruelty. None protested the actions of the other officers or interceded on King's behalf. The public outcry led to the resignation of Police Chief Daryl Gates and prompted an investigation of Los Angeles police practices and corruption.

You probably can easily recall that incident. When you saw it on videotape, replayed over and over on television, what conclusion did you draw? Were the policemen guilty of police brutality? Did they use unwarranted and excessive force? Were you outraged? Did you condemn their actions?

Watching the videotape presented indisputable proof that the officers outnumbered, surrounded, and physically assaulted King.

They struck him repeatedly when he was down. They struck him while he twisted about in pain. And they struck him despite his begging for mercy. One newspaper columnist likened their beating him with nightsticks to a butcher tenderizing steaks. The reality of police misconduct was clear. Yet, in the first trial, the officers were found not guilty by an all-White jury! The verdict of not guilty for the officers seemed to fly in the face of reason, or did it?

Attorneys who defended the police officers knew that a defense based on "he said, she said" could not be made on the basis of the videotape. After all, the entire American public was witness to the atrocity. They chose, however, to take another tack: to define the reality of the incident for jurors and the public. They did this, I believe, by presenting arguments that touched off biases and fears related to Black men.

1. Because the trial was held in a primarily White and affluent community (Simi Valley) in Southern California, jurors were prone to hold unconscious biases and fears of Black men, who were, in the minds of many White folks, prone to violence, likely to engage in crime, and subhuman animals.

2. Rodney King had a history of criminal behavior, and police officers described him as acting as if he was on drugs and not susceptible to being controlled by ordinary physical means. This point was frequently alluded to during the trial and in the press.

3. The police officers, the defense asserted, were in fear of their lives, because a "crazed individual" who did not feel the pain of the blows could retaliate unless subdued.

4. King's rolling about on the ground and his attempts to avoid the blows were portrayed as attempts to resist. One of the basic tenets of police work, the lawyers argued, was the importance of physically controlling a suspect.

In general, King was portrayed as an out-of-control animal, potentially high on drugs, immune to pain, resisting and threatening the officers, and dangerous unless subdued. But most of all, he was Black!

The defendants, in contrast, were portrayed as credible law enforcement officers, law abiding like their White jurors, fearful for their lives, trying to protect the public, and if they made an error in judgment, it was an honest mistake.

Would you buy this reality? The jurors seemed to have bought it, and their verdict reflected it. Rodney King was defined as the problem, not the actions of the officers. The defense argued that if King would have only obeyed the law and not resisted, then his "apparent mistreatment" would not have occurred. In addition, the officers were only doing their duty and acted appropriately in light of the dangerous circumstances they found themselves in. The defense knew that if this reality could be sold to the jurors, then excusing White criminal behavior was a foregone conclusion, and the only possible verdict was not guilty.

The unfairness of this first verdict led to a huge riot, with dozens of people being killed and injured and large-scale destruction of property. In the name of justice, fortunately, the federal government prosecuted the officers in a second trial for violating the civil rights of King. In that second trial, the officers were found guilty.

THE RACIAL REALITY
OF WHITE AMERICA

In his book, *Even the Rat Was White*, Robert Guthrie, an African American psychologist, wrote a treatise that challenged the profession of psychology as being historically biased.[1] As you may know, much of the knowledge base of psychology is said (tongue in cheek) to be founded on "rat psychology," or principles of learning derived from the study of rats (hence the title of the book). The point

Guthrie was making was that the history of psychology is a White Euro-American one that neglects the contributions of psychologists of color. A similar assertion has been made about the history taught to our children in schools.

Though this is an extremely important point, the book's powerful title suggests an even more meaningful question: Who owns history? The answer you give has profound impact on each and every one of us. Inevitably, the group that "owns history" controls the gateway to knowledge construction, truth and falsity, the definition of normal and abnormal, and ultimately the nature of reality. In the United States, it is White Euro-Americans like you who own the history from which your racial reality is based.

When the contributions of various racial/ethnic groups are neglected or distorted in history, social studies, and other educational textbooks, when our mass media and other socialization sources combine to perpetuate our miseducation, when the contributions of your group are glorified over others, and when children are socialized and educated to accept and believe the historical legacy of the dominant society, then we set up conditions that privilege one group while oppressing another.

In simple terms, the racial reality of White America is a biased and bigoted one, transmitted through our educational system and the informal but powerful stream of socialization practices of families, peer groups, neighborhoods, churches, mass media, and other organizations. Our education system and these other entities define your group (Whites) as superior and another group (people of color) as inferior and undesirable, and then they constantly reinforce this message until it becomes reality for our citizens.

This can be said to be the true racial reality of White America! And unless you are liberated, you may be trapped by this false illusion.

In Chapter Three, we defined cultural oppression as possessing two complementary processes. It imposes unpleasant or undesirable conditions on certain groups or individuals, and it deprives them of conditions necessary for psychological or physical well-being. In essence, the racial reality of White America results in cultural oppression through an imposition of unwanted and undesirable roles or labels on persons of color, which results in deprivation. The case of Japanese Americans during World War II is a primary example of this process.

Several years ago, while residing in the San Francisco Bay Area, our local newspaper published a letter to the editor from a White citizen about the internment of Japanese Americans during World War II. It was sparked by the previewing of a PBS film, *Rabbit in the Moon*, about the unjustified and damaging effects that the incident had on Japanese Americans.[2] The letter reflects the racial reality of many White Americans in the community. It is reproduced here to illustrate how misinformation fosters and perpetuates insensitivity, bias, bigotry, and harm toward groups of color. More important, it provides convenient rationalizations to mistreat a specific group of Americans and labels it something other than racism.

Letter to the Editor

The film *Rabbit in the Moon* . . . is just the latest of a proliferation of articles and media programs which emphasized the victimization of Japanese-Americans during WWII, but which fail to provide the context in which it occurred.

We see only that Japanese-Americans were victimized by a racist populace. And thus the children, and perhaps even their parents, accept this distorted history as truth.

No one wants to cause discomfort among our loyal Japanese-American friends of today, who are now generations away from those 60 years ago. But to present this distorted history of the internment camps, without portraying the necessities of the time, is an injustice to the implied perpetrators—other Americans who suffered equally and may have given up hope.

Fairness and balance require that our children learn the following. Most Japanese-American friends of 60 years ago were quite different from our Japanese-American friends of today. If not direct immigrants themselves, they were the first generation of native Japanese.

Japanese Emperor Hirohito was more than a political and military leader. Japan's blend of politics and religion made him, literally, a deity whom his people worshipped. To give their lives for their emperor was an honor. Obviously, some of our then newly arrived Japanese-Americans would have divided loyalties.

Japan's attack on America plunged us into a war we had no reason to believe we would win. Nor was there reason to believe we would be spared the barbarism which Hirohito's armies had already visited on the Philippines, Singapore, and China. In Nanking alone, 800,000 Chinese civilians were viciously murdered, the city and surrounding villages burned.

Those who cite racism, rather than national security, as motivation for the camps fail to note that Chinese-Americans were not interned.

California, where many military bases and shipyards were located, also had the largest immigrant Japanese population. The impossibility of keeping troop movements secret from local citizens made security of utmost importance. Posters abounded, warning all that "Loose Lips Sink Ships." Each and every letter home from our fighting men, no matter how personal, was censored. They arrived with big stripes blacking out any words which might reveal their location or dates of movement.

Of course, justice required that an effort be made to distinguish between the loyal and possibly disloyal Japanese-Americans. But war is not just. All of our manpower was absorbed by wars going on in the Pacific and Europe at the same time, and at home by the tremendous production of war equipment necessary to win it.

We did not have the luxury of the time or personnel to discern those loyal Japanese from those who were not. Nor were we in a position to take chances. And so, good and loyal Japanese-Americans suffered. So did good and loyal Caucasian Americans. That's war.

When describing so passionately the loss of liberty of those Japanese-Americans, balance requires our children be taught what was happening to those not interned in safety, with their families, as were the Japanese.

Caucasian American fathers, too, lost their liberty. That's what happens in the military. But they also lost their physical safety, they lost their families—some for years at a time. And too many lost their lives.

Filmmaker Emiko Omori complains that "Our family and community fell apart." So too, for the many Americans.

Our children should learn that 16 million men between 18 and 35 years old were in uniform. Over a million were killed or wounded. That, when the entire U.S. population—both sexes of all ages—was 130 million.

These men, in the prime of life, weren't in the service for 18 months or two years. It was "for the duration" necessary to win.

It was a desperate war—one in which all nationalities and races of people lost.

The currently fashionable emphasis on the internment camps, without context, and the implications of racism do nothing to enhance race relations. Let's get over it. As did the generation which actually lived through it.[3]

This letter is representative of not only the racial reality of many White Americans during World War II but also the reality that continues to the present day. If you lack information about what really happened and if you accept the belief of potential spying from Japanese American citizens, then you might also come to believe as the writer of the letter did. Her letter prompted a number of other letters from outraged Asian Americans in the community. I, too, was so disturbed by the historical inaccuracies that I felt compelled to respond.

Rebuttal Letter

I read with dismay the comments of [the woman who wrote a letter to the editor] to the film *Rabbit in the Moon*, a story about the incarceration of Japanese-Americans during World War II. She takes the filmmaker to task for offering a "distorted history" of the camps and not "portraying the necessities of the time" which justified depriving the civil rights of more than 110,000 Japanese-Americans, two-thirds citizens by virtue of birth. Not only is her historical analysis flawed, but her distorted and biased outlook is dangerous. Let me briefly outline some reactions to her letter.

1. Nowhere in her letter does she ever acknowledge that an injustice was perpetrated against a specific population of U.S citizens. Her silence on this point is deafening. [The woman who wrote the letter] simply dwells on providing rationalizations for why the atrocity was carried out by the U.S. government and advises: "Let's get over it." I would like to pose the following questions: Does she truly believe the incarceration was justified? Does she realize that the actions against the Japanese-Americans were in violation of the ideals of the Declaration of Independence, Bill of Rights, and the Constitution? Does she believe that people are guilty until proven innocent? The prospect of affirmative responses to these questions is, to say the least, frightening.

2. Furthermore, who owns "history and the truth"? [The woman who wrote the letter] seems to believe that her historical accounts are more accurate, that U.S. actions were generated by a real threat, and that racism was not a factor (because "Chinese-Americans were not interned"). She needs to read the historical documents more closely, not what is primarily in textbooks but in government papers indicating that high officials knew Japanese-Americans were not a threat. She needs to know that Chinese-Americans were frequently assaulted during the

Japanese "spy hysteria" which swept the country. She needs to realize the United States was not only at war with Japan, but with Germany and Italy as well. Why were the Italian-Americans and German-Americans also not incarcerated? Did skin color have anything to do with it?

3. [The woman who wrote the letter] states that "fairness and balance" require a broader analysis. I am in agreement. Thus it seems important that she study the treatment of Asian-Americans even prior to the outbreak of WWII. There she will find that the history of Asian-Americans is the history of prejudice and discrimination. The Chinese Exclusion Act of 1882; large scale massacres of the Chinese in Los Angeles (1851) and Wyoming (1885); the meaning of the phrase "not a Chinaman's Chance"; the "Gentlemen's Agreement" to restrict Japanese immigration; the 1913 Alien Land Law which forbid the Japanese to own land; and the pervasive anti-Oriental feeling known as "the Yellow Peril" seem not to have penetrated the consciousness of [the woman who wrote the letter]. It is clear that anti-Asian sentiment was present leading up to the war with Japan, and to claim that racism was not a factor flies in the face of historical reality.

In closing, I hope that [the letter writer] realizes that remembering the internment experience is to accept responsibility for rectifying past injustices, making sure that such undemocratic actions never happen again, and helping us create a more inclusive and equitable society. "Getting over it" is not a luxury this nation can afford. We must learn from the lessons of the past.

While unpleasant for some, we must never forget how we unfairly seized the land of the American Indian people and forced them onto reservations; we can never forget the enslavement of African-Americans; we must never forget the Holocaust; and we must never forget the internment of Japanese-Americans.[4]

These two letters describe realities that occupy two extremes of a continuum. On the one end are many White Americans whose knowledge base and historical facts are either inaccurate or lacking, and on the other end are groups of color struggling to have their voices heard regarding the legitimacy of those facts. These differences in worldview would not be so disturbing were it not for the fact that the group able to define its reality more forcefully has the power to impose it on those less powerful. In the case of Japanese Americans, it resulted in taking away their property, uprooting their families, and destroying their family structures, but more important, depriving them of their civil liberties.

It is clear that the person who wrote the letter to the editor also suffers from two common notions that remain invisible to her: that "all Asians are the same" and that persons of color are not "Americans" but aliens more loyal to another country. Her argument to support her assertion that racism was not a factor in the incarceration was that Chinese Americans during World War II were not likewise interned. This is a strange twist of logic because she fails to acknowledge that China was an ally of the United States while Japan was an enemy. Her inability to distinguish between the Japanese and Chinese indicates a basic process of prejudice. Likewise, her constant emphasis on "divided loyalties" of the Japanese Americans reflects a common tendency of White Americans to view persons of color as aliens in their own land (à la Wen Ho Lee).

Even attempts to correct this injustice and tell the "rest of the story" have not penetrated the consciousness of White America. Letters such as these reveal the obliviousness and ignorance to events and findings that followed the incarceration.

1. In 1982, for example, secret documents were uncovered that revealed that agencies concerned with U.S. national security consistently concluded that Japanese Americans had committed no acts of espionage or sabotage and there was no factual basis for intern-

ment. FBI Director J. Edgar Hoover, the Federal Communications Commission, and the U.S. Navy all wrote that claims of a national security threat were not supported or were pure and simple "falsehoods." These documents only came to light when a group of attorneys representing Fred Korematsu successfully reopened his 1944 Supreme Court case that had upheld the internment. When these hidden documents came to light, they reversed the conviction of Korematsu and ruled that the government had intentionally suppressed evidence, withholding it from the Supreme Court.

2. To the letter writer's claim that racial prejudice was not at play, it is important to note that the Congressional Commission on Wartime Relocation and Internment of Civilians provided the following context for the actions of the U.S. government: "In sum, Executive Order 9066 [that resulted in the internment of 120,000 Americans of Japanese ancestry] was not justified by military necessity, and the decisions that followed from it . . . were not founded upon military considerations. The broad historical causes that shaped these decisions were race prejudice, war hysteria and a failure of political leadership."[5]

3. Propelled by indisputable evidence of wrongdoing and injustice perpetrated against a whole segment of citizens, President Reagan in 1987 issued a formal apology to Japanese Americans and signed a bill approved by Congress awarding reparations. Likewise, Fred Korematsu was recognized as a loyal American who resisted the undemocratic actions of his government by being awarded the Presidential Medal of Freedom.

THE CHANNELS THAT SHAPE OUR RACIAL REALITIES

Have you ever wondered why you hold certain beliefs and not others about people of color? Why do you believe in the superiority of White America? How are your racial realities shaped? Through what mechanisms or channels do you acquire your worldview?

It is my belief that there are three primary channels by which you are socialized, resulting in the acquisition of societal values, attitudes, knowledge, biases, and stereotypes. If bigotry and prejudice are learned, then it might be helpful to speak not only about the "racial curriculum" that each of you is taught but also about the means by which this occurs. The three most potent instruments by which you acquire your racial reality are schooling and education, the mass media, and peers and social groups (families, friends, churches, and formal and informal organizations).

Schooling and Education

Were you ever taught that Columbus discovered America? Were you ever taught that the incarceration of Japanese Americans was a national security necessity? Were you ever taught about the contributions of the Chinese in the United States, their building of the transcontinental railroad, mining of gold, and so forth? Were you ever taught that many of the framers of the Constitution of the United States owned slaves?

Our educational system has too long been dominated by the attitudes, values, beliefs, and the knowledge construction of one race and class of people (White Americans). Whether it is psychology, biology, history, anthropology, religion, economics, science, or philosophy, the Euro-American worldview is the basic foundation from which the discipline is viewed. If, indeed, our educational system is also racialized, then the knowledge base is often constructed in such a manner as to justify racism and colonialism.

It does this by omission, fabrication, distortion, or selective emphasis of information, which is designed to emphasize the contributions of White Western civilization over all other groups. The result is that schools become sites that perpetuate myths and inaccuracies about persons of color. Let me use the field of the social sciences to illustrate these assertions.

In another text, I reviewed literature that indicated how the social sciences have failed to create a realistic understanding of various ethnic groups in America.[6] It has done this to persons of color by ignoring them, maintaining false stereotypes, and distorting their lifestyles. The field has historically ignored the study of Asians in America, reinforced negative views of African Americans by concentrating its studies on unstable Black families instead of on the many stable ones, focused primarily on psychopathological problems encountered by Mexican Americans, and referred to Native Americans as "problem people." The historical use of science in the investigation of racial differences seems linked to White supremacist notions and has been referred to as *scientific racism* by many scientists of color. The basic equation behind non-White inferiority is genetic inferiority. Many examples can be cited:

- 1840 census figures (fabricated) were used to support the notion that Blacks living under "unnatural conditions of freedom" were prone to anxiety.

- It was emphasized by slave owners and supported by scientists that mental health for Blacks was contentment with subservience.

- Influential medical journals presented fantasies as facts, supporting the belief that the anatomical, neurological, or endocrinological aspects of Blacks were always inferior to those of Whites.

- The Black person's brain was smaller and less developed than White brains.

- The dreams of Blacks were more juvenile in character and not as complex as Whites.

- Good Blacks were faithful and happy-go-lucky.

- Black persons were more prone to mental illness because their minds were so simple.[7]

Likewise, G. Stanley Hall, often referred to as the father of child psychology, is said to have stated that Africans, Indians, and Chinese were members of adolescent races and in a stage of incomplete development. In most cases, the evidence used to support these conclusions was fabricated, extremely flimsy, or distorted to fit the belief in non-White inferiority.

Frighteningly, a recent survey found that many of these stereotypes continue to be accepted by White Americans: 20 percent publicly expressed a belief that African Americans were innately inferior in thinking ability, 19 percent believe that Blacks have thicker craniums, and 23.5 percent believe that Blacks have longer arms than Whites. One wonders, however, how many White Americans hold similar beliefs privately but because of political correctness or social pressures do not publicly voice them! Do you share any of these beliefs?

Even White social scientists who rejected the genetic-deficit model tended to perpetuate a view of minorities as culturally disadvantaged, deficient, or deprived. In 1962, Riessman's widely read book, *The Culturally Deprived Child*, argued against the biological inferiority of minority groups.[8] He attributed poor performance on academic tests and in classroom learning to the lack of advantages of middle-class culture (education, books, toys, formal language, and the like). The problem with his well-intentioned argument was fourfold: the term *culturally deprived* means lacking a cultural background, which is impossible because everyone inherits a culture; the term causes conceptual confusions that adversely affect social policy planning, educational policy, and research because it blames the culture for problems; cultural deprivation is equated with deviation from and superiority of White middle-class values; and it justifies infusing White middle-class values into the cultural values, families, and lifestyles of persons of color. In essence, cultural-deprivation concepts in education ultimately mean that persons of color "lack the right culture" and that White culture is better!

Again, I emphasize how American schools have become mono-cultural environments that dispense a White Euro-American racial reality to our children. In many cases, it tends to benefit White students while invalidating the reality of students of color. If our society is to free itself from the racialization of our worldview, then its educational system and school environments must become truly multicultural in content and process.

The Mass Media

How much television do you watch? Do you believe most news reported in the papers? Do you listen to rap music and watch MTV? Have you ever paid attention to the types of racial messages being communicated? Did you ever question their accuracy?

Like schools, the mass media (television, motion pictures, radio, recorded music, newspapers, and magazines) are a powerful force in shaping the racial reality of White America. Children Now, a nonpartisan and independent voice for America's children, conducted a national survey of children from the ages of ten to seventeen, which included African Americans, Asian Americans, Latinos, and Whites.[9] The study was extremely valuable because most studies have concentrated on adults, but an important question was how children receive the media's race message. Their findings can be summarized by the following:

- Regardless of race, all children were more likely to associate positive qualities with White characters (have more money, are well educated, are leaders, do well in school, and are more intelligent) and negative qualities with minority characters (break the law and are poor, lazy, and goofy).

- Whites and African Americans say they see people of their race on television, whereas Latinos and Asians are much less likely to see members of their own race.

- Children think that Whites usually play the roles of boss, secretary, police officer, and doctor in television, whereas African Americans play criminal and maid and janitor.

- Across all races, children agree that news media portray African American and Latino people more negatively than Whites and Asians, particularly when the news is about young people.

- Large majorities of African Americans, Asians, and Latinos feel there should be more people of their race as newscasters, whereas Whites feel there are enough White newscasters.

In general, it is clear from research that children are affected by and influenced about how race is portrayed in the media. Media provide interpretive information and images by selecting those to be included or excluded; helping viewers (movies and television), listeners (radio and music), and readers (newspapers and magazines) organize the data through selected and repetitive themes; supporting certain values and attitudes and condemning others; and providing models for behavior.

The absence of minority group members suggests that persons of color are not worthy of viewers' attention and that they are less important than White Americans. The stereotypical portrayals or negatively valued roles indicate that minorities are not worthy of respect and that they are dangerous, criminal, and less capable. This suggests that viewers' ideal models should be White.

The interplay of media portrayals of relationships between crime and race has a very long history that can be used to trigger fears and biases. In 1989, Charles Stuart, a wealthy furrier, accused a phantom Black man of shooting and wounding him severely and killing his pregnant wife. Stuart later was accused of killing his own wife and admitted to making up the story to deflect suspicion from him.

In 1994, headlines were made when Susan Smith (White) claimed that a car jacker had kidnapped her two young sons. She described the kidnapper as a Black man, waving a handgun, and wearing a knit cap and flannel shirt, who forced her out of her car. Later she admitted to strapping her sons into the car and driving it into a lake where they drowned.

In both cases, prior to the truth coming out, the press, radio, and television were filled with sensationalistic stories of the assailants, who were described as animalistic, as monstrous animals, and as the dregs of society. Interestingly, studies of stereotypical press portrayals of African American males throughout history follow a similar characterization. They are described as beastly, loathsome, and violent and as thugs and degenerates. Both Susan Smith and Charles Stuart seem to have learned their racial lessons well. By yelling "Black man," the racial curriculum perpetrated by the mass media inevitably predisposes us to associate African Americans with all that is evil and beastly.

It is not my purpose to conduct an extended and sophisticated analysis of the role that media play in our racial reality. The examples given are not even the tip of the iceberg in understanding the vast influence of the many aspects and dimensions of mass media. Television programs, movies, recorded music, radio, newspapers, magazines, and the many forms of media transmit an enormous body of material regarding race, ethnicity, interracial relationships, and culture. Much of this information is fiction, but it is often confused with fact and knowledge. It is nevertheless clear that media are a powerful force in the social construction of your knowledge about race, culture, and ethnicity.

Peers and Social Groups

Think back over your life. How did you form your opinions and feelings about other races? If you are like most people, your actual contacts with people of color were probably few and very brief. As a result, your information (the racial curriculum) was probably based on secondary sources. I have already mentioned two of them. Among the most powerful in the formation of your racial reality is the information that comes from peers, family, friends, and important social groups and organizations. What messages did you receive about race and racism from school, at work, in church, and from family? Try to apply the following examples to your own personal life. Have you had similar experiences?

At a fraternity sports party, a group of White males were sitting around their living room during a late Sunday afternoon, chugging down beer after beer tapped from a keg. They had just finished watching the first half of a football game and were obviously quite inebriated. Excitedly talking about the last play from scrimmage that resulted in an incomplete pass, one of the boys exclaimed, "Them niggers can't play quarterback!" This brought out a howl of laughter, and another member said, "That's because they're just jungle bunnies!" More laughter erupted in the room and others produced a flurry of racial slurs: "monkey," "coon," "burr head," "Oreo," and "Uncle Tom"! Each slur brought on laughter and renewed attempts to outdo one another in finding the most degrading reference to Blacks. As they exhausted their list, the game became a form of free association with Blackness. "Black pussy," "black sheep," "criminal," "rapist," "castration," "welfare family," "cattle prod," and so on, they shouted. It was clear that some of those in the group were quite uncomfortable with the game, but said nothing and chuckled at the responses anyway.

In high school and college I pursued a guy named Dong, a biracial Vietnamese American. His father was a White American former soldier who married a Vietnamese woman during the war. I thought he was cute and would frequently visit his home where the mother would cook us weird food that smelled weird as well. I did not think of him as being from a different race, because he wasn't Black. When my folks found out about our relationship, they expressed great displeasure. "We don't associate with those kind of people," my dad would emphatically state. My mother would conveniently forget to give me phone messages from Dong. During this brief period of time, my mother would frequently tell me the story of her sister, Ann, who married a Latino man, which resulted in her family disowning her. I would argue that she was wronged, but my mother would only say, "You can always find someone of your own kind." At family functions, I began to notice my uncle's chauvinistic and racist jokes. Whenever I protested, they would only accuse me of being a White liberal and that someday I would understand. To preserve family harmony, I simply remained silent during our family functions. I can't remember why my short-lived relationship with Dong ended. I just know it was easier not to be involved with him.

———————

It was a late summer afternoon. A group of White neighborhood mothers, obviously friends, had brought their four- and five-year-olds to the local McDonald's for a snack and to play on the swings and slides provided by the restaurant. They were all seated at a table watching their sons and daughters run about the play area. In one corner of the yard sat a small Black child pushing a red truck along the grass. One of the White girls from the group approached the Black boy and they started a conversation. During that instant, the mother of the girl exchanged quick glances with the other mothers, who nodded knowingly. She quickly rose from the table, walked over to the two, spoke to her daughter, and gently pulled her away to join her previous playmates. Within minutes, however, the girl again approached the Black boy and both began to play with the truck. At that point, all the mothers rose from the table and loudly exclaimed to their children, "It's time to go now!"

It goes without saying that significant others such as peers, families, and friends teach you a societal curriculum that contains beliefs, attitudes, and behavior related to race and race relations. Likewise, work sites, neighborhood organizations, and national ones like the Boy Scouts all combine to influence your attitudes and actions. In the just-cited examples, the social construction of knowledge about race, ethnicity, and culture is clear.

1. Being a person of color is "less than" being White. For the fraternity boys to so easily come up with racial slurs indicates not only that they have learned their lessons well regarding bigotry but also that being Black is associated with inferiority. The association of inferiority is also present in the family that discourages their daughter from an interracial relationship with the biracial Vietnamese boy and by the mother's discouraging her daughter from even playing with someone of a different race.

2. To speak against racial prejudice and discrimination may result in ostracism or lack of support from significant others. As noted in the previous example, the young girl chose not to speak against family members who told racial jokes or to disagree with family members about their biases in order to preserve family harmony. Those in the fraternity who might not harbor racial prejudice said nothing and even chuckled at the racial slurs being

bandied about. Would you remain silent in such a situation? Remember, remaining silent is a form of approval and complicity.

3. Separation of the races is not only desired but also important. When one realizes that White children as young as four and five are being discouraged from associating with members of another race, then one can understand how deeply ingrained these lessons become as they are reinforced throughout your development.

IMPACT OF THE RACIAL CURRICULUM ON PERCEPTIONS AND BELIEFS

A 1994 Harris Poll commissioned by a national conference (formerly known as the National Conference of Christians and Jews) found that the racial curriculum of our society has affected the reality of both White Americans and persons of color.[10] For example, two of their primary conclusions were that Whites continue to minimize the plight of minorities and that racial/ethnic groups continue to experience mistrust, envy, and misunderstandings toward one another.

Perceptions of White Americans

1. Whites believe that minorities are doing better than they really are in contradiction to standards-of-living data and the social-psychological costs of discrimination experienced by persons of color.

2. More than half the Whites surveyed believe that equality has been achieved.

3. Although White folks express willingness to work together to protect children from gangs and violence, find solutions to racial problems, and help feed, clothe, and house the homeless, they are hindered by mistrust, suspicions, and distrust of minority groups.

Perceptions of Persons of Color (including interethnic)

1. There is tremendous resentment of Whites by all minority groups.

2. Two-thirds of minorities think Whites "believe they are superior and can boss people around," "are insensitive to other people," "control power and wealth in America," and "do not want to share it with non-Whites."

3. More than 40 percent of African Americans and Hispanics and one of every four Whites believe that Asian Americans are "unscrupulous, crafty, and devious in business."

4. Nearly half the Hispanic Americans surveyed and 40 percent of African Americans and Whites believe that Muslims "belong to a religion that condones or supports terrorism."

5. Blacks think they are treated far worse than Whites and worse than other minority groups when it comes to getting equal treatment in applying for mortgages, in the media, and in job promotions.

6. Only 10 percent of African Americans—a staggeringly low number—believe that the police treat them as fairly as other groups.

7. African Americans believe that everyone else is treated with more equality and especially that Asian Americans are doing better.

It becomes quite obvious that our educational system, mass media, peers, social groups, and organizations are powerful channels by which you learn your lessons about race and race relations. Although it is clear that White supremacy and racism are learned through these avenues, it is also clear that they can be used to combat racism, enhance group understanding, and engender more sensitivity to cultural differences. This will be the focus of our discussion in a forthcoming chapter.

✍ What You Can Do to Overcome Racism

Use the following exercises to gain insight into your own racial reality.

Exercise Number 1

This exercise rates your comfort level with racial/ethnic groups.

1. Assessing your interracial contacts might be helpful in revealing just how much or how little of your knowledge and feelings toward people of color is formed from actual personal experience. Do this exercise.

Rate the comfort level associated with each group. Use the following scale: 1 = very comfortable; 2 = mildly comfortable; 3 = neutral; 4 = mildly uncomfortable; 5 = very uncomfortable.

Rank order the group you have the most actual contact with (1 = most contact) to that with the least (5 = least). It is important to note that I am referring to actual interpersonal contacts at work, school, neighborhood, and organizations.

In the next column, estimate the percentage of time over a one-week period that you have with persons of color.

Racial/ Ethnic Group	Comfort Level	Rank Order of Contacts	Percentage of Contact per Week
African Americans	_____	_____	_____
Asian Americans	_____	_____	_____
Latino/Hispanic Americans	_____	_____	_____
Native Americans	_____	_____	_____
White Americans	_____	_____	_____

2. Is there a correlation between the comfort level and the percentage of contacts you have with a particular group? What do you think it means?

3. Look at the comfort level scores. Can you explain why one group is more comfortable for you than the other? For example, some Whites find Asian Americans more within their comfort range than, let's say, Black Americans. Why? Explore and discuss this with others.

4. Does any aspect of this surprise you? For example, does it surprise you to discover how many or how few contacts you have with members of another race or ethnic group?

5. In light of the fact that you have so few contacts with some groups, what does it suggest to you about your role in the acquisition of accurate information?

Exercise Number 2

In this chapter, we mentioned a study conducted by Children Now on the impact of television on children's perceptions of race. An interesting assignment is to keep a one-week journal of all television programs that you watch (news, talk shows, movies, comedies, biographies, sporting events, and so forth). This exercise can be conducted on formal or informal bases. As a classroom assignment, for example, the instructor might wish to quantify the study by identifying specific categories and their meanings. For most readers, an informal survey can be quite revealing. Here is an example of what can be done.

- Over the course of a week, how many times were various racial/ethnic minority groups portrayed (in entertainment programs, news, and so on)? Just obtain a count. Which groups (including White Americans) were highly represented? What group was least likely to be on TV?

- Can you characterize the portrayals? For example, were the characters portrayed positively or negatively? Were stereotypes involved?

- What roles did minorities generally play? What about Whites?

- Take a count by race of newscasters, game show hosts, commentators, and so forth. Were there disparities?

If a group does this activity, it will certainly generate much fruit for discussion. If you have done this activity by yourself, try to think about the reasons and the potential impact of the findings on people of color and on Whites, such as you.

Exercise Number 3

On a personal level, try to identify when you first became aware of a particular racial group. For example, think about your childhood. When did you become aware of African Americans, Asian Americans, Latino/Hispanic Americans, and Native Americans? Was the awareness tinged with negativism, fear, rejection, and abhorrence or with positive associations?

Isn't Racism a White Problem?

In textbooks, the news media, everyday conversations, and even in lecture halls, I have often heard reference to "the Chinese problem," "the Black problem," "the Indian problem," "the immigrant problem," or "the minority problem." You may have also used such language. Rarely do I hear reference made to "the White problem." Unfortunately, people of color in our society are frequently seen as problematic or are experienced as problems. Such is the case when Rudyard Kipling, an English writer, coined the phrase "White man's burden" in 1899.[1]

From a social-psychological perspective, an uncritical acceptance of such language leads to a mind-set that blames the victim. W. Ryan, in his book *Blaming the Victim*, identifies a common phenomenon in our society: victims are often accused of having brought on the negative consequences they suffer.[2] A powerful example is the following: a woman who is raped in our society is often accused of having enticed the rapist to rape her ("She wore seductive clothing," "She should not have been on that side of town," "She led the attacker on," and so forth), or it is argued that the perpetrator should be excused because her *no* was really a *yes* or because "any red-blooded man would have done the same thing in that situation."

Likewise, the negative consequences suffered by minorities because of racism are attributed to their own shortcomings. How many of you, for example, have inferred that high unemployment and poverty rates among Latinos and African Americans are due to their laziness; low educational attainment among minorities is due to intellectual inferiority; or the incarceration of nearly 120,000 Japanese Americans during World War II (two-thirds were U.S. citizens by virtue of birth) could be justified for national security reasons. It seems strange that you are less prone to consider external reasons for these results: prejudice, racism, discrimination, and oppression.

Part of the problem is a tendency to focus on what Thomas Parham calls "an analysis of the oppressed" (victim analysis) as opposed to an analysis of the oppressor.[3] We know much about the consequences of racism on the victims already; we know little, however, about the oppressor and the hidden dimensions of racism. By focusing your attention on the effects of racism instead of the causes, White Americans effectively avoid paying attention to factors that continue injustice. Likewise, you are able to escape personal responsibility for making changes and avoid being blamed for causing or perpetuating injustice.

If we accept the premise that many of the negative consequences suffered by persons of color are due to White racism, would it not be more correct to speak about "the White problem"? As many of you have already surmised by the title of this chapter, I believe that racism is a White problem and not a people-of-color problem! Before we continue, however, it is important for readers such as you to note that this phrase is not an attack on White people. I want to make a clear distinction between White Euro-Americans (as a people) and the ideology of White supremacy. It is the latter that represents the oppressive stable arrangements and practices through which collective actions are taken (government, business, unions, schools, churches, courts, and police) and by which rewards and career opportunities are conferred on White folks while foreclosing those for racial minorities. White supremacy decides who deserves training and skills, medical care, formal education, political influence, productive employment, fair legal treatment, decent housing, and so forth. Although White people are not the enemy, White supremacy is most likely to be reflected by the beliefs and actions of Euro-Americans.

Earlier, I made the assertion that it is impossible for any of us not to inherit the racial biases and assumptions of our forebears. White Euro-Americans are culturally conditioned into oppressor roles without their informed consent. At the very least, social-psychological studies lend credence to the fact that the majority of White Americans are prejudiced or racist, although most are unknowingly so. What is disturbing, however, was the study by Pettigrew that concluded that even though Whites may express a rejection of racial injustice, they remain reluctant to act on measures necessary to eliminate inequities![4]

My position on racism is this. You do not have to be actively racist to contribute to the racism problem. Inaction, itself, is tacit agreement that racism is acceptable; and because White Americans enjoy the benefits, privileges, and opportunities of the oppressive system, they inevitably are racist by both commission and omission. As a result, it is my contention that White racism is truly a White problem and that it is the responsibility of my White brothers and sisters to be centrally involved in combating and ending racial oppression.

WHAT IS WHITE SUPREMACY?

Just what is White supremacy? The concept itself is so antagonistic to our notions of freedom, equality, and social justice that few of you would ever consider yourselves to be White supremacists. Frankly, the overwhelming majority of you aren't, not the overt conscious type anyway. You usually associate White supremacy with groups like the neo-Nazis, the Klan, or the skinheads, groups you despise and condemn. Yet the power of White supremacist ideology is so deeply ingrained in our society that its operation is nearly invisible. Let's take a few moments to define and analyze how it manifests itself in your daily lives and in the institutions you support.

White supremacy is a doctrine of White racial superiority that justifies discrimination, segregation, and domination of persons of color based on an ideology and belief system that considers all non-White groups racially inferior. There are some key elements in this definition that need elaboration. First, because it is a doctrine, White supremacy rests on a set of interlocking beliefs and principles that are taught and inculcated into people. Such a socialization process occurs through education, the media, and how your family and friends transmit beliefs related to racial superiority to you. Second, the teachings are characterized by beliefs that White people and by extension your culture are superior to non-White groups. Third, the beliefs are not necessarily based on reason, but on faith and dogma. Fourth, the doctrine is manifested in individual, institutional, and cultural sanctions and ultimately discriminates, segregates, and oppresses persons of color.

In our society, the actors involved in the manifestations of White supremacy tend to be at three levels: *individual level*—dominant group members (White Americans) discriminating against persons of color (target group); *institutional level*—structures, policies, and practices that unfairly treat persons of color; and *cultural level*—imposition of White Euro-American cultural heritage on other groups while negating or destroying the cultural heritage of minority groups. To help you understand more clearly the operation of White supremacy, I would like to introduce a new concept called *ethnocentric monoculturalism*.

White supremacy is a specific manifestation of ethnocentric monoculturalism, because the latter is broader and provides a framework to understand all forms of group oppression. The defining difference is the ability (power) of one group in a particular society to oppress another group on a large scale and on a systemic basis. For example, it is possible for the dominant group in Japan, Latin

America, or Africa to oppress their culturally different citizens on the basis of skin color as well.

ETHNOCENTRIC MONOCULTURALISM

Ethnocentric monoculturalism is a singular attitude or belief that one's race, culture, or nation is superior to all others, accompanied with the power to impose this expression on a less powerful group. In the United States, ethnocentric monoculturalism appears in the form of White supremacy and racism. As a result, racism in the United States must be viewed as a White problem because it is White Euro-Americans who are primarily responsible for the oppression of people of color, and consequently they are responsible for making changes. To understand the insidious and hidden nature of racism, it is important for you to understand the five components of ethnocentric monoculturalism.

Component One—Belief in Superiority

Ask yourself these questions: Are you proud to be an American? Do you believe that living in this country is more desirable than living in any other part of the world? Do you believe that the United States is the most advanced nation in the world? If you answered yes to these questions, you are not alone in your beliefs and feelings. You have also, however, fulfilled one of the primary ingredients of ethnocentric monoculturalism, a belief in your group's superiority. Even using the term *American* to refer to only citizens of the United States is ethnocentric. The Americas include Latin America and South America. Even North America encompasses Canada. Residents in these countries also can lay claim to the title "American."

It is not unusual for you to take great pride in yourself, your family, your friends, your group, and your country. It is both a natural and common phenomenon to be taught to view your cultural heritage, your values, and your way of life as positive and desirable. As a result, most of us possess a strong belief in the superiority of our group's cultural heritage (history, values, language, traditions, arts and crafts, and so forth). The group norms and values that you share in your society with others are generally viewed positively, and descriptors often used to refer to your group and nation are "more advanced" and "more civilized." Each of us possesses conscious and unconscious feelings of superiority, and we strongly believe that our way of doing things is the best way.

In the United States, White Euro-American culture is seen as not only desirable but also normative. Physical characteristics such as being light complexioned, blond haired, and blue-eyed; cultural characteristics such as belief in Christianity (single-god concept), individualism, Protestant work ethic, and capitalism; and linguistic characteristics such as Standard English, being objective by controlling emotions, and the written tradition are highly valued components of Euro-American culture. People possessing these traits and adhering to these norms are perceived more favorably and often are allowed easier access to the privileges and rewards of the larger society. This latter consequence has been termed *White privilege*, a concept that will be discussed in a future chapter.

Component Two—Belief in the Inferiority of Others

The second component of ethnocentric monoculturalism is a belief in the inferiority of other groups' entire cultural heritage, which extends to their customs, values, traditions, arts and crafts, and language. This represents the other side of the superiority coin. If you harbor a belief in your own group's superiority, it becomes the standard by which others are judged. If throughout your life being fair complexioned, adhering to a belief in Christianity, and speaking "good English" are considered both desirable and normative, then individuals who are dark skinned, believe in a different god, or who speak with an accent would be seen as less desirable or inferior.

We often use descriptors like "less developed," "uncivilized," "primitive," or even "pathological" to describe groups or societies that differ from us. The lifestyle or ways of doing things by the group are considered inferior. Physical characteristics such as dark complexion, black hair, and brown eyes; cultural characteristics such as belief in non-Christian religions (Islam, Confucianism, polytheism—many gods, and so forth), collectivism, present time orientation, and the importance of shared wealth; and linguistic characteristics such as bilingualism, non-Standard English, speaking with an accent, use of nonverbal and contextual communication, and reliance on the oral tradition are usually seen as less desirable by the society.

Psychological studies consistently reveal that individuals who are physically different, who speak with an accent, and who adhere to different cultural beliefs and practices are more likely to be evaluated negatively in our schools and workplace. People of color may be seen as less intelligent, less qualified, more unpopular, and as possessing more undesirable traits.

Component Three—Power to Impose Standards

All groups and societies are to some extent ethnocentric—that is, they feel positively about their cultural heritage and way of life. The defining feature of ethnocentric monoculturalism, however, is power: the power to impose the values and standards of one group on another. Power is the ability to act on the needs, desires, beliefs, and values of one entity in order to influence, control, and define the existence of another. Philosopher Friedrich Nietzsche believed that a primary human motivation was the *will to power,* and psychiatrist Alfred Adler also believed this to be a basic human condition. Although all human interactions may involve the exercise of power (attempts to influence), an imbalance in its distribution can lead to abuse. An abuse of power can be seen in the overt actions of fascists, tyrants, ruthless executives, child molesters, spousal abusers, and racists who exercise unchecked power. These observations led Lord Acton in 1887 to state, "Power tends to corrupt, and absolute power corrupts absolutely." We usually associate power with overt actions such as military might, but the truth is that power is often covert, invisible, and hidden.

In the United States, it is White Euro-Americans who possess the tools and hold the power to influence, mistreat, invalidate, and oppress other groups. The issue here is not to blame but to speak realistically about how our society operates. Minorities can be biased, can hold stereotypes, and can strongly believe that their way is the best way. Yet, if they do not possess the power to impose their values on others, they hypothetically cannot oppress. It is power or the unequal status relationship between groups that defines ethnocentric monoculturalism. Ethnocentric monoculturalism is the individual, institutional, and cultural expression of the superiority of one group's cultural heritage over another and the possession of power to impose those standards broadly on the less powerful group. Because minorities, in general, do not possess a share of economic, social, and political power equal to that of Whites in our society, they are generally unable to truly discriminate on a large-scale basis. The damage and harm of oppression is likely to be one-sided: from majority to minority group.

Component Four—Manifestation in Institutions and Our Society

As part of the cultural conditioning process, our society imparts and enforces ethnocentric values and beliefs on its citizens through the programs, policies, practices, structures, and institutions of the society. For example, chain-of-command systems, training and educational systems, communication systems, management systems, and performance appraisal systems often dictate and control our lives. They attain untouchable and godfather-like status in an organization. Because most systems are monocultural in nature and demand compliance, racial/ethnic minorities and women may be oppressed. Psychologist James Jones labels institutional racism as a set of policies, priorities, and accepted normative patterns designed to subjugate, oppress, and force the dependence of individuals and groups on a larger society.[5] It does this by sanctioning unequal goals, unequal status, and unequal access to goods and services. Institutional racism has fostered the enactment of discriminatory statutes, the selective enforcement of laws, the blocking of economic opportunities and outcomes, and the imposition of forced assimilation and acculturation on the culturally different.

The consequences of institutional bias can be seen in housing patterns; segregated schools; segregated churches; White control of newspapers, radio, and TV; the selection process for sites for freeways, expressways, and low-cost housing; and the biased historical legacy in our educational curriculum. Comedian and social activist Dick Gregory makes this blunt but candid observation:

> Basically, Black folks in America do not hate White folks. We hate this stinking White racist system with these stinking White racist institutions, not you. . . . Individual racism we're not worried about. It's this damn institutionalized racism that's choking us to death. Here's what Black folks is talking about today: a White racist system that keeps me locked in a Black ghetto all my life so I've got to develop a different culture to survive with the rats and roaches. And when I break out and come to your institutions, you give me the wrong tests. You don't ask me about the ghetto. You ask me about the Eiffel Tower.[6]

Component Five—The Invisible Veil

Although the consequences of ethnocentric monoculturalism may be clearly visible, how it operates is less visible. That is one of the primary reasons why victim blaming occurs, because if the real causes are hidden, people have a tendency to attribute bad outcomes to those who are suffering: "They must have done something wrong to deserve it." Several social-psychological principles can explain the invisible phenomenon of ethnocentric monoculturalism.

First, because people are all products of cultural conditioning, their values and beliefs (worldview) represent an *invisible veil* that operates outside the level of conscious awareness. As a result, people assume universality—that everyone regardless of race, culture, ethnicity, or gender shares the nature of reality and truth. This assumption is erroneous but seldom questioned because it is firmly ingrained in our worldview.

Elsewhere I have defined a worldview as to how individuals perceive their relationship to the world (nature, institutions, other people, and so forth). A worldview is a product of a person's cultural upbringing and life experiences. Some have described it as our philosophy of life, how we think the world works, or our conceptual framework. It is an all-encompassing filter that determines how we think, define events, make decisions, and behave. In the United States, the Euro-American worldview is normative and represents the default standard by which judgments are made regarding normal-abnormal, desirable-undesirable, good-bad, and healthy-unhealthy.

Second, because all of us live, play, and work within organizations, those policies, practices, and structures that may be less than fair to minority groups are invisible in controlling our lives. These represent systemic barriers that mirror the nature of race relations in the United States. For example, high-status positions are usually White dominated, whereas minority groups and women occupy low-status positions. The dominance of White men in management and other leadership positions poses a structural problem for underrepresented groups because evaluation of minorities is likely to be distorted or to reflect Euro-American standards.

In addition, applying a common standard in evaluating employees is oftentimes seen as equal and fair treatment. After all, we are not discriminating against anyone. But suppose the standards used for promotion, for example, favor one group over another? Wouldn't that be unfair? Herein lies one of the basic ironies that contribute to the invisible veil of ethnocentric monoculturalism: the assumption that equal treatment is fair treatment and that differential treatment is discriminatory (biased) treatment. Let's use an example to illustrate this erroneous belief.

All of us who have sons and daughters applying to college know that one of the basic criteria used to evaluate the merits of student applications is performance on the Scholastic Assessment Test (SAT). Suppose a university uses a cutoff score of 690 on the math section of the exam (out of 800 points—placing students at the 90+ percentile) for admission. Now if we look at the crop of freshman students admitted to the university, we would find that few Black or Latino students are represented. We would not, however, conclude that the university has discriminated against students of color but rather that those students did not make the grade. We have treated everyone the same regardless of race, color, gender, sexual orientation, or religious affiliation. The conclusion that we have acted fairly may be true, depending on whether the standard used is in itself both unbiased and predictive of academic success.

Suppose, however, that we find that students of color who score between 590 and 690 do equally well at the university if they are admitted. In this scenario, a case could be made that the use of scores on the SAT is not predictive of college success and unfairly discriminates against minority applicants. We will return to this issue shortly, but the conclusion in this example is that equal treatment may be discriminatory treatment. The unfair differential impact on minority groups becomes difficult to attribute to bias because "we are treating everyone the same."

HISTORICAL LEGACY OF WHITE RACISM

Perhaps the greatest obstacle to a meaningful movement toward an eradication of White racism in our society is the failure to understand your unconscious and unintentional complicity in perpetuating unfairness and discrimination via your personal ethnocentric values and beliefs and the society's biased institutional policies and practices. The power of racism is related to the invisibility of powerful forces that control and dictate your life. In a strange sort of way, we are all victims. Minority groups are victims of oppression. Majority group members are victims unwittingly socialized into oppressor roles.

The thesis that you are socialized into a racist society can be seen throughout history. Oppression and White racial supremacy have been reflected as early as the uneven application of the Bill of Rights in favor of White immigrants and their descendants as opposed to minority populations. Some 226 years ago, Britain's King George III accepted a "declaration of independence" from former subjects residing in this country. This proclamation was destined to shape and reshape the geopolitical and sociocultural landscape of the world many times over. The lofty language penned by its principal architect, Thomas Jefferson, and signed by those present was indeed inspiring: "We hold these truths to be self-evident, that all men are created equal."

Yet as we now view the historical actions of that time, we cannot but be struck by the paradox inherent in those events.

- First, all fifty-six of the signatories were White males of European descent, hardly a representation of the current racial and gender composition of the population.

- Second, the language of the declaration suggests that only men were created equal, but what about women?

- Third, many of the founding fathers were slave owners who seemed not to recognize the hypocritical personal standards they used because they considered Blacks to be subhuman.

- Fourth, the history of this land did not start with the Declaration of Independence or the formation of the United States of America. Yet our textbooks continue to teach us an ethnocentric perspective—Western civilization—which ignores over two-thirds of the world's population.

- Fifth, it is important to note that those early Europeans who came to this country were immigrants attempting to escape persecution (oppression) but in the process did not recognize their own role in the oppression of indigenous peoples (American Indians) who had already resided in this country for centuries.

- Last, in 1778, the U.S. Constitution contained the following clause: "Representatives and direct taxes shall be apportioned among the several states . . . according to their respective numbers, which shall be determined by adding to the whole number of free persons . . . and excluding Indians not taxed, three-fifths of all other persons [slaves]."

This passage has become known as the "three-fifths clause" (art. 1, sec. 2), which defined the Black slave as property and three-fifths of a man; the American Indian, however, was completely written out of the Constitution. In other words, the clause legalized institutional racism for nearly a hundred years.

The conclusion is inescapable: the so-called natural and inalienable rights of individuals expressed by European and European American history seem to have been intended for White Americans only. When one considers the colonization and exploitation of Third World countries, the forced removal of Native Americans from their lands, the enslavement and segregation of African Americans, the incarceration of Japanese Americans during World War II, the immigration restrictions on persons of color throughout history, and the English-only movement in the United States, then the inevitable conclusion can only be explained through White racism. Even more frightening is that these acts were not perpetrated by a few racist individuals but by the whole governments of North Atlantic cultures!

I do not take issue with the good intentions of the early founders, nor do I infer in them evil and conscious motivations to oppress and dominate others. Yet the history of the United States has been the history of oppression and discrimination against racial/ethnic minorities and women. Western European cultures, which formed the fabric of the United States of America, are relatively homogeneous when compared not only with the rest of the world but also with the increasing diversity in this country. This Euro-American worldview continues to form the foundations of our educational, social, economic, cultural, and political systems. Its very invisibility allows us to deceive ourselves into believing that racism is greatly exaggerated, that good people do not discriminate, and that our institutions operate fairly and in an unbiased manner. Yet for White folks, such as you, overcoming racism and bias means making the invisible visible no matter how unpleasant. It means that White Euro-Americans must realize that they benefit not only from the many proud accomplishments of their ancestors but also from their shameful acts.

What You Can Do to Overcome Racism

Test your own attitudes and values in the following exercises.

Exercise Number 1

Ethnocentric monoculturalism has several components. The first characteristic is a strong belief in the superiority of your cultural heritage and country. In general, feeling good about your culture and the traditions of your society are imbued with a philosophy of life containing many values. These operate automatically in your life decisions.

Rate yourself on the following statements on a continuum from 1 being "disagree strongly" to 4 being "agree strongly." Write in the number that best fits your reaction.

Philosophical Values Inventory

1. Success in this society results from hard work. _____

2. People are masters of their own fate. _____

3. Immigrants to this country should assimilate and acculturate. We should be a melting pot. _____

4. America is the land of opportunity for all. _____

5. There is no better country to live in than the United States. _____

6. We are the most technologically advanced and developed nation in the world. _____

7. The most qualified person should get the job. _____

8. The cream always rises to the top. _____

9. We should be a color-blind nation. _____

10. Individualism and capitalism make for a better life. _____

Scoring Key: scores > 30 = strong positive adherence to U.S. cultural values and philosophy; scores = low positive endorsement of U.S. cultural values and philosophy; scores 21–29 = mixed valuation of U.S. cultural values and philosophy.

What score did you obtain on this instrument? Remember, scoring high or low is not necessarily good or bad. It simply identifies the values you consider important and those that you feel positively about. The problem comes when the basic assumptions related to these items are hidden from you and they are used to evaluate other groups as being good or bad, and desirable or undesirable. If this is the case, ethnocentric monoculturalism may become operative.

Exercise Number 2

Unmasking Assumptions and Values: Look at each of the ten statements in the philosophical values inventory. What basic value or assumption do they contain? Although some of these will be presented in the forthcoming chapters, try to make the assumptions more explicit. Remember, as long as these assumptions remain invisible, they control your assumptions and evaluations of others. Here are some hints for your work.

Possible Assumptions Inherent in Items

1. Success or failure is attributable to individual effort.

2. Outcomes in life are controllable.

3. Assimilation and acculturation are for Whites only.

4. Opportunity abounds in America for everyone.

5. The United States is the best country in the world.

6. Technology and science are desirable.

7. Merit is the key to advancement and success.

8. Competence will always be rewarded.

9. We are better off to eliminate racial distinctions because differences are divisive.

10. Individualism and capitalism are much better than collectivism and socialism.

Given these possible assumptions, can you present counterarguments? Would it surprise you that many people of color would take issue with these assumptions? What implications does this have for race relations? How might racial/ethnic minority groups feel oppressed by the operation of these assumptions in our society?

Exercise Number 3

Understanding the operation of oppression and ethnocentric mono-culturalism is well illustrated in three videos that are available in educational institutions and oftentimes in the public library. The following were produced by and can be obtained from the Television Race Initiative, sponsored by PBS.

1. *Blink*, by Elizabeth Thompson, is the story of racial hatred and violence as told through the eyes of Greg Withrow, once a fanatical White supremacist. It indicates how class differences and conflict serve to mask the effects of generational racial prejudice and violence.

2. *Of Civil Wrongs and Rights: The Fred Korematsu Story*, by Eric Paul Fournier, is the tale of Fred Korematsu, interned during World War II, and his battle with the U.S. Supreme Court. The story of civil injustice as manifested via ethnocentric monoculturalism is a study of the triumph of human dignity.

3. *In Whose Honor?* by Jay Rosenstein, is the story of Charlene Teters, a Spokane Indian, who struggles to make the public understand the demeaning use of Indian mascots and symbols for sports teams. Although the Washington Redskins, Atlanta Braves, and Cleveland Indians claim to honor Native Americans, Teters reveals the disrespect of cultural rituals and the devastating impact on Natives.

Try to view these films with others so they can be discussed as a group.

6

What Does It Mean to Be White?

What does being White mean?
  Have you ever asked yourself that question?
  If not, why haven't you?
  If you have, what was your answer?
  Recently, in preparation for a documentary on "The Invisibility of Whiteness," I posed this question to White strangers in the middle of downtown San Francisco. The following are some representative responses generated from the exercise.

Forty-Two-Year-Old White Businessman

Q: What does it mean to be White?

A: Frankly, I don't know what you're talking about!

Q: Aren't you White?

A: Yes, but I come from Italian heritage. I'm Italian, not White.

Q: Well then, what does it mean to be Italian?

A: Pasta, good food, love of wine (obviously agitated). This is getting ridiculous!

Themes: Denial or conflicted feelings about being White. Claims Italian heritage but is unable to indicate more than superficial understanding of ethnic meaning. Expresses annoyance at the question.

<u>*Twenty-Six-Year-Old White Female College Student*</u>

Q: What does it mean to be White?

A: Is this a trick question? . . . I've never thought about it. . . . Well, I know that lots of Black people see us as being prejudiced and all that stuff. I wish people would just forget about race differences and see one another as human beings. People are people and we should all be proud to be Americans.

Themes: Never thinks about being White. Defensive about prejudicial associations with Whiteness. Desires to eliminate or dilute race differences. Believes people are people and everyone should be proud to be American.

<u>*Sixty-Five-Year-Old White Male Retired Construction Worker*</u>

Q: What does it mean to be White?

A: That's a stupid question!

Q: Why?

A: Look, what are you . . . Oriental? You people are always blaming us for stereotyping and here you are doing the same to us.

Q: When you say "us," whom are you referring to?

A: I'm referring to Americans who aren't colored. We are all different from one another. I'm Irish but there are Germans, Italians, and those Jews. I get angry at the colored people for always blaming us. . . . When my grandparents came over to this country, they worked twenty-four hours a day to provide a good living for their kids. My wife and I raised five kids, and I worked every day of my life to provide for them. No one gave me nothing! I get angry at the Black people for always whining. . . . They just have to get off their butts and work rather than going on welfare. At least you people (reference to Asian Americans) work hard. The Black ones could learn from your people.

Themes: Believes question stereotypes Whites and expresses resentment with being categorized. Views White people as ethnic groups. Expresses belief that anyone can be successful if they work hard. Believes African Americans are lazy and that Asian Americans are successful. Strong anger directed toward minority groups.

Thirty-Four-Year-Old White Female Stockbroker

Q: What does it mean to be White?

A: I don't know (laughing), I've never thought about it.

Q: Are you White?

A: Yes, I suppose so (seems very amused).

Q: Why haven't you thought about it?

A: Because it's not important to me.

Q: Why not?

A: It doesn't enter into my mind because it doesn't affect my life. Besides, we are all individuals. Color isn't important.

Themes: Never thought about being White because it's unimportant. People are individuals and color isn't important.

These are not atypical responses given by White Euro-Americans when posed with this question. When I asked the same question to people of color, their answers tended to be more concrete.

Twenty-Nine-Year-Old Latina Administrative Assistant

Q: What does it mean to be White?

A: I'm not White, I'm Latina!

Q: Are you upset with me?

A: No . . . it's just that I'm light, so people always think I'm White. It's only when I speak that they realize I'm Hispanic.

Q: Well, what does it mean to be White?

A: Do you really want to know? . . . Okay, it means you're always right. It means you never have to explain yourself or apologize. . . . You know that movie *Love Is Never Having to Say You're Sorry?* Well, being White is never having to say you're sorry. It means you think you're better than us.

Themes: Strong reaction to being mistaken for being White. Claims that being White makes people feel superior and is reflected in their disinclination to admit being wrong.

Thirty-Nine-Year-Old Black Male Salesman

Q: What does it mean to be White?

A: Is this a school exercise or something? Never expected someone to ask me that question in the middle of the city. Do you want the politically correct answer or what I really think?

Q: Can you tell me what you really think?

A: You won't quit, will you (laughing)? If you're White, you're right. If you're Black, step back.

Q: What does that mean?

A: White folks are always thinking they know all the answers. A Black man's word is worth less than a White man's. When White customers come into our dealership and see me standing next to the cars, I become invisible to them. Actually, they may see me as a well-dressed janitor (laughs) or actively avoid me. They will search out a White salesman. Or when I explain something to a customer, they always check out the information with my White colleagues. They don't trust me. When I mention this to our manager, who is White, he tells me I'm oversensitive and being paranoid. That's what being White means. It means having the authority or power to tell me what's really happening even though I know it's not. Being White means you can fool yourself into thinking that you're not prejudiced, when you are. That's what it means to be White.

Themes: Being White means you view minorities as less competent and capable. You have the power to define reality. You can deceive yourself into believing you're not prejudiced.

Twenty-One-Year-Old Chinese American Male College Student (ethnic studies major)

Q: What does it mean to be White?

A: My cultural heritage class was just discussing that question this week.

Q: What was your conclusion?

A: Well, it has to do with White privilege. I read an article by a professor at Wellesley. It made a lot of sense to me. Being White in this society automatically guarantees you better treatment than minorities and unearned benefits and privileges. Having white skin means you have the freedom to choose the neighborhood you live in. You won't be discriminated against. When you enter a store, security guards won't assume you will steal something. You can flag down a cab without the thought they won't pick you up because you're a minority. You can study in school and be assured your group will be portrayed positively. You don't have to deal with race or think about it.

Q: Are White folks aware of their White privilege?

A: Hell no! They're oblivious to it.

Themes: Being White means having unearned privileges in our society. It means you are oblivious to the advantages of being White.

THE INVISIBLE WHITENESS OF BEING

The responses given by White Euro-Americans and persons of color are radically different from one another. Yet the answers given by both groups are quite common and representative of the range of responses my students give in my diversity and multicultural classes. White respondents would rather not think about their Whiteness, are uncomfortable or react negatively to being labeled "White," deny its importance in affecting their lives, and seem to believe that they are unjustifiably accused of being bigoted by virtue of being White.

Strangely enough, "Whiteness" is most visible when it is denied, when it evokes puzzlement or negative reactions, and when it is equated with normality. Few people of color react negatively when asked what it means to be Black, Asian American, Latino, or a member of their race. Most could readily inform the questioner about what it means to be a person of color. There seldom is a day, for example, in which I am not reminded of being racially and culturally different from those around me. Yet Whites often find the question about their Whiteness quite disconcerting and perplexing.

It appears that the denial and mystification of Whiteness for White Euro-Americans are related to two underlying factors. Let me use an analogy to make my points. First, most people seldom think about the air that surrounds them and how it provides an essential life-giving ingredient, oxygen. We take it for granted because it appears plentiful; only when we are deprived of it does it suddenly become frighteningly apparent.

Whiteness is transparent precisely because of its everyday occurrence, its institutionalized normative features in your culture, and the fact that you are taught to think of your lives as morally neutral, average, and ideal. As a person of color, I do not find Whiteness to be invisible because I do not fit the normative qualities that make it invisible. If I were a fish, oxygen would also be required for my survival. However, the medium to deliver it must be water, not air. As a person of color, I perceive the atmosphere that symbolically represents White culture as quite noticeable, and although it is nurturing to White Euro-Americans, it may prove toxic to my existence.

Second, Euro-Americans often deny that they are White, seem angered by being labeled as such, and often become very defensive. "I'm not White, I'm Irish." "You're stereotyping, because we're all different." "There isn't anything like a White race." In many respects, these statements have validity. I imagine that many of you have made similar statements at one time or another. Yet many of you would be hard-pressed to describe your Irish, Italian, German, or Norwegian heritage in any but the most superficial manner. One of the reasons is related to the processes of assimilation and acculturation. Although there are many ethnic groups, being White allows you to assimilate.

Even though persons of color are told to assimilate, this psychological process is meant for Whites only. Assimilation and acculturation are processes that assume a receptive society. For racial minorities, they are told in no uncertain terms that they are allowed only limited access to the fruits of our society. Consequently, the accuracy of whether Whiteness defines a race is largely irrelevant. What is more relevant is that Whiteness is associated with unearned privilege—advantages conferred on White Americans while excluding persons of color. It is my contention that much of the denial associated with being White is related to the denial of White privilege, a topic we will deal with in the next chapter.

PEOPLE OF COLOR UNDERSTAND WHITE PRIVILEGE BETTER THAN WHITES

Although asking White folks about their Whiteness may prove beneficial at some levels, accepting their answers as truth is unlikely to elicit a deeper understanding of racial reality. This is not meant as a put-down of you but acknowledges the fish-out-of-water analogy. To get at the issue of White privilege, it may be best to seek answers from persons of color. After all, if you want to understand oppression, should you ask the oppressor or the oppressed? If you want to learn about sexism, do you ask men or women? If you want to learn about racism, do you ask Whites or persons of color? If you want to understand homophobia, do you ask straights or gays? Studies support the contention that the most accurate assessment of bias comes not from those who enjoy the privilege of power but from those who are most disempowered.[1]

There are two basic assumptions that I make concerning the province of Whiteness. First, people of color understand White people better than White folks understand people of color. Although this statement is supported by studies, it is also something readily derived from common sense. People of color operate within a White world and are forced to operate within that context. We are taught your language, your history, your culture, your thoughts, and your feelings from the moment of our birth or from the time we arrive in the United States. We attend your all-White schools, are exposed to a Euro-American curriculum, work for White-controlled places of employment, and are subjected to a White justice system. We are also exposed to your biases and prejudices.

You, however, seldom have much experience with people of color. Though you may claim to have minority friends, you do not socialize together, nor do you have much intimate contact with persons of color once you leave your places of employment. Even though you may attend ethnic celebrations, dine in minority community restaurants to sample ethnic foods, or participate in fundraising for "good causes" related to ethnic arts and humanitarian goals, you often remain on the outskirts of the groups you hope to help or understand. You are acquainted with only the most superficial cosmetic workings of ethnic minority groups.

Therefore the knowledge base of racial minorities comes primarily from a distorted picture of persons of color picked up from the media and from an educational system that teaches you falsely that Columbus discovered America, the pioneers settled and tamed the West, and Christians civilized the heathens. Unlike your minority counterparts, your social, psychological, and economic survival is not based on the ability to understand minority groups. You have the privilege of disengaging from the minority community or minority individuals should you feel uncomfortable or tire of those associations. People of color do not enjoy that luxury!

This statement leads us to our second point, what Robert Terry calls "the parable of ups and downs."[2] The "ups" are in power and control, seldom worry about the "downs," are willing to allow some token downs to occupy moderate positions of influence, associate primarily with one another, and define the downs as less intelligent and capable. The downs spend time trying to explain their "downness" to the ups (who find it difficult to believe), are forced to justify their existence to the ups, and are constantly vigilant to the thoughts and actions of the ups. Terry states:

> The bad news is that when we're UP it often makes us stupid. We call that "DUMB-UPNESS." It's not because UPS are not smart. It's that UPS don't have to pay attention to DOWNS the way DOWNS have to pay attention to UPS. DOWNS always have to figure out what UPS are UP to. The only time UPS worry about DOWNS is when DOWNS get uppity, at which time they're put DOWN by the UPS. The UPS' perception is that DOWNS are overly sensitive; they have an attitude problem. It is never understood that UPS are underly sensitive and have an attitude problem.

White privilege allows those in power to impose their definitions of reality on persons of color, thereby invalidating their experiences. Let me give a personal example of what has been called *micro-invalidations* and *micro-aggressions*. Several years ago, I was invited to keynote a conference held in Washington, D.C. Arriving into Dulles Airport, I hailed a cab to reach my hotel. During the trip, the driver engaged me in an animated discussion of the recent Holyfield-Tyson heavyweight championship title fight. You will recall that the fight generated much public discussion because of the behavior of Mike Tyson, who bit off a piece of Holyfield's ear and was subsequently disqualified. After some friendly bantering about the incident, the cabdriver turned to me and stated, "You know, you speak excellent English—no accent at all!"

During the same evening, after delivering my keynote, I was surrounded by members of the audience who wanted to ask other questions or to meet me. One White woman shook my hand and complimented me on the frankness of my remarks. The following exchange ensued:

Q: Dr. Sue, where were you born?

A: Portland, Oregon.

Q: No, I meant, where were you really born?

A: Portland, Oregon.

Q: I'm sorry (smiling and chuckling) . . . I mean, what country were you born in?

A: The United States.

Q: Oh! (long pause) I hope you have a good visit . . . (appears embarrassed and scurries away).

Late that evening, on my way to dinner with a colleague, we entered a fancy restaurant in the downtown D.C. area. My friend Dave, a White Euro-American, and I approached the hostess. Even though I made the reservation and was standing in front of my friend, the hostess only acknowledged my presence with a quick smile but addressed Dave only. Upon being seated, the waiter quickly handed Dave the wine menu without hesitation. Dave was given the honor of the wine tasting as well and was the person to whom the waiter recounted the list of entrée specials that evening and to whom the waiter gave special attention (women are usually able to relate to this example better than men). Despite the fact that I had made the reservations and had intended to treat Dave that evening, the waiter obviously assumed that my friend was the person in charge. My only consolation that evening was that Dave also received the check!

How should one view these three incidents? Let me give you my interpretation. The cabdriver's compliments about my speaking excellent English and the female attendee's inquiry about my country of birth are reminders that many continue to view me as an alien in my own country. The mind-set evidenced by these two White individuals reveals a deeper, albeit unconscious, belief that people who are visible racial/ethnic minorities are foreigners. These two examples of micro-invalidations occur all too frequently: only White people speak good English and minorities are seen as immigrants, not legitimate citizens.

The "land of the free and the home of the brave" is the rightful place of White Euro-Americans only! "If you don't like it here, go back to China!" "If you don't like it here, go back to Africa!" "If you don't like it here, go back to Mexico." Why is it that we never hear the statement, "If you don't like it here, go back to Europe (England, Ireland, Germany, Italy, and so on)"? The answer is obvious: White Americans are the legitimate citizens of the United States, whereas people of color are only immigrants and transients (not rightful heirs).

In the parable of the ups and downs, I suppose many would consider my perception and subsequent interpretation to be that of a down. Yet Whites (ups) would have a different view of the entire situation: "The taxi driver was making polite conversation; shouldn't you have simply accepted the compliment without making such a big deal out of it?" "The female conference attendee was only being friendly. Why can't you accept the fact that she was sincerely interested in you and made a simple mistake?" Whereas my experiential reality tells me that stereotyping and bias are entering these inter-actions, Euro-Americans are denying and invalidating my beliefs and experiences. Who is correct? Before we try to answer that ques-tion, let us return to an analysis of my experiences with the restau-rant staff.

When the check came from our waiter, I took it from Dave's side of the table (he already knew I was treating him that evening). Throughout our restaurant experience, I did not share my impres-sions with Dave about what had transpired. At the end of the meal, however, I took the opportunity to make my thoughts known. I casually voiced my observations, expecting his understanding and support. These actions, I concluded, were evidence of unconscious and unintentional biases. To my surprise, my trusted colleague told me "not to be oversensitive" or "paranoid"! He invalidated my ex-perience and implied that I had misinterpreted the actions of the restaurant staff.

Our discussion of the matter became quite heated, with my accusing Dave of being insensitive and with his accusing me of be-coming obsessed with "your racism stuff." He even challenged me to ask our waiter over and raise the issues with him. I did not do this because it represented a no-win situation for me. If I asked him over, the waiter would certainly become defensive and deny the accusa-tion. Instead he would probably give many reasons for his behavior: Dave was seated closer to the waiter's station, so he got the menu first, or whoever was handed the wine list was a random process and had nothing to do with race. The quandary confronting persons of color is this: How does one prove unconscious and unintentional bias when the perpetrators truly believe their actions were moti-vated by other reasons?

What was even more disturbing was the behavior of my col-league. As I reflected on this incident, I became aware of my friend's behavior from the moment we had entered the restaurant until we finished the meal. He was oblivious to his preferential treatment, did not think twice about being acknowledged first, seemed to assume it was natural that he was the one in control, and enjoyed his treatment throughout the meal.

It suddenly dawned on me that unearned White privilege is seen as a source of strength and that it provides Euro-Americans with the permission to deny its existence and use it to dominate others! I realized the insidious and seductive effect of White privilege on White Euro-Americans. Why should you want to give up a world that is made for you? The benefits that accrue to you by virtue of your Whiteness serve to keep you satisfied and to enlist your unwitting complicity in maintaining unjust social arrangements. If Whiteness as unearned privilege and advantage is predicated on White supremacy and the oppression of people of color and if Whites benefit from it, then a frightening conclusion must be drawn: Whites have a stake in racism. To be White is to benefit from racism!

As a result, pointing out these unfair benefits to them evokes guilt and defensiveness: just as it did with my colleague. Incidents like this point to several disturbing aspects about White privilege: the group with power ultimately defines reality; even the most well-intentioned White persons, be they neighbors, coworkers, or friends, may have great difficulty seeing how their Whiteness enables them to benefit from the oppression of others; and micro-invalidations and micro-aggressions do great psychological harm to racial/ethnic minorities by denying their realities.

THE EQUATING OF WHITENESS WITH BEING HUMAN

Consider some of these views commonly expressed by White Americans.

- "People are people." "We are all human beings." "We're all Americans." "We're all the same under the skin."

- "We should emphasize our similarities, not our differences." "I don't see color at all." "We should be a color-blind society." "Everyone should be treated the same."

- "We should all learn to blend in." "If you immigrate to this country, you should assimilate and acculturate." "When in Rome, do as the Romans do." "We are a melting pot."

These statements reveal several distorted underlying thoughts and premises of current Euro-American thinking. First, there is an explicit assumption that people are people, and we are all human beings who share many similarities with one another. Second, differences are divisive, negative, and act as barriers to human relationships. Third, the ultimate goal of assimilation and acculturation is exemplified in the melting pot concept; everyone should desire and work to become the same. Like all familiar sayings that arise from history and age-old usage, there is much truth to them. The problem, however, lies in the dual but antagonistic meaning of these statements.

Yes, it is important to learn the language and culture of the society you reside in, but should it be at the cost of losing your cultural heritage and group identification? Yes, differences can prove divisive, but isn't it related more to how people perceive differences than to the differences themselves? For example, is skin color the problem or is it society's perception of color that is at fault? Yes, stressing commonalities is important, but does that mean differences are bad, deviant, or wrong? Yes, we are all the same under the skin and are all human beings, but why is being human defined from a White perspective? Yes, we should treat everyone the same, especially if differential treatment is discriminatory in nature. But can treating everyone the same result in unfairness? These are loaded questions when we probe into how Whiteness has infiltrated the answers. Let me briefly address the myth of the melting pot concept.

The Myth of the Melting Pot: For Whites Only

As mentioned earlier, prior to the formation of the United States of America, many White Europeans immigrated to this country to escape oppression in their own homelands. There are numerous reasons for this large-scale movement of people, but as more and more White immigrants came to the North American continent, the guiding principle of blending the many cultures together became codified into such terms as the *melting pot* and *assimilation and acculturation*. The most desirable outcome of this process was a uniform and homogeneous consolidation of cultures, in essence for everyone to become the same.

The ultimate hope was that these early immigrants would forge a new national identity in which there would exist a shared language, culture, and history. As the many groups began to coalesce, a general American culture began to emerge, which served as a reference point for immigrants and their children: the middle-class cultural patterns of largely Protestant, Anglo-Saxon, and White ethnics from European countries (Britain, Germany, Ireland, Italy, and so forth).

If there is anything that can be termed *White culture*, it is the synthesis of ideas, values, and beliefs coalesced from descendants of White European ethnic groups in the United States. Although I acknowledge the dangers and limitations of overgeneralizing, I think it's accurate to say that the European-American worldview can be described as possessing some of the following values and beliefs: rugged individualism, English language, mastery and control over nature, a unitary and static conception of time, religion based on Christianity, separation of science and religion, and competition. If the merging of European cultures into an American one was the result of assimilation and acculturation, you may ask, how is the melting pot concept a myth?

First, the melting pot seems to have been meant for White Euro-Americans only. A basic important tenet of assimilation and acculturation is the existence of a receptive society—that is, once a person has learned the language and customs of the group and now accepts those desired values, that person should become a full member of the society, with all the rights and privileges that follow. But despite how acculturated people of color become, they are never fully accepted by the dominant culture. Persons of color are constantly reminded of their inferior status and told in no uncertain terms that they are not welcomed or desired.

Although most White immigrant groups were confronted with prejudice and oppression when first arriving in America, their experiences in the United States have been qualitatively different from the experiences of non-White people. In a significant way, European immigrants over the past century and racial minorities face opposite cultural problems. The new Europeans were seen as not "American" enough, and they were pressured to give up their strange and threatening ways and to assimilate. Although it might have taken several generations, the offspring that were successful in this process could usually expect to become accepted citizens. African Americans, Asian Americans, and Latino Americans were second-class Americans. They were seldom welcomed and were told to "stay in your place" and were not allowed into the mainstream culture of the privileged, even when "fully acculturated."

Second, there is something insidiously pathological about the melting pot concept in its assumption that groups should assimilate. Bea Wehrly, a counselor-educator, states, "Cultural assimilation, as practiced in the United States, is the expectation by the people in power that all immigrants and people outside the dominant group will give up their ethnic and cultural values and will adopt the values and norms of the dominant society—the White, male Euro-Americans."[3]

Many psychologists of color, however, have referred to this process as *cultural genocide*, an outcome of colonial thought. Persons of color, more than their White brothers or sisters, are aware of the frightening implications of this expectation. Rather than a voluntary process, it is one of forced compliance, an imposition of the standards of the dominant group on the less powerful one. So the melting pot (a seemingly harmless and neutral concept) is in actuality a justification for political imposition. The European colonization efforts toward the Americas, for example, operated from the assumption that the enculturation of indigenous peoples was justified because European culture was superior. Forcing the colonized to adopt European beliefs and customs was seen as "civilizing" them.

In the United States, this practice was clearly seen in the treatment of Native Americans, where their lifestyles, customs, and practices were seen as backward and uncivilized, and attempts were made to make over the "heathens." Such a belief is also reflected in Euro-American culture and has been manifested in attitudes toward other racial/ethnic minority groups in the United States as well. "Racial/ethnic minorities would not encounter problems if they would just assimilate and acculturate." Unfortunately, the dilemma facing people of color is that of being sold a false bill of goods: "If you assimilate, you will bear the fruits of our society."

Third, many of my White brothers and sisters are fond of saying, "When in Rome, do as the Romans do. Shouldn't people who immigrate to this country or those who reside in it, acculturate? After all, when I travel abroad, I have to accept the ways of another country. This is only common sense." Let us, for the moment, assume that assimilation is desirable and that becoming a part of your country of residence is important. The question I ask you is this: Shouldn't we, therefore, all become Native Americans? Further, why aren't we?

Answering these two questions brings us into the realm of sociopolitical discussions of power. It is clear that assimilation is not a concept of equality, but one of power. Who has the power to determine the direction of assimilation? The early immigrants to the North American continents imposed their will on the indigenous people of the land. They had no inclination or thoughts to assimilate or acculturate to the customs and norms of the American

Indians. True assimilation and acculturation is based on an equal-status relationship: different groups have equal influence on one another.

In summary, the melting pot concept is a sham! It is a White Euro-American concept meant for Whites only. The myth of the melting pot is predicated on several false assumptions: a receptive society, an equal-status relationship between culturally different groups, and the society's morally and politically neutral character. In reality, the melting pot is a lie used to mask White supremacy and White privilege. Its goals are to perpetuate an imbalance of economic, social, and political power, to control the gateways to power and privilege, and to determine which groups will be allowed access to the benefits, privileges, and opportunities of the society. One might even conclude that the ideal of "melting" is to become as White as possible.

The Deception of Whiteness as a Universal Identity

"Derald, why are you always talking about cultural differences? When I look at you, I don't see you as an Asian American at all. You're no different than me. We're both Americans. Why can't we simply relate to one another as human beings? After all, there is only one race in this world. It's called the human race" (White Euro-American colleague).

I have increasingly come to understand the hidden meaning of these statements. In most cases, there is an implicit equation that a human being is the same as being White. The speaker is usually saying something like this: "Differences are divisive, so let's avoid acknowledging them and seek out our commonalities. I'm uncomfortable with racial differences, so let's pretend they don't exist. To keep me comfortable, just pretend to be White. Meet me on my ground and we'll do fine."

According to this stance, being a human being or an American is the same as being White. Whiteness surrounds the use of these terms, and on a conscious and unconscious level, there is an aversion to seeing race, color, or differences. Color blindness uses Whiteness as the default key and represents a racially motivated defense. The pretense by White Americans of not seeing color is motivated by the need to appear free of bias and prejudice, fears that what they say or do may appear racist, or an attempt to cover up hidden biases. To be color blind not only denies the central importance of racial differences in the psychological experience of minorities (racism and discrimination) but also allows the White person to deny how his or her Whiteness intrudes upon the person of color.

White teachers, for example, frequently admonish their African American students to "leave your cultural baggage at home and don't bring it into the classroom." They have little awareness that they bring their Whiteness into the classroom and operate from a predominantly White ethnocentric perspective. I wonder how they would react if I were to say, "Why don't you leave your White cultural baggage at home?" The invisible veil of Whiteness pervades the definitions of what it is to be a human being, to be just a person, and to be an American. The message from our society is that a human being is White!

In closing this chapter, I repeat the opening question: What does being White mean? How do you feel about the following statements?

To be White means

- To be socialized into a world of White supremacy

- To inherit and benefit from a world of White privilege

- To knowingly or unknowingly have a stake in the perpetuation of White racism

- To deny the reality of people of color and to define reality from a White perspective

- To be oblivious to your own biases and prejudices

- To be right

- To possess the luxury of not exploring yourself as a racial/cultural being

- To be able to equate a human being with being White

- To be an oppressor with the power to force your will on persons of color

More important, being a White American means living in a world of self-deception, a world in which your skin color is an asset and all other colors are a liability.

☞ What You Can Do to Overcome Racism

Try the following exercises.

Exercise Number 1

In the last chapter, you were asked to fill out a philosophical values inventory and to deconstruct the basic assumptions inherent in those ten statements. In light of our discussion on what it means to be White, reanalyze your answers. Have they changed significantly? In what ways have they changed? Are the assumptions clearer now? If you were to retake the inventory, would you answer differently?

Exercise Number 2

Try this exercise. Gather a group of friends, colleagues, or classmates together. Pose to them the following question: What does it mean to be White? It may be best to structure the activity before having the group answer. Divide the group up into smaller groups of three to five people.

Give them the following exercise to work on. As a group or individual, complete each phrase with as many responses as you can generate. Try your best to free-associate or brainstorm.

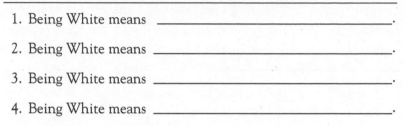

What Does It Mean to Be White?

1. Being White means _____.

2. Being White means _____.

3. Being White means _____.

4. Being White means _____.

1. Was this exercise difficult for you? Why?

2. What feelings or reactions did you experience? Why?

3. In looking at the responses, can you identify themes and their meanings?

4. What implications do these responses have for you as a White person?

5. If you are a person of color who participated in this exercise, what do the responses mean to you?

Exercise Number 3

Exercise number 2 can be used in any number of ways: to increase awareness of yourself as a racial/cultural being, to explore your own perceptions about other racial/cultural groups, and to become aware of how other groups perceive your group and themselves.

• *Objective one.* Increase awareness of yourself as a racial/cultural being. Each particular racial/ethnic group can do a similar exercise. For example, African Americans can do the same exercise by simply changing the question to "What does it mean to be Black/African American?" Asian Americans, Latino/Hispanic Americans, and Native Americans can do the same thing.

• *Objective two.* Each racial/ethnic group can also use this exercise for other groups. For example, Whites can fill in responses to "Being African American means . . . ," or African Americans can fill in responses to "Being Asian American means . . ."

- *Objective three*. This can be an eye-opening exercise for all groups. How do other groups perceive your group? For example, White Americans can profit from seeing how other racial/ethnic minority groups perceive them.

What Is White Privilege?

Now that you've read the analysis in the last chapter, it seems important to give you a concrete and formal definition of White privilege. White privilege is the unearned advantages and benefits that accrue to White folks by virtue of a system normed on the experiences, values, and perceptions of their group. White privilege automatically confers dominance to one group, while subordinating groups of color in a descending relational hierarchy; it owes its existence to White supremacy; it is premised on the mistaken notion of individual meritocracy and deservedness (hard work, family values, and the like) rather than favoritism; it is deeply embedded in the structural, systemic, and cultural workings of U.S. society; and it operates within an invisible veil of unspoken and protected secrecy.

THE DECONSTRUCTION
OF WHITE PRIVILEGE

White privilege continues to be a taboo topic for White people in our society. It is an unacknowledged secret that is overtly and covertly denied and protected through the use of self-deception. It protects White folks from realizing that they benefit from racism; as long as it is hidden from consciousness, you can maintain the illusion that you are not responsible for the state of race relations because you do not knowingly engage in racist behaviors. The invisible nature of White privilege serves to keep you comfortable, confident, and relatively oblivious to how it has the opposite effects on persons of color and how it harms, intimidates, oppresses, alienates, and makes for discomfort. Making the invisible visible is the first step toward dismantling the unfair and harmful nature of White privilege. The deconstruction of White privilege requires an analysis of its five basic components.

Automatically Confers Dominance Versus "I Made It on My Own"

Because you live in a society normed and standardized on White Euro-American values, most of the structures, policies, and practices of your institutions are situated in such a manner as to pave the road for White folks while creating obstacles for other groups. The United States continues to favor White, Eurocentric ways of thinking, acting, and being that do not match the reality of racial/ethnic minorities in this country. In this respect, two sides of the coin are present: on the one side, White privilege automatically confers dominance, control, and power to White Americans; and on the other side, it automatically disempowers and oppresses people of color. On the one side, it automatically advantages one group; and on the other side, it automatically disadvantages the other. Peggy McIntosh, a White Wellesley professor, in her article "White Privilege: Unpacking the Invisible Knapsack" makes this last point as well: "As a white person, I realized I had been taught about racism as something which puts others at a disadvantage, but had been taught not to see one of its corollary aspects, white privilege, which puts me at an advantage."[1]

I could probably get you to acknowledge that persons of color, women, gays and lesbians, disabled, and other marginalized groups are often put in a disadvantaged position. Most of you would further admit that being a racial minority in this society subjects you to second-class citizenship. Yet it is intriguing that most White Americans would actively deny that they are advantaged automatically by this state of affairs. In the last chapter, for example, the Black salesman who says that White customers avoid him, view him as a well-dressed janitor, and always corroborate the information he dispenses with White salespeople is clearly disadvantaged (may make fewer sales). In addition, he must constantly cope with internal feelings of micro-invalidation that strike at the core of his self-esteem. White salespeople, however, fail to see that the African American presence in the showroom actually ensures that the White salespeople will make more sales (advantaged). The fact that White customers will seek them out and treat them as more knowledgeable and trustworthy validates them as superior sales representatives. The deception resides in the belief by White folks that the superior outcome (sales) reflects their individual efforts ("I made it on my own").

Many other examples can be given. The hostess and waiter who treated my friend Dave as the person in control made him feel confident, validated, and strong; they left me, however, feeling invalidated, belittled, and frustrated. Not too long ago, a well-known Black actor, Danny Glover, with upraised hand, watched cabs whiz by him in New York City, only to stop to pick up White pedestrians a short distance down the block. Store clerks who examine the identification of Black customers attempting to cash checks with greater frequency and care than they do for White customers are another of the countless examples of such everyday occurrences.

Because White folks tend to see racism as individual acts of meanness, they seldom consider that an invisible system of White privilege has automatically conferred racial dominance to them; it advantages and validates you but disadvantages and invalidates persons of color. The system protects unfair individual acts of racial dominance by denying their race-related meanings and offering alternative explanations of reality grounded on a White Euro-American perspective.

Exists on White Supremacy Versus "I'm Not Responsible for the Oppression of Others"

White privilege could not exist without White supremacy. In Chapter Five, we defined White supremacy as a doctrine of racial superiority that justifies discrimination, segregation, and domination of persons of color based on an ideology and belief system that considers all non-White groups racially inferior. The examples just cited are clear: the Black salesperson is less competent and capable than White salespersons; my friend Dave is seen as superior and the one in charge; both the Black actor and the Black customers are less trustworthy and prone to potential crime. But White supremacy is more all-encompassing and insidious than these individual examples. They are manifested not just in individual acts of bias and discrimination but also in the very institutional and cultural foundations of our society.

White supremacy and oppression go hand in hand. In his book *Pedagogy of the Oppressed*, Paulo Freire describes the ability of the dominant culture to control minorities through the ability to define their identities and roles. Minorities are defined as criminals, delinquents, untrustworthy, less intelligent, lacking moral character, primitive, uncivilized, prone to violence, aliens, illegal immigrants, and so forth. The roles they occupy are servants, housekeepers, janitors, or generally lower positions in our society.[2]

To maintain the conformance and silence of persons of color, White supremacy as a doctrine and belief is instilled through education and enforced by biased institutional policies or practices that punish those who dare raise their voices in objection to their second-class status. You are taught that Columbus discovered America, that the pioneers settled the West, that the internment of Japanese Americans was based not on racism but on national security, and that the Lewis and Clark expedition gave the United States a claim to the Oregon territory. You are taught to believe in the notion that differences are deviant, in the myth of the melting pot, in positive portrayals of White folks, and in negative portrayals of minority groups. A particularly noteworthy and powerful example of White supremacy was the *manifest destiny* argument in the 1840s: all land owned by Native Americans was decreed by God to belong to White people.

The irrational sense of entitlement is a dominant feature of White privilege. And even more insidious are the benefits that accrue to White folks from these historical events. Unless you are the indigenous peoples of this land, you benefit from the past injustices of those who took the land from the early inhabitants. Pretense and mystification about these facts only serve to perpetuate White supremacy. When my White brothers and sisters, for example, claim that they should not be blamed for the past actions of their ancestors (taking land from American Indians, enslaving Blacks from Africa, segregating Latinos, and taking businesses from Japanese Americans during their internment), they miss a vital point. They still benefit from the past injustices of their forebears!

So even if you are completely free of conscious racial prejudices and desire to forgo or disclaim White privilege, you still receive benefits automatically, and unintentionally. If you profit from White privilege, whether knowingly or unknowingly, then you serve an oppressor role.

Predicated on Favoritism Rather Than Meritocracy Versus "The Most Qualified Ought to Get the Job"

In referring to President George W. Bush, syndicated columnist Molly Ivins once commented, "George Bush was born on third base and believes he hit a triple." This statement represents the ultimate illusion of meritocracy, that those who occupy a favored position achieved their status through individual effort and merit alone. If you accept the concept of White privilege, then you must entertain the more realistic notion that many White folks did not succeed because of superior ability but due to favoritism. George Bush did not become president of the United States solely because of hard work or superior intellect but was born into a privileged family, given favored status by a White society (all his life attending the best White schools, living in the best White neighborhoods, obtaining the best White jobs, having to only deal with a White police force, and so forth), and had opportunities not available to persons of color. Using the baseball analogy, whereas President Bush started on third base, most persons of color cannot even make it to the batter's box!

In the United States, our society arose from the cherished concept of *rugged individualism*; it is part of the Protestant ethic that believes there is a strong relationship between ability, effort, and success. People who succeed in our society work harder, have more skills, or are more competent. People who fail to achieve much in our society are seen as lazy, less capable, or less intelligent. Democratic ideals such as "equal access to opportunities," "everyone can make it in society if they work hard enough," "liberty and justice for all," "God helps those who help themselves," and "fulfillment of personal destiny" are culturally conditioned into your thinking. Behind these phrases lies one major assumption: everyone operates on a level playing field. In the presence of White privilege, however, the playing field is tilted in such a way as to be an uphill trek for persons of color and a downhill one for Whites.

The idea that you are the "master of your own fate" unfairly blames minority citizens for their inability to achieve more in this society. It fails to take into consideration the systemic forces of racism, prejudice, and discrimination and the operation of White privilege. People of color who suffer in poverty and unemployment and who live in the ghettos or barrios are blamed as suffering from deficiencies in their lifestyles or as possessing personal inadequacies.

Yet the reasons may not be internal but external: denied jobs, refused apartments, stopped-and-searched, declared uneducable, and told by a society that they are incompetent, untrustworthy, less intelligent, and culturally deprived. There is a triple purpose to the existence of White privilege: to advantage White Americans, to disadvantage persons of color, and to attribute causes to individual deficiencies, thereby relieving White society of responsibility for perpetuating inequality. The ultimate conclusion drawn from an understanding of White privilege is that your achievement as a White person may not be due so much to meritocracy as to unearned advantages and benefits. Likewise, the lower achievements of persons of color may not be due to personal inadequacies but to the unfair operation of White privilege.

Embedded Systemically in Society Versus "The Cream Always Rises to the Top"

I have already presented arguments challenging the belief that those with greater competence, superior skills, good work ethic, and high intellect automatically benefit from the rewards of society: "the cream always rises to the top." White privilege is not confined just to the individual perceptions or actions of Euro-Americans. Indeed, I have tried to make the case that institutional and cultural manifestations of White privilege are more harmful because they are systemically embedded in our society and have large-scale effects that dwarf individual actions of prejudice or discrimination.

Discriminatory benefits that favor Whites are seen in all facets of our society: bank lending practices, access to health care, housing, jobs, education, media portrayals, law enforcement, and court decisions that mete out justice. I am not talking about a few individuals hurt by White privilege but about literally millions of marginalized persons in our society. The existence of institutional racism shields the operation of White privilege through what I call standard operating procedures (SOPs), which represent the rules, habits, procedures, and structures of organizations that oppress persons of color while favoring Whites. Two examples can be given to illustrate the pervasiveness of White privilege. Let us trace the institutional and societal SOPs pertaining to Felix Hernandez (Latino) and Randall Clay Jr. (White), two hypothetical figures but very representative of situations that constantly present themselves in the work site.

The Case of Felix Hernandez

Born and raised in the barrios of Los Angeles, Felix is the eldest of six children, whose mother and father migrated from Mexico to the United States several years before his birth. Both parents have no more than a fifth-grade education; the father works as a laborer and the mother as a housekeeper. Attempts to better their economic situation by trying to start a landscaping business met with failure, especially because banks would not lend Mr. Hernandez the necessary start-up funds. The father was considered not creditworthy, and the bank would not accept their home as collateral; it was in a neighborhood that seemed immune to the housing-appreciation boom in Los Angeles.

From the age of twelve, Felix worked at different odd jobs to help pay the mortgage and support the family. In addition to working part-time throughout middle and high school, he had financial responsibilities that extended his community college education to four years. Because he came from a poor community, the schools he attended were considered among the worst in the state; there was a high turnover rate of teachers and students, testing scores were low, physical facilities were in bad need of repair, school supplies and computers were nearly absent, and both delinquency and truancy were high.

In addition, Felix was exposed to a curriculum that seldom portrayed his group positively but was strong in reflecting the contributions, achievements, heritage, and cultures of White America. Oftentimes Felix found himself resentful and alienated from the material. Worst yet, he expended great psychological efforts to fight off viewing himself and his group as inferior.

At a young age, he was labeled a "yellow bird" by teachers and placed into special classes that were more custodial than educational. Another group of students were labeled "blue birds" and tracked into college prep course work. When Felix's mother observed that most of the students in the yellow-bird track were Brown or Black and nearly all those in the blue birds were White, she strenuously objected. The school psychologist attempted to appease her by administering several standardized IQ tests. The results, according to the psychologist, revealed that Felix was actually worse than expected. His scores were consistent with students in educable mentally retarded classes. From that point on, teachers expected little from Felix.

Despite his inferior education, Felix graduated from junior college, received a bachelor's degree in business from a four-year state college, and obtained an MBA at the age of thirty-five from a relatively unknown private school that many considered a "diploma mill." He was the first and only one in his family to obtain a college education and an advanced degree. He has been employed for the past five years as a project manager for a small computer software firm operated by Taiwanese-born partners.

The Case of Randall Clay Jr.

Born into an upper-middle-class family in Los Angeles, Randall Clay is the eldest of three children. His father was employed as a middle manager for a major technology company prior to starting his own software-computing firm. In her former life, Mrs. Clay was an elementary school teacher but is now a full-time homemaker. Mr. Clay credits his successful rise in business to hard work, good planning, and business acumen. After obtaining his bachelor's from the University of California-Los Angeles (UCLA), he saved money and purchased a fixer-upper in an affluent neighborhood of Los Angeles and saw his equity appreciate at an astounding pace. Years later, he used his home as collateral for a major loan from the bank to start his own business. Because of his high income, savings, and the location of his home, Mr. Clay was considered an excellent credit risk by the bank.

As a youngster, Randall attended the best public schools in Los Angeles; there was no formal tracking, the high school prided itself in producing college-bound graduates, teachers seldom left the district, student dropout rates were low, and the student body was relatively homogeneous (few students of color attended). The physical surroundings were more like a college campus, supplies and computer equipment were plentiful, and teaching was considered superior. Randall could relate well to the primarily Euro-American curriculum, never felt alienated, and worked hard throughout the high school years. Although he had considered a part-time job to increase discretionary funds for social activities, his father always stated, "School is your job; . . . just get a good education" and subsequently increased Randall's allowance.

Teachers seldom doubted Randall's intellectual abilities. Counselors gave him vocational and career advice, recommended his taking advanced placement (AP) classes, and even helped him select appropriate colleges. Though Randall received multiple offers from top-tier colleges, he chose to attend his father's alma mater, UCLA, majoring in business administration. He finished in four years and then attended the University of California-Berkeley, where he obtained an MBA at the age of twenty-five. Upon Randall's graduation, Mr. and Mrs. Clay expressed admiration for their son's accomplishments and praised Randall for his dedication and hard work. During Randall's job search, Mr. Clay had simply placed a call to colleagues at his former place of employment. Within a week after Randall's interview with the company, he was hired into a middle-management position at a high starting salary.

Afterword

Imagine that the lives of both of these men intersected several years later. In their aspirations to move up the career ladder, Felix and Randall applied for the director's position with a large nationally known Silicon Valley computer company. Though both were on the shortlist, the company offered the position to Randall because of his impressive academic credentials and the institutions he had attended, because of his greater experience in working for a "big national firm," because he seemed skilled in being able to supervise large groups of employees, because he "fit in better" with the corporate culture, because he had better letters of reference, and because he appeared, despite his youth, more accelerated than other candidates.

Although a few were impressed with Felix, the interviewers felt that he would have difficulty fitting into their corporate culture; despite his excellent grades, several questioned the quality of his education, his "small-time" experience in a local firm, and the apparent lack of leadership experience.

Did the "cream rise to the top"? That's an important question for you to ask. Certainly, if you were to inspect the résumés of both men, Randall Clay would appear to be clearly the superior candidate. He went to more competitive schools, earned better grades, took a harder curriculum (AP courses), finished his education at a faster pace, earned his MBA from a nationally renowned institution, had more work experience with a multinational corporation, supervised many more employees, and had greater work responsibilities.

In contrast, Felix Hernandez went to schools that had poor academic reputations, received mediocre grades, did not take AP courses in high school (none were offered), obtained his master's degree from a nationally unranked professional school, required an above-average amount of time to complete higher education, and his work experience was limited to a local start-up company. Indeed, as the project manager, Felix supervised only three employees on his team and did lack experience in supervising a large labor force.

What are hidden in the analysis of the résumés are the SOPs (institutional and societal policies, programs, practices, and structures) that have disadvantaged Felix and advantaged Randall. The SOPs may be applied equally to all groups but serve to maintain the status quo.

- Systemic societal forces that produce segregation, allowing only certain groups to purchase homes in affluent neighborhoods, resulting in differential worth of real estate

- Bank lending practices that consider creditworthiness on the basis of location, inevitably discriminating against minority communities

- Inequitable school financing in which property taxes of wealthy communities produce greater educational resources than poorer communities

- Segregated schools that dispense inferior education to one group, but advantaged education to another

- Biased curricula, textbooks, and materials that affirm the identity of one group while denigrating others

- Educational testing that is normed and standardized on a White-middle-class population, resulting in culturally biased test instruments used to track minority students into non-college-bound classes

- Teachers and counselors with expectations, attitudes, and racial perceptions that result in beliefs that students of color are less capable, often resulting in a self-fulfilling prophesy among minorities that it is true

- School tracking systems that may unfairly perpetuate inequities in education

- Hiring policies and practices that utilize the "old boy's network" to recruit and hire prospective employees

I therefore ask the question again: Did the "cream rise to the top"? It would seem from this analysis that another argument can be made. In light of the numerous hurdles placed in the path of Felix, his achievements can only be considered laudatory. And although Randall was obviously bright and hardworking, his trek to the top was paved with many advantages; foremost among them is a society structured in such a way as to benefit Whites.

The Unspoken and Protected Secret Versus "We Should Be a Color-Blind Nation"

The "invisible Whiteness of being" maintains its viability precisely because it is a protected and seldom spoken secret. In 1972, Ralph Ellison's book *Invisible Man* described the *invisible man syndrome*, where racial issues and color are diluted, ignored, or considered irrelevant.[3] When originally formulated, the concept of a color-blind society was seen as the answer to discrimination and prejudice: Martin Luther King, for example, advocated judging people not by the color of their skin but by their internal character.

Many White Americans, however, have distorted or conveniently used color blindness as a means of color denial or more accurately *power* denial. An understanding of White privilege ultimately unmasks a dirty secret kept hidden by White Americans: much of what they have attained is unearned, and even if they are not overtly racist, Whites cannot choose to relinquish benefits from it. In his own racial awakening, Robert Jensen, a White professor of journalism writes:

> I know I did not get where I am by merit alone. I benefited from, among other things, white privilege. That doesn't mean that I don't deserve my job, or that if I weren't white I would never have gotten the job. It means simply that all through my life, I have soaked up benefits for being white. I grew up in fertile farm country taken by force from non-white indigenous people.

I was educated in a well-funded, virtually all-white public school system in which I learned that white people
like me made this country great. There I also was taught
a variety of skills, including how to take standardized
tests written by and for white people.

There certainly is individual variation in experience.
Some white people have had it easier than me, probably
because they came from wealthy families that gave them
even more privilege. Some white people have had it
tougher than me because they came from poorer families. White women face discrimination I will never
know. But, in the end, white people all have drawn on
white privilege somewhere in their lives.[4]

Getting White privilege out of the closet is difficult and resisted
for several reasons.

• *The white-out phenomenon.* White privilege mimics the norms
of fairness, justice, and equity by whiting out differences and perpetuating the belief in sameness. The denial of power imbalance,
unearned privilege, and racist domination is couched in the rhetoric
of equal treatment and equal opportunity. As mentioned earlier, the
programs, policies, and practices of institutions may be monocultural. They are applied equally to all groups, so organizations and
policymakers believe they are not discriminating and are being emi-
nently fair. Educational policy regarding IQ testing, use of college
admission test scores, and hiring and promotion criteria in employment decisions are applied equally across all groups. As in the case
of Felix and Randall, however, they have damaging differential
impact on persons of color. Unfortunately, the belief in equal treatment masks the fact that the universal standards are White.

• *Pretense of innocence.* As long as White Americans view
racism, unfairness, and discrimination as residing in individual acts
and believe that they did not overtly discriminate or consciously
condone private acts of racism, they can alleviate guilt and respon-

sibility for its existence. "I didn't own slaves; don't blame me for the sins of my forefathers," and "I didn't take part in the internment of the Japanese Americans" are prototypical statements of this posture. The pretense of innocence is a conspiracy among Whites to deny the pain and suffering experienced by people of color, but more important, it's to absolve them of personal responsibility for perpetuating injustice and allow them to remain passive and inactive. Viewing racism as not deeply embedded in our culture and institutions but only in individual manifestations allows Whites to pretend that racism does not exist on a systemic level. They need not take collective action and risk possible censure from family, friends, and coworkers for revealing the ugly secret of White privilege.

• *Living a false White reality.* White Americans have power precisely because they are able to define reality. The authors of a report released in April 2001, *Off Balance: Youth, Race, and Crime in the News,* analyzed broadcast, magazine, and newspaper coverage of crime reporting from 1910 to 2000.[5] Blacks are overrepresented in the media as criminals and underrepresented as victims in proportion to the true crime statistics for their race. This imbalance in coverage creates a situation whereby persons of color are inaccurately perceived, whereas Whites are viewed as law-abiding. Indeed, the term *young Black male* has become synonymous with criminal.

Unfortunately, the reality that Whites live is a false one, clouding their ability to see themselves or their group in an accurate manner. The school shootings of children in Colorado, Oregon, Arkansas, Pennsylvania, Mississippi, and California have made Littleton and Santee household names. After the killing of two White children by a classmate, the mayor of Santee, California, stated, "We're a solid town, a good town, with good kids, a good church-going town, an All-American town." Interestingly, this reaction typifies the puzzlement of many White communities. "How could such a dreadful thing happen in our community?"

A recent FBI report indicates that there is no profile of a school shooter. Yet persons of color see a clear profile. These shootings of students by fellow classmates have occurred in primarily White suburbs and rural communities. White boy after White boy after White boy have been the shooters. There is plenty of violence in urban communities and schools, but it appears that White America can only see crime in minority communities. Tim Wise, a Nashville-based writer, reports the following facts: White children, not those in the urban ghetto, are most likely to use drugs. They are seven times more likely to use cocaine than Blacks, eight times more likely to have smoked crack, ten times more likely to have used LSD, seven times more likely to have used heroin, twice as likely to binge drink, and twice as likely to drive drunk. White youth, ages twelve to seventeen, are more likely to sell drugs and twice as likely to bring a weapon to school as Black males![6] Few Whites are aware of these statistics. It is obvious that White denial allows one to see White communities as healthy while minority communities are labeled easily as violent, dangerous, and infused with crime.

A LIST OF WHITE PRIVILEGE ADVANTAGES AND DISADVANTAGES

Having defined White privilege, its meaning, and its function in Euro-American society, a more specific list may help you understand precisely how it may be manifested in your everyday reality. The following is a list compiled from the writings of White women and men whose personal journey to understanding and combating racism resulted in an awakening to their own White privilege: Peggy McIntosh, Sara Winter, Robert Jensen, and Mark Maier.[7]

1. *Advantage:* When you attend school, you can be assured that your race will be portrayed positively; the curriculum will reflect your

heritage and contributions to your nation; you will be told that you made this nation what it is today. (*Disadvantage:* The contributions of racial/ethnic minorities are often ignored in the educational literature; they are portrayed negatively as problem people or in stereotypical fashion.)

2. *Advantage:* When you hail a cab, you don't have to worry about not being picked up because of your race, let alone even think about this matter. (*Disadvantage:* A recent study conducted by *Dateline* indicates that 25 percent of New York City taxi drivers will not pick up Black customers.)

3. *Advantage:* When you go for a job interview, you never worry or even think about how being White may be held against you. You are assured that employers will not presume you are less competent or capable because of your race. (*Disadvantage:* Studies support the fact that persons of color are often viewed as suspect in their qualifications, whereas Whites are not subjected to a similar evaluation because of their skin color.)

4. *Advantage:* When you read a magazine or newspaper or watch television, you are likely to see people of your race widely represented in different roles and at different levels. (*Disadvantage:* Minorities are consistently underrepresented in media; when portrayed, they usually are in lower-level positions.)

5. *Advantage:* When you apply for a loan, write a check, or use your credit card, you can count on your skin color not to work against you in determining reliability or creditworthiness. (*Disadvantage:* Persons of color are often suspected as poor credit risks, as not having financial resources, or of being less trustworthy in monetary transactions.)

6. *Advantage:* You will not, as a White person, feel obligated or be expected to "give something back to the White community" or to extend yourself outside work hours to bring others of your race into the opportunity structure. (*Disadvantage:* Persons of color are often singled out as being responsible for their group or as

representatives of their race. As a result, they are saddled with the additional expectation that they are obligated to "give back" to the community.)

7. *Advantage:* You can generally purchase a home in most neighborhoods and feel welcomed or at least be treated neutrally. (*Disadvantage:* Even with the financial means, many persons of color are made to feel unwelcome in many neighborhoods—they represent the wrong elements, will increase crime, or will lower the market value of homes in the neighborhood.)

8. *Advantage:* If a traffic cop stops you while driving, you can be pretty sure you were not targeted or profiled because of being White. (*Disadvantage:* Recent results of a New Jersey investigation of traffic stops suggest that racial profiling is all too prevalent. Among African Americans and Latinos, being stopped by police is called DWB, or "driving while Black or Brown.")

9. *Advantage:* You can arrange, most of the time, to be among people of your own race. (*Disadvantage:* White folks have the luxury of arranging to be among members of their own race, to disengage from other racial groups, and to avoid dialogue or confrontation. People of color have no such luxury. They operate in a society that is made for and run by White folks.)

10. *Advantage:* You can choose public accommodation without fearing that people of your race cannot get in or will be mistreated. (*Disadvantage:* Traveling throughout the country and seeking stays in local motels or even larger hotels, many people of color continue to be denied accommodations or made to feel unwelcome.)

11. *Advantage:* You can choose blemish cover or bandages in "flesh" color and have them more or less match your skin. (*Disadvantage:* This is a statement that brings home the point of how our society is structured and created primarily for Whites only.)

12. *Advantage:* You can remain oblivious of the language and customs of persons of color, who constitute the world's majority, without feeling in your culture any penalty for such oblivion. (*Dis-*

advantage: Persons of color cannot survive in this society by ignoring the language and customs of White folks. They are constantly vigilant and painstakingly aware of how their survival means understanding the minds and institutions of their oppressors.)

13. *Advantage:* You can criticize our government and talk about how much you fear its policies and behavior without being seen as a cultural outsider. (*Disadvantage:* Any critical statements by persons of color toward the United States are likely to be seen as coming from a foreigner. "If you don't like it here, go back to China, Mexico, or Africa.")

14. *Advantage:* When you enter a department store and browse through sales items, you can be assured that the security guards will not pay extra attention to your presence or follow you throughout the store. (*Disadvantage:* Persons of color are more likely than Whites to be perceived as criminals or "up to no good.")

15. *Advantage:* When you look at people on the organizational hierarchy, you are likely to see many others of your own race. People like you will be represented at higher levels. (*Disadvantage:* In an organizational hierarchy, people of color are more likely to occupy the lower rungs of the employment ladder.)

16. *Advantage:* You are seldom likely to be mistaken for a janitor. (*Disadvantage:* Persons of color are seldom perceived as leaders, as authoritative and knowledgeable.)

17. *Advantage:* You can purchase posters, postcards, picture books, greeting cards, dolls, toys, and magazines featuring people of your race. (*Disadvantage:* White Euro-American society continues not to reflect social and demographic reality.)

18. *Advantage:* When you hunt for an apartment, apply for a job, or seek admission to a club, you don't have to worry that your race will make you appear threatening. (*Disadvantage:* Again, persons of color are more likely to be perceived as untrustworthy.)

19. *Advantage:* You can criticize the United States government or its various institutions without fear that you will be perceived as

a foreign subversive or radical who is intent on overthrowing the government. (*Disadvantage:* Because persons of color are often perceived as aliens to begin with, voicing dissatisfaction with the country reinforces the belief that they are subversives.)

20. *Advantage:* The ultimate White privilege, however, is your ability to acknowledge your unearned privileged status but at the same time ignore its meaning. (*Disadvantage:* The ultimate White hypocrisy is to recognize that your privileged position was unfairly earned on the backs of minorities but to ignore its meaning. This, perhaps, is the most frustrating issue confronting people of color. Why, if you recognize White privilege, do you continue to do nothing?)

What You Can Do to Overcome Racism

Try the following exercises.

Exercise Number 1

Do you benefit from White privilege? Take the following inventory. Mark each of the following statements "true" or "false."

White Privilege Inventory	True	False
1. I can obtain legal or medical help without my race working against me.		
2. I am seldom placed in a position where I am asked to speak for my race.		
3. If I want, I can always arrange to be in the company of people of my race.		
4. When I enter a department store to shop, I can be assured that security guards will not follow me or suspect me of shoplifting.		

White Privilege Inventory	*True*	*False*
5. Store personnel will not be suspicious of my financial resources when I cash a check or use my credit card because of my race.	_____	_____
6. When I am stopped by a traffic officer, I never worry that racial profiling was involved.	_____	_____
7. I never worry whether my children will be given curricular material that show people of my race or if people of my race will be portrayed positively.	_____	_____
8. The person in charge is generally a person of my race.	_____	_____
9. Coworkers will never suspect that I obtained my job because of my race rather than my good qualifications.	_____	_____
10. If I am loud in public or disturb the peace, my race is never put on trial.	_____	_____

1. If you marked most of these to be true, you are the recipient of White privilege. What does that mean for you?

2. As we did in the last section of this chapter, for each statement identify the advantages that you experience because of your Whiteness. Now outline the disadvantages that people of color suffer because of White privilege.

Exercise Number 2

This chapter identified five components of White privilege: it (1) automatically confers dominance to one group, (2) owes its existence to White supremacy, (3) is premised on individual meritocracy rather than favoritism, (4) is embedded in the systemic workings of U.S. society, and (5) operates within an invisible veil.

In the cases of Felix Hernandez and Randall Clay Jr., we outlined how White privilege is embedded in the systemic workings of society, characteristic number four. As an exercise, can you do the same for the other four components? The other four components are listed in one column. Now how do they apply to both individuals? Use the following outline to discuss and record how White privilege is operating.

Components of White Privilege	Felix Hernandez	Randall Clay Jr.
1. Automatically confers dominance		
2. Manifested in White supremacy		
3. Based on favoritism instead of meritocracy		
4. Invisible		

Exercise Number 3

Think about these questions or discuss them with others.

1. If you accept the fact that White privilege exists, how does that make you feel? Are you guilty about it? Do you feel uncomfortable?

2. Realizing that White privilege exists, what does that mean for you?

3. If you believe that White privilege is unfair and a travesty to society, what do you plan to do about it? Try to list the actions you would take to dismantle White privilege. Does the task seem overwhelming? Are you having difficulty coming up with solutions?

4. What does giving up White privilege mean? Is it even possible for a White person to "disown" White privilege? What does this mean for you?

Part II
Overcoming the Problem

How Do You Develop a Nonracist White Identity?

When my White students begin to really grasp the meaning of White privilege and how thoroughly it is entrenched in our everyday lives, they often ask me what can be done to overcome or minimize it. This is a very difficult question to answer because it requires not only massive societal changes but also much personal work and commitment. Fortunately, recent work by psychologists on *White racial identity development* provides some fruitful answers. On a personal level, the question is, How do you develop a non-racist White identity.

To help answer this question, let us look at the case of Miriam Cohen (not real name), a participant in one of my workshops who submitted the following personal journey of her racial awakening. Much of the dialogue has been reconstructed and altered slightly, but it captures the essence of her reported dilemmas.

The Case of Miriam Cohen

Miriam Cohen, a young and single White teacher, had recently graduated from a prestigious eastern university in teacher education. Because of her expressed desire to teach disadvantaged students, she accepted a teaching position in an inner-city school district that included a heavy concentration of low-income African American students. Some of her White friends had suggested that she accept one of numerous other positions she had been offered, particularly one in an affluent community with a reputation for superb schools. Miriam decided against going elsewhere, because "these people need help." Her professors commended her public service interest and social justice commitment to helping minorities. Within a period of several months, Miriam had two rather disturbing experiences in working at the high school. The first involved the parents of a Black male student who was failing to turn in homework assignments and seemed resistant to her authority. Miriam had asked for a parent-teacher conference to discuss their son's problem. Needless to say, she found it extremely difficult to establish rapport with them. Not only did they seem to minimize the issues regarding their son, but they seemed to view her with suspicion. They implied that Miriam could not possibly understand them or their son because she was White. During the session, the husband mentioned that he played in a local jazz band, and his wife often acted as a backup singer.

As Miriam's undergraduate major had been dramatic arts (she even had a course on the contributions of Black entertainers), she saw this as a good opportunity to establish a sense of commonality with the parents. She directed the conversation toward African American movie stars, singers, and athletes. At this juncture, the wife became noticeably agitated and stated, "Stop that shit, honey! You're not Black and you never will be."

Miriam was surprised at the wife's reaction and apologized to the couple for offending them. She tried to explain that she was just trying to establish a relationship with them and that she was not unfamiliar with minority experiences. "After all, I'm a Jew, and I know what oppression is. I'm also a woman, like you, and have experienced sex discrimination as well." At this point, the couple rose from their seats, stated that they were wasting their time, and left the room.

The second incident occurred with an African American male substitute teacher who taught in the classroom next to her. He was a handsome, muscular individual who obviously prided himself on his physical appearance. He had been divorced from his wife for nearly a year and obviously found Miriam attractive. One afternoon, after classes, they shared a cup of coffee in the faculty lounge, where they struck up a friendly conversation. He seemed very warm, open, and sincere in explaining his recent divorce and the pain he had to endure. He had been married to a White woman, who he claimed had "used him" and who he had discovered was a racist. He described a domestic situation in which his ex-wife had brought unwarranted charges of domestic violence against him, and he was forced to plead guilty in exchange for probation and counseling because "those Whites will give me a bum rap if it goes to trial."

Obviously emotional and agitated, the teacher blurted out, "All of you Whites are racist. What do you care about me?" At these statements, Miriam tried to reassure the teacher that not all Whites are bigoted, that she cared about Black people, and that she wouldn't be teaching at the school unless she cared. The anger and agitation seemed to drain from the teacher when this was said, and he seemed to open up more fully.

He talked about his boyhood experiences of discrimination, how his ex-wife had hurt him, how he couldn't find a permanent teaching job because of racism, and how he felt so lonely and isolated. "Sometimes I feel like I'm worthless, that no one cares about me. What woman would want an unemployed Black man?" Again, Miriam reassured the Black teacher that everyone was worthwhile and that he was no different.

Looking up at Miriam, the teacher asked, "Do you really mean that?" Miriam responded in the affirmative. This was followed by a series of other questions, "Do you think women would find me attractive? Do you find me attractive?"

Although Miriam answered all of these questions honestly, she felt very uncomfortable at this point. She was totally unprepared for what happened next. The teacher moved his chair next to her, placed his right hand on her knee, and asked, "Do you really like me?" Miriam recalls that she felt frozen and trapped. She did not answer the question but firmly removed the hand from her knee and shifted her chair away. At these actions, the following exchange took place.

Black Teacher: You Whites are all the same, say one thing, mean another! You're just another racist bitch!

Miriam: I'm not racist. This is . . . we're teaching colleagues.

Black Teacher: You think I'm hitting on you. Well, maybe I am. What's wrong with a man liking a woman? I'm not against interracial relationships, but you seem to be!

Miriam: There's nothing wrong with it, but our relationship is professional. (Stammering) I, I, mean . . . I mean, it would not be collegial.

Black Teacher: (lowering voice) You mean if we weren't colleagues you would consider going out with a Black man?

Miriam: Yes, well . . . ah (stammering), ah, maybe.

Black Teacher: Well, my teaching assignment for this school will end next week when the regular teacher returns. We can get it on then, OK?

This case raises some rather complex questions that are often reenacted in one form or another in interracial relationships. I wouldn't be surprised if you have experienced similar situations. Miriam's stage of White racial identity clouds her ability to fully understand how she also contributed to the misunderstandings that developed between her and the Black parents and between her and the Black male substitute teacher.

An understanding of Miriam's dilemma can be distilled into two main questions: Who is Miriam Cohen as a racial/cultural being? and What does being White mean to Miriam? It is my contention that Miriam's unresolved racial biases and prejudices, cultural conditioning, and the invisibility of her Whiteness are culprits intruding into her relationships with people of color. They are also representative of the dilemma faced by many White Americans in the United States. Let us look more closely at Miriam's predicament and try to draw out some lessons in the hope of improving our understanding of race relations.

First, it is clear that Miriam's image of herself is that of an unbiased individual who does not harbor racist thoughts and feelings; she perceives herself as working toward social justice and possesses a conscious desire to better the life circumstances of those less fortunate than she is. As evidence of her commitment, she chose employment linked to an inner-city school district with a heavy concentration of racial/ethnic minority students. These are certainly admirable qualities and on the surface are quite commendable. Yet Miriam seems to evidence a naïveté that I have observed in many younger White Euro-Americans. She is what many persons of color would call a "White liberal," motivated by "White guilt." She fails to understand the almost paternalistic manner in which she wants to "help these people." I seriously question whether she is free of personal biases and prejudices and how much she really understands her own motives and behavior.

Second, being a White person in this society means chronic exposure to ethnocentric monoculturalism as manifested in White supremacy. It is difficult, if not impossible, for you not to inherit the racial biases, prejudices, misinformation, deficit portrayals, and stereotypes of your forebears. To believe that you are somehow immune from inheriting such aspects of White supremacy is to be arrogant, naïve, or engaging in self-deception. Such a statement is not intended to assail Miriam's integrity but to suggest that she too has been victimized. It is clear that no one was born wanting to be racist, sexist, or homophobic. Misinformation is not acquired by free choice but imposed through a painful process of cultural conditioning. Although Miriam is not consciously aware of her own biases and preconceived notions regarding African Americans, they are definitely affecting her ability to be an effective teacher and a colleague with people of color.

Her decision to teach minority students, her misguided attempts to form rapport via reference to Black entertainers, and her inability to deal with the prove-to-me-you're-not-a-racist game all seem to support a *reaction formation*—an attempt to unconsciously deny aspects of her potential biases. She is so wound up in living out her "unbiased" image of herself that she allows her hang-ups to affect her relationships. The ultimate fear confronting Miriam is to be accused of being racist. As a result, her behavior and reactions are guided by an attempt to deny this possibility, at the cost of being inauthentic. One lesson I suggest is this: as long as you deny your own racism or deny that racism exists, then the greater the difficulty in developing an authentic and positive White identity.

Third, if Miriam and other White folks are to become authentic racial beings, they must free themselves from the cultural conditioning of their past and move toward the development of a nonracist White identity. As we have seen from the last few chapters, many of you seldom consider what it means to be White in our society. Such a question is vexing to you because you seldom think of race as belonging to you, nor do you think of the privileges that come your way by virtue of your white skin. Charles Ridley, an African American psychologist, points out the psychological process involved in this self-deception: "Unintentional behavior is perhaps the most insidious form of racism. Unintentional racists are unaware of the harmful consequences of their behavior. They may be well intentioned, and on the surface, their behavior may appear to be responsible. Because individuals, groups, or institutions that engage in unintentional racism do not wish to do harm, it is difficult to get them to see themselves as racists. They are more likely to deny their racism."[1]

I do not wish to appear harsh or accusatory, but Miriam appears to be an unintentional racist: she is unaware of her biases, prejudices, and discriminatory behaviors; she perceives herself as a moral, good, and decent human being and finds it difficult to ever see herself as racist; she does not have a sense of what her "Whiteness" means to her; and her teaching and interpersonal relationships with people of color are likely to be more harmful (unintentionally) than helpful.

These conclusions are often difficult for White folks to accept because of the defensiveness it is likely to engender and the feelings of blame. Yet I ask that you not be turned off to the message and the assertions of this chapter. I ask you to continue your multicultural journey in this chapter as we turn to recent research on White racial identity development.

THE PROCESS OF WHITE RACIAL IDENTITY DEVELOPMENT

Conferences on "Whiteness" have begun to spring up in different parts of the country; many of them are sponsored by academia, professional groups, and local community organizations. In the past, such gatherings would be seen as threatening and associated with rednecks and hood-wearing White-power groups. Yet if you were to enter one of these gatherings, you would note the presence of attendees dressed no differently than you or me. If you were to listen to speakers, the topics and conversations would be a major surprise: The Unfairness of White Privilege, How to Develop a Nonracist White Identity, We Are the Oppressors, The Color of White, or The Psychology of Being White. Instead of emphasizing White pride, there is almost a tendency to apologize for being White and a definite intent to denigrate the shameful racial heritage of White Americans.

The new and contemporary interest in Whiteness, wherein White folks gather to enlighten one another, to confess their racist "sins," and to admonish others to do likewise can only be described as ironic. Most of the people involved in such activities tend to be academics, social service workers, teachers, and students. All profess to talk about their racial awakening, the realization that they have oppressed people of color, and that the road to liberation must entail abandoning their racist upbringing and developing a non-racist White identity.

In reality, writings on White privilege, on the need for White Americans to own up to their bias and prejudices, and on the need to understand oneself as a racial being have been echoed consistently in the past. The voices of these early writers, however, have always been drowned out or marginalized. The early writings on this issue seldom made it into popular magazines, professional journals, or other respected publishing outlets. Instead they were published primarily in non-mainstream outlets, where those already converted read them. In the rare instance where they came to the attention of mainstream readers, they were often discarded as "histrionic trash from sellouts."

Recently, a number of multicultural experts in the field of education and psychology have begun to emphasize the need for you to deal with Whiteness as a sociodemographic racial category and to examine your own racism. They point out that most White Americans are willing to admit that being a member of a minority group subjects members of the group to a different experience than White folks. The experience or reality of people of color is far different from the White experience in America. Understanding this experience and how it affects you is, according to multicultural specialists, locked up in the process of White racial identity development.

Early studies, for example, have found that the level of White racial identity awareness was predictive of racism: the less aware you are of your White identity, the more likely you are to exhibit increased levels of racism; and White women were less likely to be racist. Many believe that women tend to be less racist than men because of women's greater experiences with discrimination and prejudice. Evidence also exists that multicultural competence (ability to communicate, teach, manage, and supervise effectively in a cross-cultural sense) is correlated with your White racial identity attitudes. Because developing multicultural sensitivity is a long-term developmental task, the work of many researchers has gradually converged on a conceptualization of the process of racial/ethnic identity development for White Euro-Americans.

The process of healthy identity development for you as a White person, according to psychologist Janet Helms, involves a two-phase process: abandoning your White racism and working to develop a nonracist identity.[2] Acceptance of this developmental process is based on several important assumptions that I have repeatedly stressed. These assumptions are often difficult for White Americans to accept because they are invisible and out of conscious awareness. Yet if you are to understand what being White in the United States means, it is important to entertain their legitimacy.

- First, racism is a basic and integral part of U.S. life and permeates all aspects of your culture and institutions. This statement should be clear in light of our analysis of White supremacy, White privilege, and ethnocentric monoculturalism.

- Second, in keeping with my previous assertions, you are socialized into U.S. society and therefore inherit the biases, stereotypes, and racist attitudes, beliefs, and behaviors of the society. Although it is an unpleasant conclusion for you, it is inescapable that you are racist, whether knowingly or unknowingly, intentionally or unintentionally.

- Third, the level of White racial identity development in an interracial encounter (understanding and working effectively with minorities) affects the process and outcome of your relationships. You have already seen how Miriam Cohen's stage of development affected her relationships with African American students, parents, and colleagues.

- Fourth, how you perceive yourself as racial beings seems to be strongly correlated with how you perceive and respond to racial stimuli. Consequently, your race-related reality represents major differences in how you view the world.

- Fifth, White racial identity development seems to follow an identifiable sequence—that is, there is an assumption that White Americans who are born and raised in the United States may move through levels of consciousness regarding their own identity as racial beings.

- Last, the most desirable development is one where you not only accept your Whiteness but also define it in a nondefensive and nonracist manner. This must be an active and constant ongoing process, where you do so without guilt but with a determined understanding that to deny the humanity of any one person is to deny the humanity of all.

Phase One—Naïveté

Though none of you enters this world as an empty slate, it is also clear that none of you is born with preconceived notions, stereotypes, racial bigotry, or hatred. Your early childhood is generally marked with a naïve curiosity about race. There is a tendency to be innocent, open, and spontaneous regarding racial differences.

I remember one story that an African American woman told me about a young White male child who had never before met a Black person in the flesh. She was interviewing for a job as a cook with a White couple and was seated on their living room sofa. The young child played on the floor several feet away and slowly but purposely rolled his truck closer and closer to her. When it rolled up against the woman's leg, he hastily retrieved it but moved next to her. As the White couple and the African American woman continued their conversation, the young child reached over and with his right forefinger rubbed her leg. He then looked at his finger, obviously interested in whether the black color would rub off on it. Needless to say, the White couple froze with horror at the actions of their son.

Examples like this are not atypical for very young children. I'm sure that readers such as you could recount numerous examples of incidents similar to this one. A young White child who has almost no personal contact with Asian Americans, for example, may see a Vietnamese man in a supermarket and loudly comment on the shape of his eyes or "unusual" physical features. Other than the embarrassment and apprehensions of adults around the child, there is little discomfort associated with this behavior for the youngster.

As a young child, you may notice differences, but the awareness of their social meaning attached to race, bias, and prejudice is either absent or minimal. Such an open and naïve orientation becomes less characteristic of you as the socialization process progresses. Studies reveal that racial awareness and the burgeoning social meanings occur between the ages of three and five years. The negative reactions of your parents, relatives, friends, and peers toward issues of race begin to convey mixed signals to you. This is reinforced by the educational system and mass media that instill racial biases in you and propel you into the conformity stage.

Phase Two—Conformity

As you have seen, the naïveté phase ends quickly because of the social messages about race that bombard you from the moment of birth. Nevertheless characteristics of this early stage are maintained throughout the stage of conformity. For example, you can continue to be very naïve about the meaning and implications associated with race and racism. Although there is increasing awareness of racial differences, there continues to be minimal awareness of you as a racial being and subsequently a strong belief in the universality of values and norms governing behavior.

Two major but diametrically opposed belief systems are being planted in your psyche. First, you are taught about the virtues of democracy—that everyone was created equal, that the nation was built on the foundations of freedom, that equal access and opportunity are the building blocks of our society, and that prejudice, discrimination, and bigotry are not only distasteful but evil. From your early schooling, you are told that racism is not only illegal but also morally bad. The good, decent, and moral citizen, like you, does not discriminate on the basis of race. These beliefs are deeply ingrained in your self-image and identity. To be accused of being a racist in our society is to have your personal integrity maligned.

Yet processes that are more insidious and powerful teach you that minority groups are inferior and deserve their inferior treatment. The White parent who quickly locks the car doors while driving through a Latino neighborhood, the mother who discourages a child from playing with Black schoolmates, the young child who overhears racial epithets, and the negative portrayal of minorities in the media all lead to one damning conclusion: persons of color are the dregs of our society and should be avoided. The conformity phase is marked by your acceptance of White superiority and minority inferiority. Consciously or unconsciously, you begin to believe that White culture is the most highly developed, and all others are primitive or inferior.

Contradictory beliefs can exist in your psyche because of your ability to compartmentalize your attitudes, beliefs, and behaviors. You may believe that you are not racist yet believe that minority inferiority justifies discriminatory and inferior treatment. Or you may believe that minority persons are different and deviant yet believe that "people are people" and that differences are unimportant.

The primary mechanisms operating here are denial and compartmentalization. For example, Whites deny that they belong to a race, which allows them to avoid personal responsibility for perpetuating a racist system. You have difficulty in seeing or are unable to see the invisible veil of cultural assumptions, biases, and prejudices that guide your perceptions and actions. You believe that White Euro-American culture is superior and that other cultures are primitive, inferior, less developed, or lower on the scale of evolution.

It is important to note that in this phase of development, you are unaware of these beliefs and operate as if others universally share them. You believe that differences are unimportant and that "people are people," "we are all the same under the skin," "we should treat everyone the same," and "problems wouldn't exist if minorities would only assimilate" and that discrimination and prejudice are something that others do. Your orientation professes color blindness, and it is encapsulated in a cocoon of ethnocentrism.

Because of naïveté and encapsulation, it is possible for two diametrically opposed belief systems to coexist in your mind: there is an uncritical acceptance of White supremacist notions, which relegates minorities into the inferior category with all the racial stereotypes, and there is a belief that racial and cultural differences are considered unimportant. This allows you to avoid perceiving yourself as a dominant group member or as having biases and prejudices. In her own White racial awakening, Peggy McIntosh stated the following:

> My schooling gave me no training in seeing myself as an oppressor, as an unfairly advantaged person, or as a participant in a damaged culture. I was taught to see myself as an individual whose moral state depended on her individual moral will. . . . Whites are taught to think of their lives as morally neutral, normative, and average, and also ideal, so that when we work to benefit others, this is seen as work which will allow "them to be more like us."[3]

The primary mechanism used in encapsulation is your denial: denial that people are different, denial that discrimination exists, and denial of your own prejudices. Instead the locus of the problem is seen to reside in the minority individual or group. Minorities wouldn't encounter problems if they would assimilate and acculturate (melting pot), if they would value education, or if they would only work harder.

The conformity stage is marked by your conscious belief in the democratic ideal—that everyone has an equal opportunity to succeed in a free society, and those who fail must bear the responsibility for their failure. White Euro-Americans become the social reference group, and the socialization process consistently instills messages of White superiority and minority inferiority throughout your upbringing. The underemployment, unemployment, and undereducation of marginalized groups in our society are seen as support that non-White groups are lesser than Whites. Because everyone has an equal opportunity to succeed, the lack of success of minority groups is seen as evidence of some negative personal or group characteristic (low intelligence, inadequate motivation, or biological and cultural deficits). Victim blaming is strong as the existence of oppression, discrimination, and racism are denied. Whereas the naiveté stage is brief in duration, the conformity stage can last a lifetime.

Phase Three—Dissonance

In the conformity phase of development, you are unlikely to recognize the polarities of democratic principles of equality and the unequal treatment of minority groups. Such obliviousness may eventually break down when you become aware of inconsistencies. For example, a White person becomes conflicted over irresolvable racial moral dilemmas that are frequently perceived as polar opposites: believing you are nonracist, yet not wanting your son or daughter to marry a minority group member; believing that "all men are created equal," yet seeing society treat people of color as second-class citizens; and not acknowledging that oppression exists, yet witnessing it (beating of Rodney King and the unwarranted perse-cution of Wen Ho Lee).

Conflicts between loyalty to one's group and to humanistic ideals may manifest in various ways. You become increasingly conscious of your Whiteness and may experience dissonance, resulting in feelings of guilt, depression, helplessness, or anxiety. Statements such as, "My grandfather is really prejudiced, but I try not to be" and "I'm per-sonally not against interracial marriages, but I worry about the chil-dren" are representative of personal struggles occurring in the White person. This type of conflict is best exemplified in the following passage from Sara Winter:

> When someone pushes racism into my awareness, I feel guilty (that I could be doing so much more); angry (I don't like to feel like I'm wrong); defensive (I already have two Black friends. . . . I worry more about racism than most whites do—isn't that enough); turned off (I have other priorities in my life with guilt about that thought); helpless (the problem is so big—what can I do?). I HATE TO FEEL THIS WAY. That is why I mini-mize race issues and let them fade from my awareness whenever possible.[4]

Movement into the dissonance phase occurs when you are forced to deal with the inconsistencies that have been compart-mentalized or encounter information and experiences at odds with your denial. In most cases, you are forced to acknowledge your Whiteness at some level, to examine your own cultural values, and to see the conflict between upholding humanistic nonracist values and exhibiting contradictory behaviors. For example, you may con-sciously believe that "all men are created equal" and that you "treat everyone the same" but suddenly experience reservations about hav-ing African Americans move next door or having your son or daugh-ter involved in an interracial relationship. These more personal experiences bring you face-to-face with your own prejudices and biases. In this situation, thoughts that "I am not prejudiced," "I treat everyone the same regardless of race, creed, or color," or "I do not discriminate" collide with your denial system.

Or some major event (assassination of Martin Luther King, viewing the Rodney King beating, and so forth) may force you to realize that racism is alive and well in the United States. The increasing realization that you are biased and that Euro-American society does play a part in oppressing minority groups is an unpleasant one. Dissonance may make you feel guilty, ashamed, angry, and depressed. Rationalizations may become the manner used to exonerate your own inactivity in combating perceived injustice or personal feelings of prejudice: "I'm only one person, what can I do?" or "Everyone is prejudiced, even minorities." As these conflicts ensue, you may retreat into the protective confines of White culture (encapsulation of the previous stage) or move progressively toward insight and revelation (resistance and immersion stage).

Whether you regress is related to the strength of positive forces pushing you forward (support for challenging racism) or negative forces pushing you backward (fear of some loss). For example, challenging the prevailing beliefs of the times may mean risking ostracism from White relatives, friends, neighbors, and colleagues. Regardless of your choice, there are many uncomfortable feelings of guilt, shame, anger, and depression related to the realization of inconsistencies in your belief system. Guilt and shame are most likely related to the recognition of your role in perpetuating racism in the past. Or guilt may result from your fear of speaking out on the issues or taking responsibility for your part in a current situation.

For example, you may witness an act of racism, hear a racist comment, or be given preferential treatment over a minority person but decide not to say anything for fear of violating racist White norms. Oftentimes you may delude yourself with rationalizations: "I'm just one person. What can I do about it?" This approach is one frequently taken by many White people in which they rationalize their behaviors by the belief that they are powerless to make changes. There is a tendency to retreat into White culture. If, however, others (may include some family and friends) are more accepting, forward movement is more likely.

Phase Four—Resistance and Immersion

If you progress to this stage, you will begin to question and challenge your own racism. For the first time, you begin to realize what racism is all about, and your eyes are suddenly opened. Racism becomes noticeable in all facets of your daily life (advertising, television, educational materials, interpersonal interactions, and so on). A major questioning of your own racism and that of others marks this phase of development. In addition, increasing awareness of how racism operates and its pervasiveness in U.S. culture and institutions is the major hallmark at this level of development. It is as if you have awakened to the realities of oppression; see how educational materials, the mass media, advertising, and the like portray and perpetuate stereotypes; and recognize how being White has allowed you certain advantages denied to various minority groups.

You are likely to experience considerable anger at family and friends, institutions, and larger societal values that are seen as having sold you a false bill of goods (democratic ideals) that were never practiced. Guilt is also felt for having been a part of the oppressive system. Strangely enough, the person is likely to undergo a form of racial self-hatred at this stage. Negative feelings about being White are present, and the accompanying feelings of guilt, shame, and anger toward oneself and other Whites may develop.

The *White-liberal syndrome* may develop and be manifested in two complementary styles: the paternalistic protector role or the overidentification with the minority group. In the former, you may devote your energies to an almost paternalistic attempt to protect minorities from abuse. A strong argument can be made that Miriam Cohen, for example, evidences many of the characteristics in this stage. You may actually even want to identify with a particular minority group (Asian, Black, and so forth) in order to escape your own Whiteness. You will soon discover, however, that these roles are not appreciated by minority groups, and you will experience rejection.

Again, you may resolve this dilemma by moving back into the protective confines of White culture (conformity stage), again experience conflict (dissonance), or move directly to the introspective stage. In many cases, you may develop a negative reaction toward your own group or culture. Although you may romanticize people of color, you cannot interact confidently with them because you fear making racist mistakes. This discomfort is best exemplified in a passage by Sara Winter:

> We avoid Black people because their presence brings painful questions to mind. Is it OK to talk about watermelons or mention "black coffee"? Should we use Black slang and tell racial jokes? How about talking about our experiences in Harlem, or mentioning our Black lovers? Should we conceal the fact that our mother still employs a Black cleaning lady? . . . We're embarrassedly aware of trying to do our best but to "act natural" at the same time. No wonder we're more comfortable in all-White situations where these dilemmas don't arise.[5]

The discomfort in realizing that you are White and that your group has engaged in oppression of racial/ethnic minorities may propel you into the next stage.

Phase Five—Introspection

This phase is most likely a compromise of your swinging from an extreme of unconditional acceptance of White identity to a rejection of Whiteness. It is a state of relative quiescence, introspection, and reformulation of what it means to be White. You realize and no longer deny that you have participated in oppression, that you benefit from White privilege, and that racism is an integral part of U.S. society. However, you become less motivated by guilt and defensiveness, accept your Whiteness, and seek to define your own identity and that of your social group. This acceptance, however, does not mean a less active role in combating oppression. The process may involve addressing these questions: What does it mean to be White? Who am I in relation to my Whiteness? Who am I as a racial/cultural being?

The feelings or affective elements may be existential in nature and involve feelings of lack of connectedness, isolation, confusion, and loss. In other words, you know that you will never fully understand the "minority experience" but feel disconnected from your Euro-American group as well. In some ways, the introspective phase is similar in dynamics to the dissonance phase in that both represent a transition from one perspective to another. The process used to answer the questions just posed and to deal with the ensuing feelings may involve a searching, observing, and questioning attitude. Answers to these questions involve dialoguing with and observing your own social group and actively creating and experiencing interactions with various minority group members as well.

Asking the painful question of who you are in relation to your racial heritage, honestly confronting your biases and prejudices, and accepting responsibility for your Whiteness are the culminating outcomes of the introspective stage. New ways of defining your White Euro-American social group and membership in that group become important. The intense soul-searching is most evident in Sara Winter's personal journey as she writes:

> In this sense we Whites are the victims of racism. Our victimization is different from that of Blacks, but it is real. We have been programmed into the oppressor roles we play, without our informed consent in the process. Our unawareness is part of the programming: None of us could tolerate the oppressor position, if we lived with a

day-to-day emotional awareness of the pain inflicted on other humans through the instrument of our behavior. . . . We Whites benefit in concrete ways, year in and year out, from the present racial arrangements. All my life in White neighborhoods, White schools, White jobs and dealing with White police (to name only a few), I have experienced advantages that are systematically not available to Black people. It does not make sense for me to blame myself for the advantages that have come my way by virtue of my Whiteness. But absolving myself from guilt does not imply forgetting about racial injustice or taking it lightly (as my guilt pushes me to do).[6]

There is realization that your Whiteness has been defined in opposition to people of color, by standards of White supremacy. By being able to step out of this racist paradigm and redefine what her Whiteness meant to her, Sara Winter is able to add meaning to developing a nonracist identity. The extremes of good and bad or positive and negative attachments to White and to people of color begin to become more realistic. You no longer deny being White, honestly confront your racism, understand the concept of White privilege, and feel increased comfort in relating to persons of color.

Phase Six—Integrative Awareness

Reaching this level of development is most characterized by understanding self as a racial/cultural being, developing awareness of sociopolitical influences with respect to racism, developing an appreciation of racial/cultural diversity, and rooting out buried and nested racial fears and emotions. A nonracist White Euro-American identity begins to emerge and becomes internalized. You begin to value multiculturalism, are comfortable around members of culturally different groups, and feel a strong connectedness with members of many groups. Perhaps most important is your inner sense of security and strength, which needs to develop and is needed to

function in a society that is only marginally accepting of integra-
tively aware White persons.

The integrative awareness stage is the result of forming a new
social and personal identity. With the greater comfort in understanding yourself and the development of a nonracist White identity comes a commitment to social action as well. You accept
responsibility for effecting personal and social change without
always relying on persons of color to lead the way.

> To end racism, Whites have to pay attention to it and
> continue to pay attention. Since avoidance is such a basic
> dynamic of racism, paying attention will not happen nat-
> urally. We Whites must learn how to hold racism reali-
> ties in our attention. We must learn to take responsibility
> for this process ourselves, without waiting for Blacks'
> actions to remind us that the problem exists, and with-
> out depending on Black people to reassure us and forgive
> us for our racist sins. In my experience, the process is
> painful but it is a relief to shed the fears, stereotypes,
> immobilizing guilt we didn't want in the first place.[7]

The racist-free identity, however, must be nurtured, validated,
and supported in order to be sustained in a hostile environment.
You will be constantly bombarded by attempts to resocialize you
into the oppressive society. Increasing awareness of your own
Whiteness, reduced feelings of guilt, acceptance of your role in perpetuating racism, and renewed determination to abandon White
entitlement lead to an integrative status. You become increasingly
knowledgeable about racial, ethnic, and cultural differences, value
diversity, and are no longer fearful, intimidated, or uncomfortable
with the experiential reality of race. Development of a nonracist
White identity becomes increasingly strong. Indeed, you begin to
feel comfortable with your nonracist White identity, do not personalize attacks on White supremacy, and can explore the issues of

racism and personal responsibility without defensiveness. In other words, you can "walk the talk" and actively value and seek out interracial experiences. Characteristics of this stage can be found in the personal journey of Mark Kiselica:

> I was deeply troubled as I witnessed on a daily basis the detrimental effects of institutional racism and oppression on ethnic-minority groups in this country. The latter encounters forced me to recognize my privileged position in our society because of my status as a so-called Anglo. It was upsetting to know that I, a member of White society, benefited from the hardships of others that were caused by a racist system. I was also disturbed by the painful realization that I was, in some ways, a racist. I had to come to grips with the fact that I had told and laughed at racist jokes and, through such behavior, had supported White racist attitudes. If I really wanted to become an effective, multicultural psychologist, extended and profound self-reckoning was in order. At times, I wanted to flee from this unpleasant process by merely participating superficially with the remaining task . . . while avoiding any substantive self-examination.[8]

This status is different from the previous one in two major ways: it is marked by a shift in focus from trying to change people of color to changing the self and other Whites, and it is marked by increasing experiential and affective understanding that were lacking in the previous status. This later process is extremely important. Indeed, Helms believes that a successful resolution of this stage requires an emotional catharsis or release that forces you to relive or reexperience previous emotions that were denied or distorted. The ability to achieve this affective and experiential upheaval leads to a euphoria or even a feeling of rebirth and is a necessary condition to developing a new nonracist White identity. Again, Sara Winter states:

Let me explain this healing process in more detail. We must unearth all the words and memories we generally try not to think about, but which are inside us all the time: "nigger," "Uncle Tom," "jungle bunny," "Oreo"; lynching, cattle prods, castrations, rapists, "black pussy," and black men with their huge penises, and hundreds more. (I shudder as I write.) We need to review three different kinds of material: (1) all our personal memories connected with blackness and black people including everything we can recall hearing or reading; (2) all the racist images and stereotypes we've ever heard, particularly the grossest and most hurtful ones; (3) any race related things we ourselves said, did or omitted doing which we feel bad about today. . . . Most whites begin with a good deal of amnesia. Eventually the memories crowd in, especially when several people pool recollections. Emotional release is a vital part of the process. Experiencing feelings seems to allow further recollections to come. I need persistent encouragement from my companions to continue.[9]

Though Sara Winter speaks primarily about the internally racist messages regarding African Americans, her process of healing is also applicable to all marginalized groups.

Phase Seven—Commitment to Antiracist Action

Integrative awareness is a major step in combating your racism, but it is not enough. Phase seven is most characterized by social action. If you have reached this stage, there is likely to be a consequent change in your behavior and an increased commitment toward eradicating oppression as well. It requires courage on your part to act in a manner that speaks to social justice. Seeing a wrong and actively working to right it require moral fortitude and direct action. Objecting to racist jokes; trying to educate family, friends, neighbors, and coworkers about racial issues; taking direct action to eradicate racism in the schools, the workplace, and in social policy often put you in direct conflict with other Whites.

You will, however, become somewhat immune to social pressures for conformance because your reference group begins to change. In addition to family and friends, you will begin to actively form alliances with persons of color and other liberated Whites. They will become a second family to you, giving you validation and en-couraging you to continue the struggle against individual, institutional, and societal racism. Some actions associated with phase seven include the following:

- Searching out valid information on race and racism

- Actively seeking out interracial relationships and experiences

- Being open to discussing racial issues with acquain-tances of color

- Expressing positive racial messages to family members, friends, and coworkers

- Standing against racist comments and jokes

- Joining or forming community or professional groups that work on behalf of multiculturalism, diversity, and antiracism

- Planning, coordinating, conducting, or attending antiracism forums with other interested parties

- Voting for candidates who share your vision of multiculturalism and antiracism

- Supporting public policies that allow for equal access and opportunity

- Advocating for a multicultural curriculum in your schools

Developing a healthy White racial identity, therefore, can be summarized as consisting of four components. First, you must actively place yourself in new and oftentimes uncomfortable situations that impel you to question yourself as a racial/cultural being and to increase awareness of racial issues, especially racism. Second, change must occur in the form of new insights, attitudes, and behaviors that lead to a realization of your role in the perpetuation of racism. Third, considerable and continuing energies must be devoted to the maintenance of a healthy White racial identity. In other words, change is not enough in the face of societal forces that serve to squelch or punish dissent. Fourth, you must take action to eradicate racism when you see it. This requires considerable courage, but I believe you must do it. Along with this change, however, must be a determination to stand against the toxicity of racism, no matter how unpleasant the process. These four important components will form the basis of our next chapter.

What You Can Do to Overcome Racism

Try your hand at the following exercises.

Exercise Number 1

Overcoming your racism means an awareness of yourself as a racial/cultural being. Earlier in this chapter, I presented the case of Miriam Cohen. Reread the case and answer these questions by yourself or discuss them in a group situation.

1. Why did Miriam's attempt to relate to the African American couple fail? Why did her mention of Black entertainers and use of Black phrases seem to turn the couple off?

2. Doesn't Miriam have a valid point that Jews and women are also oppressed groups? Shouldn't this allow us to understand and relate to one another in a more meaningful fashion? Why did it seem to have the opposite effect? Miriam's

emphasis on her being a woman and a Jew did not seem to validate the couple's Black experience. Rather, it seemed to negate it. Why did it do so?

3. Miriam seemed easily manipulated by the African American male teacher. Although the teacher was obviously attempting to seduce Miriam and probably treated most women in a sexually objectified manner, a strong case can be made that Miriam also contributed to the problem. For example, the prove-to-me-you're-not-a-racist game instigated by the Black teacher seemed to tap into an especially vulnerable aspect of Miriam. Can you discern what that might have been?

4. African Americans are often suspicious of the motives of White helping professionals. Are White teachers, for example, authentic in their desire to help, or are they doing it for some other reasons? What do you think was behind Miriam's desire to teach at an inner-city school? In what way did her motives interfere with her ability to work effectively with African American students, parents, and colleagues? How would you have worked through the suspicions in both cases?

Exercise Number 2

Personalizing the phases of White racial identity development is very important, so it does not simply become an intellectual exercise. Reflect on your own White identity development with respect to the characteristics of each phase. What phase do you believe you are at? Can you give specific examples from your life experiences or events for each of the phases? Phase seven is perhaps the most difficult for you because it links awareness to action.

Phases of White Racial Identity	My Experiences
1. Naïveté	_____
2. Conformance	_____
3. Dissonance	_____
4. Resistance	_____
5. Introspection	_____
6. Integrative Awareness	_____
7. Antiracist Action	_____

In looking at your response, what implications does it have for you in your fight to overcome racism?

Exercise Number 3

It goes without saying that phase seven, commitment to antiracist action, is most difficult for White folks to attain. Try to list as many things that you could do to overcome racism at the individual, organization, and societal levels. This exercise is most productive when done in a brainstorming session by a group.

9

What Must You Do
to Combat Racism?

I f the forces that foster and perpetuate racism are deeply embedded in your personal makeup, your institutional policies and
practices, and the culture of your society, how can you possibly make
a difference? The prospect of developing a healthy White racial
identity may seem overwhelming to you. This realization often leads
to a feeling of hopelessness.

"The problem of racism is so big that it seems hopeless. What
can I do to combat the forces of bigotry? Where do I begin? After
all, I'm only one person. Further, even you say that becoming nonracist is complex and difficult to achieve. I have few minority acquaintances. Most of us prefer to stick with our own group. How
can I or any other White person possibly learn about other groups
when we seldom have meaningful contact with one another?"

When I was invited to testify before President Clinton's Race
Advisory Board, this was precisely the issue they wanted me to address. My message that afternoon was that there is much you can do.
You must not become paralyzed by these difficult questions and
observations, because they only serve to foster inaction by giving you
an excuse not to challenge others and yourself. Although the battle
against prejudice and discrimination must be a systemic national
effort, there is much that can be done on an individual basis.

Developing a healthy White racial identity means becoming
liberated from your racist social conditioning and developing the

ability to truly understand the meaning and implications of racism. To accomplish this task, you must actively place yourself in situations that challenge your biases and preconceived notions. You cannot wait for time to solve our racial problems or leave it to future generations, because racism belongs to us, not to our descendants. None of you can passively wait for the state of race relations to improve or solely rely on others to help deal with your own racial hang-ups.

Unfortunately, the liberation process is too often unplanned and occurs by happenstance—that is, you do not consciously or deliberately place yourself in situations that force you to interact with others who are different than your group, nor do you plan educational activities that enhance your development. Many of my White friends and colleagues changed not because of their own efforts but because an event out of their control forced them to seriously question their values and assumptions. This statement is not meant to negate their courage in continuing the multicultural journey or to minimize those of you who have always been active allies in the battle against racism.

Few of you, however, actively seek out experiences that are unfamiliar or make you uncomfortable. How many of you, for example, have purposely gone to an all-Black function, an all-Latino function, or an all–Asian American activity? No, I am not referring to visits to Chinatown novelty stores or dining at Mexican restaurants but to some event where you were the only White person present and had to initiate contact with members of that group. If you have, then you are probably aware of what I mean. Let me have you imagine a scenario.

Imagine that you are the only White teacher to attend an educational forum full of African American educators. As you enter the room, you discover that you are the only White teacher attending. You notice that most of the Black educators are huddled in small groups engaged in animated conversation. Many questions flow through your mind: "Do they notice I'm the only White person here? Should I approach that Black couple and introduce myself? Will they be friendly toward me? Will they see me as an intruder? Is that group in the corner talking about me?" Besides having these intrusive questions, you may find yourself very vigilant: "I better be careful about what I say or do. I better join a group, or they will think I'm prejudiced and avoiding them. I hope I don't make any offensive misstatements. I better be polite and friendly and avoid any topic dealing with race. I better not mention that I employ a Black cleaning lady. I wish I could leave but better not because they will misinterpret my actions."

In light of these anxieties and the multitude of vexing questions that arise in interracial situations, why would you want to be placed in such a predicament? No wonder you avoid situations that are tinged with racial overtones. But emotional discomfort and conflict are often preconditions for personal growth and change. My work has suggested that three things must happen if you are to become liberated from your personal racism.

First, you must encounter situations, events, and experiences that challenge your preconceived notions, beliefs, or values. In general, for most White Americans, these encounters occur outside their control but are capable of shattering strongly held beliefs about race and produce new insights. As I mentioned previously, many of you were probably deeply affected when you witnessed the beating of Rodney King. But more provincial, random occurrences can be equally powerful experiences that provoke change: overhearing a racial slur about a close minority friend, witnessing how you were treated preferentially while persons of color were relegated to second-class treatment, or encountering persons of color that destroy your long-held stereotypes (an Asian American who is forceful and assertive, an obviously intelligent African American, and the like).

As an educator, however, I realize that creating the context for change can be purposefully planned and instigated as well. In my teaching, for example, I often plan exercises or assignments for my students that place them in situations that expose them to events that question their racial reality. I have them visit minority communities, make home visits, or do internships in agencies where racial/ethnic minorities comprise the majority of clients. Only recently, however, have I come to the realization that if the eradication of racism is dependent on the courses or workshops we offer, then we have lost the battle. Only if you are willing to create your own learning experiences will we have any hope of becoming a nation based on fairness and justice.

Much of this chapter is therefore based on suggestions to you, dear readers, as to what you can personally do to free yourself and become valuable allies in the struggle for equal rights. Likewise, I challenge my brothers and sisters of color to do the same. For Asian Americans, it means getting to experience the lived realities of their Black, Brown, and Red brothers and sisters. For African Americans, it means getting to experience the lived realities of their Yellow, Brown, and Red brothers and sisters. As persons of color, we need to recognize that our understanding of one another (interethnic) may be as difficult a journey as that undertaken by our White brothers and sisters.

Second, racism awareness is unpleasant and painful. Trying to calm people down, have them restrain their feelings, and discuss racial issues rationally and objectively may work against liberation. Exploring your own biases, prejudices, and race-related beliefs can be very frightening, especially when you come to the realization that you have held a false image of yourself as being bias-free. The courage to engage in activities that challenge your assumptions or that place you in situations that produce discomfort is a precondition to change. Deeply embedded emotions and feelings that are associated with belief systems, stereotypes, and fears must be uncovered.

Oftentimes the strong expression of feelings is precisely what is required to produce awareness and change. The development of a healthy White identity means that you must be able to unearth all of the nested emotions associated with racial fears; acknowledge your biases and preconceived notions; be open and honest with yourself and others; hear the hopes, fears, and concerns of all groups in this society; recognize how prejudice and discrimination hurt everyone; and seek common solutions that allow for equal access and opportunities.

Developing a nonracist identity is a monumental task because it requires honestly examining unpleasant racial realities like racial prejudice, racial stereotyping, and racial discrimination and accepting responsibility for changing yourselves, your institutions, and your society. One of the greatest difficulties that White Americans have in understanding racism is that you perceive and experience yourself as moral, decent, and fair-minded. Consequently, you often do not realize that your beliefs and actions may be discriminatory in nature.

Third, those who have gone through the struggle of becoming liberated from their social conditioning, who have begun to develop a nonracist identity, and who now actively work against injustice must continue to work toward maintaining their new identities and personal resolve. The forces that discourage you from challenging the status quo and that threaten you with a loss of social support or the fruits of your labor are never ending and enduring.

Liberated White people such as you are often threatened with ostracism, a loss of friends, being disowned by family members and relatives, and occasionally even threats of physical harm from other White folks. For example, confronting friends, colleagues, neighbors, or even relatives about the offensiveness of ethnic jokes can lead to isolation. Your friends and relatives may label you as uptight, politically correct, a bleeding-heart liberal, or lacking a sense of humor. Your presence will make them uncomfortable in future interactions, and they may avoid you, leading to a sense of isolation. The message they send is clear: unless you are one of us and get off your high horse, we don't want you around!

Or if you confront your supervisor or boss about discriminatory actions, your promotion or merit increase may be jeopardized. You become labeled as a troublemaker and begin to lose credibility. All of these counterexperiences may lead you to give up your new White identity and retreat back to a previous phase of development. It is easier to conform to the prevailing attitudes of the community, not to rock the boat, and just "go along to get along." Maintaining a healthy White identity is not an easy thing to do. It oftentimes means seeking and developing new friendships and support groups, allies who continue to validate your nonracist identity and who encourage you to continue the multicultural journey.

PERSONAL RESPONSIBILITY FOR CHANGE

Combating racism on a personal level means much soul-searching. You need to realize that racism, prejudice, and discrimination are not just intellectual concepts for objective study and "for the other person." They have very personal consequences for those who are the victims. Although many of you are willing to acknowledge that racism must be addressed at an institutional and societal level, you often avoid addressing it on a personal level and fail to identify personal growth experiences as necessary elements.

I would argue that it is difficult, if not impossible, for any of you to be race-sensitive without understanding and working through your own personal biases and prejudices. It must entail a willingness to address internal issues related to personal belief systems, behaviors, and emotions when interacting with other racial groups. There must be a personal awakening and willingness to root out biases and unwarranted assumptions related to race, culture, ethnicity, and the like. When confronting racism on a personal level, several psychological assumptions can guide you in the quest to develop a healthy nonracist White identity.

Assumption One—You Were Not Born Wanting to Be a Racist

Although psychological studies point to the fact that racism is rooted in normal psychological processes (tendency to classify similarities and differences, motivational predisposition to dominate and control, and being open to social conditioning), it is a fair statement to say that no one was born with racist attitudes and beliefs. Misinformation related to culturally different groups is not acquired by your free choice. These are imposed through a painful process of social conditioning: you are taught to hate and fear others who are different in some way.

In a strange sort of way, you are as much victims as persons of color in this respect. Like your brothers and sisters of color, you are also raised in a society that bombards you with messages regarding your superiority and the inferiority of minorities. Your victimization, however, is quite different because you are socialized into oppressor roles. It is clear that no one (Whites and persons of color) is immune from inheriting the racial biases of our forebears. When people of color are portrayed in the educational curriculum in unflattering stereotypes and untruths, when their cultural differences are viewed as inferior and deviant, and when the characteristics that define them are those related to danger and fear, it is little wonder that many White folks, such as you, grow up believing that persons of color are to be feared and avoided. This realization may help you understand that you are not to be blamed. Yet absolving yourself of guilt does not mean that you can avoid responsibility for action to change and to combat all forms of bias and discrimination.

Assumption Two—Having Racist Attitudes and Beliefs Is Harmful to You

You may be under the mistaken notion that racism is harmful only to people of color. Yet research now reveals the detrimental consequences to White Americans as well. Being an oppressor almost necessitates the diminishing of your perceptual accuracy in order to continue oppressive ways. Few oppressors are completely without remorse for their role in the degradation and dominance of others. The harm, damage, and acts of cruelty to persons of color can only continue if you diminish your own humanity; lose you sensitivity to those you hurt; become hard, cold, and unfeeling to the plight of the oppressed; and turn off your compassion and empathy for others. Dulling and diminishing your own perception is an attempt to escape the guilt and remorse associated with acts of callousness and destruction. In essence, to continue your ways means exchanging your humanity for the power, wealth, and status attained from the oppression of others.

It is therefore clear that racism serves as a clamp on your mind, distorting your perception of reality. It allows you to misperceive yourself as superior and all other groups as inferior. It allows for the systematic mistreatment of large groups of people based on self-deception and perpetuating misinformation. To live your day-to-day lives unfettered by guilt, you must deny, diminish, or avoid the full realization that you are responsible for the pain and suffering you have caused racial minorities. Yet, at some level, you must realize your complicity in perpetuating the secrecy of White privilege, that your advantage is built on the suffering of others. You must harbor great feelings of guilt that oftentimes manifest in defensiveness and outbursts of anger.

An exercise I frequently introduce to participants in my racism awareness workshops is simply to ask them this question: How many of you would ever choose to be Black? Generally, not a single White person will raise a hand in response to this question. Would you?

When I persist and ask why, we enter a dialogue that results in admissions that they perceive that being Black is to be oppressed. They readily admit that being Black means discrimination, prejudice, lack of equal access and opportunity, and so forth. If you know this, I ask, how can you possibly sit home and do nothing?

At this point in the exercise, there is often great discomfort among the participants. Many express feelings of hopelessness ("The problem is too big"), defensiveness ("I don't condone racism so why blame me"), anger ("All of us have been discriminated against, get over it"), guilt ("I guess I should do more"), and fear ("Our way of life is being threatened"). These feelings, I submit, are defensive maneuvers used by White folks to protect them from their greatest fear: "I am responsible for the pain and suffering of people of color. How can I possibly live my life day in and day out with the knowledge of my personal complicity in the dehumanization of persons of color?"

There is a concept that my Native American brothers and sisters call the *soul wound*. It refers to the intergenerational historical trauma suffered by Native American ancestors in the *trail of tears*, the genocide of Native Americans, the taking of their lands in exchange for reservations, and their continued mistreatment by the U.S. government. The legacy of the soul wound is present to this very day in Native Americans. Likewise, the enslavement of African Americans, the incarceration of Japanese Americans, and the Holocaust for Jews have left their wounds in the current generations and the future ones to come.

I believe that White Americans, like you, suffer from a soul wound as well. It is from the subconscious knowledge that you have engaged in actions that have deprived other groups of their humanity. This is the true White person's burden: the knowledge of your complicity in the systematic mistreatment of people of color. Until you acknowledge this fact, accept responsibility for your past and present actions, and actively work to do something about the injustices in our society, your soul wound will remain with you forever.

Assumption Three—People of Color Also Grow Up Acquiring Misinformation

Many persons of color may come to believe in their own inferiority, have difficulty separating their oppressive experiences from accurate information about White Americans, and acquire misinformation about other minority groups.

It goes without saying that people of color are constantly bombarded with messages that negate their identities and portray them in unflattering terms. Asian Americans are sneaky, untrustworthy, back stabbers, aliens, unassertive, passive, inscrutable, make poor leaders, and so forth. African Americans are sexually promiscuous, culturally deprived, criminals, prone to violence, intellectually inferior, good in sports, and so forth. Latino/Hispanic Americans are aliens, lazy, unmotivated, irresponsible, uneducable, and so forth. Native Americans are savages, drunkards, noncompetitive, have no conception of time, passive and unassertive, and so forth.

The problem here is related to two psychological processes, the self-fulfilling prophecy and the *stereotype threat*. In the former, if young Asian Americans, for example, encounter situations that continually reinforce stereotypes that they are passive and unassertive, then they may come to believe in the stereotypes and behave accordingly. Teachers who believe that Asian Americans are poor in interpersonal relationships, unassertive, and quiet can create conditions that make the students more withdrawn. Psychologist Claude Steele has found that stereotype threat is a powerful force that may result in poor test-taking performance even when persons of color may not accept stereotypes about themselves or members of their group.

In the case of Black students, Steele found that stereotype threat is evoked when a situation presents itself that is charged with racial implications for the individual. For example, tests of intelligence or ability are likely to trigger awareness in African Americans that they are in a situation that contains stereotypes regarding the racial inferiority of their group. The discomfort and anxiety at being seen as intellectually inferior are enough to often result in lowered test performance. That the results are not reflective of their true abilities is found in higher performance when the threat is removed.

Because of the constant oppression and invalidation experienced by persons of color, they may find it difficult to separate their issues of White racism from White folks. I recall one example that illustrates this point. Years ago, I was a faculty member of a specially funded program to train primarily counselors and therapists of color. It was an attempt to increase the number of helping professionals returning to work in the ethnic minority community. Almost all of the faculty were persons of color, except for two White professors. We had little interaction with one of them because he was a researcher whose role did not require him to have contact with us. The other White man, however, was a trainer and attended all our meetings.

Needless to say, he was treated with great mistrust and disrespect. Many of us questioned his motives. Why would a White man be involved with our project? What were his ulterior motives? The many slights, innuendos about his being unwanted, and even overt hostility failed to get him to resign from the group. It was only much later that we realized his true commitment to racial equality, when he became the most outspoken critic of the university's hidden racial biases. This experience made me realize that many White folks, such as you, are willing to help. Your motives are not necessarily self-serving, the battle for racial equality is also a part of your struggle, and you make valuable allies.

Although I have generally focused on the relationship between White Americans and people of color, it goes without saying that race relations involve interethnic ones as well: African American with Asian American, Latino American with Native American, Native American with African American, and so forth. A 1994 Harris Poll commissioned by a national conference (formerly known as the National Conference of Christians and Jews) found that racial/ethnic groups continue to experience mistrust, envy, and misunderstandings toward one another.[1]

- More than 40 percent of African Americans and Hispanics and one of every four Whites believe that

Asian Americans are unscrupulous, crafty, and devious in business.

- Nearly half the Hispanic Americans surveyed and 40 percent of African Americans and Whites believe that Muslims belong to a religion that condones or supports terrorism.

- African Americans believe that everyone else is treated with more equality and especially that Asian Americans are doing better.

In other words, the building of healthy multicultural alliances cannot occur solely on the common-enemy reaction to White supremacy. Persons of color have generally shied away from dealing with their own interethnic misunderstandings and conflicts for several reasons. First, in relationship to the larger dominant society, most minorities are not in a power position to systemically discriminate against one another. Second, there has been an unspoken rule among many minority groups: don't air your dirty laundry in public. There is great fear that the presence of conflict between two groups of color would benefit White folks because it gives them an excuse: "Why should we change, people of color are just as racist toward one another!" Third, many minorities are sensitive to the divide-and-conquer political consequences of public conflicts among racial/ethnic minorities. Conflict among minority groups serves only to benefit those who hold power.

Despite these legitimate concerns, it is clear that much stereotyping and prejudice occur among groups of color. In some communities, for example, Korean-Black and Latino-Black relations are filled with antagonisms and mistrust. As the 2000 U.S. Census reveals, the Latino population now equals the African American population and will shortly surpass it. The rapid explosion of racial/ethnic minorities means that interethnic relations will increase in importance.

Assumption Four—Ordinary Citizens Control the Tools That Result in Unjust Disparities

On March 17, 2001, several thousand counselors from the American Counseling Association gathered in San Antonio to hear the keynote address of Morris Dees, cofounder and chief trial counselor for the Southern Poverty Law Center. Dees, a southern White male, has devoted his entire professional and personal life to the struggle for civil rights. His organization has devoted its energies toward monitoring hate groups, developing ideas for teaching tolerance to children, and aiding minorities in court for civil rights. His organization successfully tried and won a historic $12.5 million judgment against White supremacist Tom Metzger and his White Aryan Resistance group in the beating death of a Black student.

Before an attentive and transfixed audience, Dees spoke of the numerous and abhorrent hate crimes that have shaken the very fiber of our nation, the bombing of the Oklahoma federal building by Timothy McVeigh, and the work of the numerous skinhead groups that the center has monitored. Throughout the speech, he made the point that these individuals believed that they were patriots, protecting a White America, and that it was White folks who have made this country great. Dees emphasized the fact that what makes America great is its diversity, and he posed several questions to the audience: Whose America is it? Is it the one envisioned by the White supremacists or the one based on equality and freedom? As human beings, aren't we better than the hate mongers who would perpetuate racial injustice?

I remember clearly the reaction of the audience. There was a standing ovation for Morris Dees, not only because of his life-long commitment to fighting injustice but also because his message made us feel good.

"We are better than that!" "We stand against hate crimes, the orthodoxy of racial hatred, and the Klan and skinheads." "We condemn acts of racial hatred and violence."

But more seductive was the strong reinforcement I sensed in people leaving that rousing event: "I am not like those hate mongers. Racists are only the skinheads and Klan. I don't discriminate. I'm not prejudiced. I believe in equality."

If we, as a nation, focus on racism as only extreme acts of hatred, then we reassure ourselves that we are not capable of prejudice, bias, and discrimination. As I have emphasized throughout this book, it isn't White supremacists who create and control the tools that result in the inequities in our society. It is people like you.

TAKING ACTION TO OVERCOME PERSONAL RACISM

Taking responsibility for change means that you must overcome the inertia and the feeling of powerlessness on a personal level. People can grow and change if they are personally willing to confront and unlearn their racist conditioning. To accomplish this task, all of you must unlearn racist misinformation, not only on a cognitive level (factual) but also on a visceral level—that is, the misinformation that has been glued together by painful emotions. You must begin to accept the responsibility for the pain and suffering you may have personally caused others.

Unlearning your biases means acquiring accurate information and experiences. Much of how you come to know about other cultures is through the media, through what your family and friends convey to you, and through public education texts. These sources cannot be counted on to give an accurate picture because they can be filled with stereotypes, misinformation, and deficit portrayals. So I propose five principles (many supported from psychological studies) to guide you in obtaining an accurate picture of culturally diverse groups.

Principle One—Learn About People of Color from Sources Within the Group

First, you must experience and learn from as many sources as possible (not just the media or what your neighbor may say) in order to check out the validity of your assumptions and understanding. Especially important is information that originates from the groups you hope to understand. Earlier, I made the point that if you want to understand racism, information from White folks may not be the most insightful or accurate sources. Acquiring information from minority-run or minority-edited radio and TV stations or publications allows you to understand the thoughts, hopes, fears, and aspirations from the perspective of people of color. It also acts as a counterbalance to the worldview expressed by White society about minority groups. Be aware that your perspective is often in marked contrast to the worldview of racial/ethnic minorities.

For the average citizen, for example, reading fiction and poetry about the culture is one way to develop knowledge of it. Try to avoid narratives that reinforce negative attitudes and stereotypes by selecting those works written by a person from within the culture. Read literature written by or for persons of the culture. This applies to both fiction and nonfiction. Whereas the professional and nonprofessional literature often portrays minorities in stereotypical ways, writings from individuals of that group may provide richness based on experiential reality. For example, there are many books (many have been on the *New York Times* best-seller list) written by minority authors about nearly every racial or ethnic group, about their history, culture, and family relationships and about topics like prejudice and racism. Reading such literature makes it possible to enter the cultural world of minorities in a safe and nonthreatening way. I recommend many in the last section of this chapter, but let me use several illustrations as to how insights and understanding can result from some powerful readings.

What are some of the racial/cultural themes you can discern from these three passages? Can you relate to them?

1. *The House on Mango Street* by Sandra Cisneros is a compelling and insightful story of Esperanza's life in a Latino neighborhood

of Chicago.[2] It is told in a series of short vignettes that is a commentary on race relations and cultural differences.

> Those who don't know any better come into our neighborhood scared. They think we're dangerous. They think we will attack them with shiny knives. They are stupid people who are lost and got here by mistake. . . . All brown all around, we are safe. But watch us drive into a neighborhood of another color and our knees go shakityshake and our car windows get rolled up tight and our eyes look straight ahead. Yeah. That is how it goes and goes.

2. The following passage comes from *The Shadowman's Way* by Paul Pitts.[3] It describes the contemporary life of a Navaho adolescent. In his description of differences between a White student and himself, he says:

> He seemed to be working to keep the conversation going. In class, I have noticed that it's important to the white kids to keep talking. It's different with Navajos, we like silence. If there's a pause in the talking, it's not uncomfortable for us.

3. This passage comes from *A Lesson Before Dying* by Ernest Gaines.[4] It is a story about an educated Black man's struggle to maintain his personal dignity in the face of racism and marginalization.

> I had come through the back door against my will, and it seemed that he and the sheriff were doing everything they could to humiliate me even more by making me wait on them. I had to put up with that because of those in the quarter, but I damned sure would not add hurt to injury by eating at his kitchen table. I tried to decide

how I should respond to them. Whether I should act like
the teacher that I was, or like the nigger that I was sup-
posed to be. . . . To show too much intelligence would
have been an insult to them. To show a lack of intelligence would have been a greater insult to me.

In the first passage, the main character speaks to the irrational
fears you may experience when you enter a minority neighborhood,
but it is muted with an understanding that people of color experience similar fears; the second passage speaks to differences in communication and learning styles between Whites and Native
Americans; and the last passage speaks to the humiliation of racism
and the struggle to maintain personal dignity in the face of forced
compliance. Such readings contain so many nuggets of truth concerning race relations and cultural differences that I often wonder
why our schools do not make better use of literature to combat bias
and increase interracial understanding.

Another safe and enjoyable way to learn about minority experiences is to attend a play, movie, musical, dance, or entertainment
event put on by ethnic minority group members. In many respects,
you will be amazed by the many universal themes they portray about
life as well as the cultural and race-related themes that deal with
their own cultures, struggles, and ethnic celebrations. In New York,
for example, the play *Harlem Song* will give theatergoers an understanding of the history and resiliency of the people of Harlem in the
face of racism.

And who could forget the major impact that the television series
Roots, by Alex Haley, had on all of us? It traced the history of a
Black man, kidnapped from Africa and enslaved in the South, and
the evolution of his family, friends, and generations that followed.
For those of you who have never seen the series, the entire dozen
or so tapes are available at almost all video rental stores. Even if you
have seen them before, share them with your family and friends. A
very rich source of information often comes from PBS. Not too long

ago, they produced a series of films shown on television that revolved around their race initiative.

In summary, literary narratives and entertainment or educational events have been used throughout human history to explore, entertain, and reveal truths about the human condition. They are powerful means to enhance the empathic response of readers, to explore issues of tolerance and understanding of different lifestyles and worldviews, and to increase sensitivity, knowledge, and awareness of culturally different groups in our society.

Principle Two—Learn from Healthy and Strong People of the Culture

Getting a balanced picture of racial/ethnic minority groups requires that you spend time with healthy and strong people of that culture. The mass media and our educational texts (written from the perspectives of Euro-Americans) frequently portray minority groups as uncivilized or pathological, as criminals or delinquents. No wonder the images you have are primarily negative. You must make an effort to fight such negative conditioning and ask yourselves what are the desirable aspects of the culture, the history, and the people. This can only come about if you have contact with healthy representatives of that group. As you seldom spend much intimate time with persons of color, you are likely to believe the societal projection of minorities as being lawbreakers, unintelligent, prone to violence, unmotivated, and uninterested in relating to the larger society.

As I emphasize in the next chapter, contact with people of color is a necessary condition to dispel your stereotypes and fears. Unfortunately, White Americans, like you, are most likely to have contact with people of color who represent only a narrow spectrum of the group, those who have gotten into trouble with society or who need special help. So contacts are usually with the homeless, antisocial indigents, and the mentally troubled. A social worker, for example, is unlikely to work with clients that are problem-free, well adjusted, successful, and with a strong family upbringing. Rather, they see dysfunctional families, homeless people, those in poverty, and those who have problems functioning independently without aid. An absence of contact with the multitude of healthy, autonomous, successful, and well-adjusted families and individuals in minority communities compounds the situation. No wonder most White Americans believe so strongly in the negative characteristics of people of color.

Overcoming your personal racial fears and discomfort around people of color is not an easy task. It requires trying out new behaviors and changing your pattern of relationships. It is hard enough to meet and become comfortable with people of your own group, but it becomes a more difficult task with people of another race or culture. Let me first give examples of what can be done to increase healthy contact with minority members.

- Frequent minority-owned businesses and get to know the proprietors.

- Attend services at a variety of churches, synagogues, temples, and other places of worship to learn about different faiths and meet church leaders.

- Invite colleagues, coworkers, neighbors, or students of color to your home for dinner or a holiday.

- Live in an integrated or culturally diverse neighborhood and attend neighborhood organizational meetings or attend or throw block parties.

- Form a community organization on valuing diversity and invite local artists, authors, entertainers, politicians, and leaders of color to address your group.

- Attend street fairs, educational forums, and events put on by the community.

Sounds easy, doesn't it? Well believe me, it's not!

As you saw in the case of Miriam Cohen in the last chapter, acting out the White-liberal guilt trip or being a "political tourist" can create resentment among people of color to what they see as an intrusion into their lives. They may view your presence in their neighborhoods as a visitor at a zoo (their communities) taking a peek at how the animals (people of color) live! How insulting! As a result, you are likely to be viewed with suspicion, hostility, and resentment. Rather than being welcomed, you are likely to be seen as an intruder with suspect motives. Indeed, under such circumstances, your presence may only lead to greater misunderstanding between you and the groups you hope to understand.

A desire to help is not enough. Indeed, your naïve good intentions can get you into great trouble and potentially pose personal danger.

Several years ago, while teaching a racism awareness course in California, I had presented to a group of graduate students in counseling about the need to become acquainted with the people you hope to serve. Most of the students were White, and I challenged them to get to know the communities of color to enhance their multicultural knowledge. They were to keep a journal of their interactions with people of color. One White student took up the challenge and decided to attend a Chinese Baptist church and a Black Baptist church in Oakland, California.

Needless to say, his experiences left him even more entrenched in his fears and apprehensions about folks of color. At both churches, he felt open hostility directed toward him. When he tried to speak with the parishioners after the service, they ignored and avoided him. He felt isolated, uncomfortable, and frightened. After the service at the Black Church, as he walked to his car, he spotted a group of Black youths standing on the corner. He recalls experiencing a panicky feeling as he quickly fumbled for his keys, dropped them on the ground, and had difficulty unlocking his door. The Black youngsters seemed to read his fears and appeared amused as he quickly drove off.

I have often used this student's experience as a case study in fail-ure. First, I would never recommend that anyone enter a minority neighborhood or any unfamiliar neighborhood without an under-standing or some knowledge of it. Second, you cannot enter as an uninvited stranger who can be seen as an interloper. Third, your presence has to be one in which you somehow contribute to the community rather than use it just for your own ends. People of color are very sensitive to being used as guinea pigs to fulfill the purposes of White needs (in this case, to fulfill a class assignment).

Where do you find cultural guides who will aid you in your desire to understand people of color? Anyone who is racially or culturally different than you can act as a cultural guide. To achieve this, you must make a concerted effort to meet and interact with visible racial/ethnic minority individuals. You may find them as a neigh-bor, coworker, or fellow student or as an acquaintance at the local gym, community committee, or interest group. Opportunities abound everywhere, but the challenge is to reach out and form a friendship with that person of color.

To be received favorably by persons of color and the community requires several conditions. You must be genuine in wanting to know folks of color. Your interactions and relationships must not be transitory and a one-shot thing. It has to be an ongoing process. For example, just to attend the Black church on a one-time basis is not to immerse yourself in the community, and it results in only cursory acquisition of knowledge. You must introduce yourself to the com-munity and to people of color in a nonhurried manner. Remember, this is a two-way process. Last, in what way will you "give back" or help those you hope to understand?

The White student, for example, might have overcome the sus-picions of the community if he had relied on an acquaintance or friend of color to serve as a liaison to the pastor or some other elder of the Church. Making friends or having someone you know of color attend with you goes a long way in your perceived legitimacy among the congregation. Often, attending with a partner or your family, especially children, will be a good way to break the ice with other parishioners. Or you could contact the pastor and share with him or her your desires and reasons for wanting to attend. Let the pastor know what you are trying to do, and be open to suggestions. In many cases, the pastor might suggest that you first make yourself known by volunteering your services in their soup kitchen, singing in the choir, and the like to increase your visibility. Such things also are powerful statements to the congregation and community that you are not a political tourist and are willing to give back to the community.

The point I am trying to make with this example is that these solutions or principles may sound easy but are complex and fraught with difficulties. These actions require humility, courage, the willingness to be vulnerable, and the perseverance to pick yourself up and start over. You must be willing to learn, to listen, to be open.

Principle Three—Learn from Experiential Reality

While going to readings, attending theater, and going to museums will help increase understanding, you must supplement your factual understanding with the experiential reality of the groups you hope to understand. These experiences, however, must be something carefully planned if they are to be successful. As you saw with the White student's attending ethnic minority churches, some form of personal connection can be most valuable in allowing entry into the benefits of interracial encounters. It may be helpful to identify a cultural guide, someone from the culture who is willing to help you understand the group, someone willing to introduce you to new experiences, someone willing to help you process your thoughts, feelings, and behaviors. This allows you to more easily obtain valid information on race and racism issues.

Early in my academic career, I was fortunate enough to meet and form a friendship with Malachi Andrews, an African American educator who taught me much about the Black experience in America. When I first joined the faculty, Malachi was aware that my research interests were related to multicultural psychology. He must have sensed that my work was purely intellectual and that my work on race relations could benefit from an experiential understanding of Black Americans. As a result, he introduced me to Black friends; we attended all-Black functions and socialized at lounges frequented by African Americans. I can remember my discomfort at being around primarily Black Americans and how I tried to mask it. Malachi helped me get in touch with my fears and apprehensions by discussions about my feelings, by forcing me not to avoid Black folks, and by allowing me to experience the full range of their humanity.

As a result, I came away with the following knowledge: cultural understanding and sensitivity cannot occur without lived experience. All of us must therefore make an effort to attend cultural events, meetings, and activities of the groups we hope to understand. This allows you to view the people interacting in their community and observe their values in action. Hearing from church leaders, attending open community forums, and attending community celebrations allow you to sense the strengths of the community, observe leadership in action, personalize your understanding, and identify potential guides and advisers.

The journey to overcome your own fears and biases has to be a step-by-step process. Immersing yourself in the environment of people who differ from you in race, culture, and ethnicity without adequate preparation may only result in a hardening of your prejudices.

Principle Four—Learn from Constant Vigilance of Your Biases and Fears

Last, your life must become a "have to" in being constantly vigilant to manifestations of bias in both yourself and the people around you. Learn how to ask sensitive racial questions of your minority friends, associates, and acquaintances. Persons subjected to racism seldom get a chance to talk about it with an undefensive and nonguilty person from the majority group. White Americans, for example, often avoid mentioning race even with close minority friends. Most minority individuals are more than willing to respond, to enlighten, and to share if they sense that your questions and concerns are sincere and motivated by a desire to learn and serve the group. When you listen undefensively, for example, to a Latino American speak about racism, both of you gain.

Several years ago, in the state of California, Proposition 209, referred to as the "anti-affirmative-action" legislation by opponents, was being strongly debated in nearly every community. The legislation would make it illegal to use race as a criterion for admission into institutions of higher education and for awarding state contracts. Feelings ran very high because the author of the legislation was a Black man who sat on the board of regents of the University of California. Proposition 209 found instantaneous support from many Whites, who quickly claimed the author as an ally. Needless to say, many persons of color perceived the Black man as being a front for the conservative elements of California and as having been co-opted by the system. Indeed, among certain groups, he was, unfortunately, labeled an "Uncle Tom" or an "Oreo" (reference to being Black outside—chocolate wafers—but White inside—crème filling.

I recall being at a reception held after a debate about the merits of Proposition 209. Most of those who attended were White folks from the community, with very few people of color. I observed a group of Whites gathered together, sipping wine, and engaged in conversation about the merits of the debate. They were very animated and freely spoke about their admiration for the author of the legislation and referred to him as "a credit to his race." Someone in the group remarked that he wished other minorities would have the courage to take a stand against special privileges as the Black author of the legislation had done. He could not understand why the ethnic minority community refused to claim him as one of their own. Another person said it would be a good idea to ask African Americans about this matter.

Shortly after this interchange, one of the hosts brought a Black woman attendee over to introduce her to the other guests. Though the group was cordial and polite to the woman, there was obvious discomfort in the group. When the Black woman apologized for interrupting their conversation and told them to please carry on, there was a moment of silent awkwardness. Then someone stated, "Oh, we were just introducing ourselves to one another."

For the rest of the evening, the conversation dealt with comments and questions about the type of work people did and other more superficial comments regarding the evening's debate. Never did the conversation ever return to the topic of affirmative action nor to the earlier conversation concerning their admiration for the author of Proposition 209. Indeed, the situation can be likened to the elephant-in-the-middle-of-the-room scenario—that is, people are well aware of the presence of the elephant but do not acknowledge or mention it. It became obvious that speaking about race or racial issues in the presence of a Black person created extreme discomfort for the group. Yet it was equally uncomfortable not to mention it at all! A valuable opportunity to learn from one another was lost in that situation.

Why did the White folks in this group have difficulty speaking about the topic of race and affirmative action when a Black person joined them? Did they make unwarranted assumptions about where the Black attendee stood on affirmative action? If you were a member of the group, what would make it difficult for you to express your true thoughts and feelings? What would make it difficult for you to ask the Black person her thoughts on the matter? If you imagine yourself in the situation, what thoughts and feelings flood your mind? Are you concerned that whatever you say or do will appear racist? Isn't the avoidance of the topic a sign of bias in itself?

The point I am trying to make is that situations like this occur frequently with similar outcomes. They are pregnant with opportunities to learn from one another and even more important to learn about yourself. When you're around people of color or when race-related issues or racial situations present themselves, ask yourself, Where are the feelings of uneasiness, differentness, or outright fear coming from? They may reveal or say something about your biases and prejudices. What makes it difficult to talk about issues of race around people of color? Why do you cross the street when you see minority youngsters approaching you? Do you do it when Whites approach you? Why do you tense up and clutch your purse more securely when a minority person enters your space? Don't make excuses for these thoughts and feelings, dismiss them, or avoid attaching some meaning to them. Only if we confront them directly can they be unlearned or dealt with in a realistic manner.

Principle Five—Learn from Being Committed to Personal Action Against Racism

Dealing with racism means a personal commitment to action. It means interrupting other White Americans when they make racist remarks or jokes or engage in racist actions, even if this is embarrassing or frightening. It means noticing the possibility for direct action against bias and discrimination in your everyday life—in the family, work, and the community. It means taking initiative to make sure that minority candidates are fairly considered in your place of employment, advocating to teachers of your children to include multicultural material in the curriculum, volunteering in community organizations to have them consider multicultural issues, and contributing to and working for campaigns of political candidates who will advocate for social justice.

For persons of color, dealing with bias and prejudice is a day-to-day occurrence. If you are to be helpful, your life must also be a constant "have to" in dealing with racism. The American Psychological Association has advocated ten very useful commonsense suggestions:

1. *Be honest.* You must develop an ability to recognize your own biases through open discussion with others. Examine your own prej-

udices, stereotypes, and values. Be willing and open to exploring your own experiences of being hurt by prejudice, but also be willing to explore the ways you have benefited from discrimination. Don't get defensive. Be open to hearing from people of color.

2. *Be a partner.* Volunteer to work on projects with groups different than your own. It's been found that working alongside a person of color as an equal does more to destroy prejudices and stereotypes. Opportunities abound, especially if you are involved in groups or organizations whose agendas deal with issues of diversity and multiculturalism. There are generally community organizations or groups that sponsor educational forums related to improving race relations or trying to instill a multicultural curriculum in the schools.

3. *Be an antiracist parent.* You must begin to raise your children to understand concepts like prejudice, discrimination, and racism. Be active in introducing your children to interacting and learning from children of color. Do it before prejudices become hardened. Take them to school-sponsored events on multiculturalism, don't discourage them from interacting with children of color, and make topics of inclusion, democracy, and antiracism a part of your everyday vocabulary.

4. *Be a role model.* Whether they want to or not, parents serve as models for their children. So being vocal in opposing racist views and practices is very important for your son and daughter to witness. Invite neighbors, colleagues, and other acquaintances of color to your home. Have children witness you, as a role model, interacting, laughing, talking, and enjoying relationships with persons of color.

5. *Be an ally.* You must reach out and become an ally of persons of color. Support victims of discrimination, be willing to join them in advocating for fair treatment, and be willing to serve as a mentor to people of color. Speak out if you see racial discrimination. When serving on committees with persons of color, help in allowing their voices to be heard.

6. *Be an activist.* When you see racial injustice, speak out and object. Be willing to challenge your family, friends, and neighbors when they make racial jokes or slurs or act in ways that indicate bias. Be vigilant not only with family and friends but also at your workplace, church, and other organizations you belong to. Work to make sure that your school district and place of employment treat groups of color fairly. Serve on groups and committees that have a multicultural agenda.

7. *Be a member.* Are you a member of the numerous organizations that stand for social justice and antidiscrimination? Join groups and organizations that stand for equality of opportunity, social justice, antidiscrimination, and antiracism. For example, explore the possibility of membership in the Anti-Defamation League, the Human Rights Campaign, the National Asian Pacific American Legal Consortium, the National Association for the Advancement of Colored People, the National Council of La Raza, the National Organization for Women, and the Southern Poverty Law Center.

8. *Be a teacher.* As a coworker, parent, neighbor, or teacher, you can teach others to value diversity and multiculturalism. The Southern Poverty Law Center, for example, can give you many examples of what ordinary citizens can do to combat hatred and bigotry. Their *Teaching Tolerance* magazine contains many good ideas and pages of references. Volunteer to be a Sunday school teacher and make sure racial equality is part of the curriculum.

9. *Be a student.* You must realize that antiracism education is a constant and ongoing process. You must educate yourself and others on a continuing and ongoing basis. Reading books, seeing movies, and going to hear minority speakers are all intended to enlighten, educate, and free us from our bigotry. Attend workshops and the many educational events on racial understanding put on at local colleges and universities, neighborhood organizations, and other groups.

10. *Be secure.* Don't be ashamed of your cultural heritage. It means, however, recognizing both the positive and negative aspects

of your group. Know your strengths and limitations. Understanding yourself as a racial/cultural being does much to reduce defensiveness and build bonds of mutual trust with others. Take an active part in defining your Whiteness in a nonracist manner and living by these newly found tenets. If you define your racial identity in such a manner, you will no longer respond with defensiveness or guilt when racism becomes an issue.[5]

What You Can Do to Overcome Racism

Try your hand at the following exercises.

Exercise Number 1

What are some novels that might be helpful in your journey to liberation? As mentioned earlier, reading texts written by minority authors can help unmask the irrational fears you possess, allow you to identify with people of color, increase empathy and understanding, and view people of color as people, not as subhuman aliens.

Although you will benefit by reading these books on your own, something you could consider is to form a reading group among your neighbors, coworkers, or other acquaintances and hold monthly meetings to discuss these texts. Some probably exist locally, and with some effort you might be able to join one. At the very least, they may be able to give you hints and tips on how to form one on your own. Group discussion and analysis of these novels can stimulate helpful and insightful dialogue. I apologize in advance for not being able to provide a brief synopsis of these novels, but page limitations prevent me from doing so. A description of these books, however, can usually be found at your local library or on the Internet.

Though there are many excellent literary works, some that readers might wish to consider are the following:

Black/African American

- *Invisible Man* by Ralph Ellison
- *I Know Why the Caged Bird Sings* by Maya Angelou
- *The Color Purple* by Alice Walker
- *Waiting to Exhale* by Terry McMillan
- *Manchild in the Promised Land* by Claude Brown
- *Black Boy* by Richard Wright
- *The Autobiography of Malcolm X* by Malcolm X (with assistance of Alex Haley)
- *Black Like Me* by J. H. Griffin (White author, but revealing)
- *Nigger* by Dick Gregory
- *Cane* by Jean Toomer
- *Go Tell It on the Mountain* by James Baldwin
- *Native Son* by Richard Wright
- *The Bluest Eye* by Toni Morrison
- *A Lesson Before Dying* by Ernest Gaines
- *Killing Rage* by bell hooks

Asian/Asian American

- *China Boy* by Gus Lee
- *No-No Boy* by John Okada
- *The Joy Luck Club* by Amy Tan

- *The Woman Warrior* by Maxine Hong Kingston

- *Obasan* by Joy Kogawa

- *Farewell My Concubine* by Pi-Hua Li and Lilian Lee

- *Donald Duk* by Frank Chin

- *Mona in the Promised Land* by Gish Jen

- *Dogeaters* by Jessica Hagedom

- *Bone* by Fae Myenne Ng

- *The God of Small Things* by Arundhati Roy

Hispanic/Latino

- *The Autobiography of a Brown Buffalo* by Oscar Acosta

- *The House of the Spirits* by Isabel Allende

- *The Rain God* by Arturo Islas

- *The House on Mango Street* by Sandra Cisneros

- *So Far from God* by Ana Castillo

- *How the Garcia Girls Lost Their Accents* by Julia Alvarez

- *The Mambo Kings Play Songs of Love* by Oscar Hijuelos

- *One Hundred Years of Solitude* by Gabriel García Márquez

- *Like Water for Chocolate* by Laura Esquivel

- *The Old Gringo* by Carlos Fuentes

- *Bless Me Ultima* by Rudolfo Anaya

- *Dreaming in Cuban* by Cristina Garcia

Native American/American Indian

- *The Shadowman's Way* by Paul Pitts

- *The Lone Ranger and Tonto Fistfight in Heaven* by Sherman Alexie

- *The Toughest Indian in the World* by Sherman Alexie

- *Ceremony* by Leslie Marmon Silko

- *Love Medicine* by Louise Erdrich

- *A Yellow Raft in Blue Water* by Michael Dorris

- *Winter in the Blood* by James Welch

- *Mean Spirit* by Linda Hogan

- *Bury My Heart at Wounded Knee* by Dee Brown

- *Custer Died for Your Sins: An Indian Manifesto* by Vine Deloria

- *Buddha in Redface* by Eduardo Duran

Exercise Number 2

There are many other ways to obtain racial/cultural information. Here are some.

1. Ethnic museums are rich in cultural information. Almost all major cities have them. Also, on your next trip to another city or while traveling abroad, make a special effort to locate those museums or points of interest that can enlighten you and your family about racial/cultural issues. African American, Native American, Asian American, Latino American, and other ethnic museums can be found by simply accessing city directories.

Years ago, while visiting Washington, D.C., I took my family to the Holocaust Museum and to a special exhibit on the internment of Japanese Americans at the Smithsonian. Even as someone whose academic life has involved studying anti-Semitism and anti-Asian sentiment, I was moved greatly by the power of the exhibits. They not only provided me with new and insightful information, but the experience also brought out my nested emotions about these two events.

2. Contact and obtain information from the many ethnic agencies, associations, and organizations in the United States: the NAACP, the Southern Poverty Law Center, the Hispanic Society of America, the Anti-Defamation League of B'nai B'rith, the Association of American Indian Affairs, the National Institute Against Prejudice and Violence, and so forth. Most of these organizations have published a multitude of papers, monographs, and books on topics related to race relations. In many cases, these contain many suggestions for increasing your awareness and knowledge of racial issues, and some even give very concrete suggestions of what can be done to combat prejudice and discrimination. Many materials are provided free of charge. These organizations would be more than happy to supply information and even to have you volunteer your services.

3. A good time to really educate yourself but also to make yourself known or more visible to a community is to attend or participate in special ethnic events or religious or ethnic holidays. These special events are usually chock-full of community and educational activities open to everyone. Many universities and organizations will put on celebrations and activities during these dates. They are generally announced in the local media. But it's important to be proactive in contacting the groups (local public-affairs arm of the local university, for example) to obtain the schedule of events. Here are just a few special dates and activities that are almost always celebrated with many events:

Ethnic/Special Groups Heritage Month Declarations

- African American Heritage Month (February)
- National Women's History Month (March)
- Asian American Heritage Month (May)
- Hispanic American Heritage Month (September)
- American Indian Heritage Month (November)

Religious, Ethnic, and Special Holidays

- Martin Luther King Jr.'s Birthday
- Lunar New Year
- Brotherhood/Sisterhood Week
- Cinco de Mayo
- St. Patrick's Day
- Indigenous Peoples Day
- Rosh Hashanah
- Yom Kippur
- Ramadan
- Hanukkah
- Christmas
- Kwanza

Conferences, Workshops, Organizational Events, Film Festivals, and Lectures on Racial/Cultural Topics

- Many professional and educational organizations hold annual conferences in major cities for their members. Paper-reading sessions, symposia, and panel presentations often include topics on race, racism, diversity, and multiculturalism. Some organizations that are likely to deal with folks of color include the American Psychological Association, the American Counseling Association, the National Association of Social Workers, the National Education Association, and so forth. For a fee, it is often possible to attend these conferences and to participate.

- Groups often advertise half-day or full-day workshops on the topics of racism and diversity. Again, these are usually put on by local, state, and national groups.

- Community organizations like churches and special-interest groups often invite renowned speakers (artists, political figures, prominent authors, educators, and the like) to speak on topics of race and racism. You can usually avail yourself of these activities. It requires making an effort to get on mailing lists, joining an interest group, or perusing the community event sections of the local newspaper.

- Film festivals and special screenings of works on race and race relations occur periodically. Sometimes a local community group will do so, but often PBS will do so as well. The Television Race Initiative that they put on several years ago was simply superb.

4. Many educational and entertainment films and videos are available on topics of racism, race, and their effects on people of color. There are literally hundreds of fiction and nonfiction films and videos that can be used to stimulate healthy discussions on racial/cultural issues. Some are broad and general and apply to all groups, such as stereotyping, racism, and prejudice. Some may be very specific to a particular racial/ethnic minority. Many of these videos and films are informative on their own, but some require some form of active analysis and discussion to process questions and sometimes strong emotions from viewers. If an opportunity for processing does not exist, the educational value can be lost. The following is a list of videos and films that I have found particularly valuable.

Nonfiction Educational Films and Videos on Subjects of Race, Racism, and Stereotyping

- *The Color of Fear*
- *Skin Deep*
- *A Class Divided*
- *Blue-Eyed*
- *Eye of the Storm*
- *Names Can Really Hurt Us*
- *All the Way Home*
- *Difficult Dialogues*

Entertainment Films (Fiction and Nonfiction)— African American

- *The Autobiography of Miss Jane Pittman*
- *Boyz N the Hood*

- *Colors*
- *The Color Purple*
- *Do the Right Thing*
- *Driving Miss Daisy*
- *Eyes on the Prize*
- *Jungle Fever*
- *Guess Who's Coming to Dinner*
- *Matewan*
- *Mississippi Masala*
- *Mo' Better Blues*
- *Roots I and Roots II*
- *Sounder*
- *To Kill a Mockingbird*
- *White Man's Burden*

Entertainment Films (Fiction and Nonfiction)— Asian American

- *Dim Sum*
- *Double Happiness*
- *Farewell to Manzanar*
- *Joy Luck Club*
- *Come See the Paradise*
- *The Wash*
- *The Wedding Banquet*

Entertainment Films (Fiction and Nonfiction)—
Latino

- *American Me*
- *The Ballad of Gregorio Cortez*
- *Born in East L.A.*
- *El Norte*
- *Like Water for Chocolate*
- *Mi Familia*
- *Milagro Beanfield War*
- *Romero*
- *Stand and Deliver*

Entertainment Films (Fiction and Nonfiction)—
Native American

- *Dances with Wolves*
- *The Last of the Mohicans*
- *The Mission*
- *Never Cry Wolf*
- *Pow Wow Highway*
- *Thunderheart*

5. Go to the local bookstore or use the Internet to access information about groups against racism. The Barnes & Noble bookstore near my apartment has large sections on cultural studies, African American studies, Asian American studies, Native American studies, Latino studies, gay and lesbian studies, and women's studies.

These sections usually contain both academic and more popular books related to topics of special populations and broader issues of racism. You don't have to choose the more academic ones, but browse through those that you find relate to your style and interests. Also, if there is a specific group or topic you wish to explore, the Internet can be very valuable and a time-saver. For example, if you simply list the topic *antiracism*, you will get literally thousands of hits that list books, organizations, activities, conferences, and so forth related to the subject.

Exercise Number 3

Monitor your racial experiences and the consequent feelings and thoughts that are aroused within you. One way is to keep a journal or diary of your day-to-day interactions or observations that involve issues of race and race relations. To be successful, however, you must become race-sensitive. When you watch TV commercials, sitcoms, or dramas that involve persons of color, try to determine the racial messages that are being sent. Are they positive or negative? What feelings are you experiencing? What thoughts? Do the same with movies, magazine articles, and newspapers. Observe interracial interactions between those around you. What about your own interracial interactions and relationships? Self-observation and monitoring can tell you much about yourself. If the messages are stereotypical and biased, and if they create unwarranted apprehensions and fears, dispute them actively. Such a journal can be kept for any period of time, weekly or monthly. After the time period, however, it is important to look at the whole picture and not just the individual incidents.

Journal Keeping—Monitoring My Racial Thoughts and Fears

1. Describe the racial incident or event. This can include a contact you had with someone of color, a movie, a commercial, or a TV program that portrayed people of color, or it can be just observing interracial interactions—for example,

overhearing a racist joke or obvious racist statements from an acquaintance, family member, or friend.

2. What was the theme or message (hidden or overt) concerning race relations?

3. What were your thoughts and feelings?

4. In light of your thoughts and feelings, what meaning does it have for you?

5. Do you have work to do on yourself? If so, list what you can do to work on correcting a bias, fear, or stereotype.

Day	Incident or Event	Theme	Thoughts and Feelings	Meaning	Corrective Action
1					
2					
3					
4					
5					
6					
7					

10

What Must Society Do
to Combat Racism?

I t is not enough for any of you, on an individual basis, to become
bias-free and culturally sensitive when the very institutions that
educate you, employ you, and govern you are themselves racist in
policy, practice, assumption, and structure. In Chapter Four, I indicated how your racial reality and your racist attitudes and beliefs are
formed from three main avenues: schooling and education, mass
media, and peers and social groups. Just as these channels can present a biased social construction of knowledge regarding race and
race relations, they also offer hope as vehicles to overcome intergroup hostility and misunderstanding and to develop norms associated with equity and social justice.

In essence, you and others must begin to substitute a multicultural curriculum that stresses equity and antiracism for the monocultural and racist one that currently exists. It must be done in your
schools, all media outlets, and in the many groups and organizations
that touch your lives. Yet to use these tools of socialization to combat racism and to reconstruct a nonbiased racial reality requires an
understanding of the conditions that would facilitate such a movement. Do we possess knowledge of the forces that would reduce or
eliminate racism?

PRINCIPLES OF ANTIRACISM

A partial answer to this question lies in the early work of Gordon Allport, a social psychologist well known for his classic book, *The Nature of Prejudice*, published in 1954.[1] Since its publication, others have conducted revealing and important work on reducing prejudice by creating conditions found to lower intergroup hostility. If you advocate breaking down racial barriers, you'll need to help produce seven conditions that seem necessary to eradicate or reduce racism. I like to refer to them as the *principles of antiracism* because the conditions they produce seem toxic to the development of prejudice and bias. Racism is most likely to diminish when you are

- Having intimate contact with people different from you

- Experiencing a cooperative rather than a competing environment

- Working toward mutually shared goals as opposed to individual ones

- Exchanging accurate information rather than stereotypes or misinformation

- Interacting on an equal footing with others rather than on an unequal or imbalanced basis

- Viewing leadership or authority as supportive of intergroup harmony

- Feeling a sense of unity or interconnectedness with all humanity

Further, it appears that no one single condition is sufficient alone to overcome bigotry. To be successful in combating racism, all conditions must coexist in varying degrees to reduce prejudice.

Principle One—Having Intimate and Close Contact With Others

Despite the fact that we are a multiracial, multiethnic, and multicultural society, we are certainly not an integrated one. Different groups continue to associate with only members of their own kind. Racial/ethnic minority communities are present in every major city in the United States. There are barrios, ghettos, ethnic enclaves, Chinatowns, Manilatowns, and Japantowns. They exist in both affluent and poor neighborhoods. There is separation along racial/ethnic lines in every part of the country. Although many of you now work side by side and attend school with people from different races, the truth is that your contacts tend to be superficial and based on prescribed roles, rules, and regulations. You maintain a form of social distance from certain groups, with race being a powerful barrier in preventing more intimate social interactions.

If you advocate breaking down racial barriers by facilitating more intimate contact between Whites and persons of color, you are probably making the following assumptions: that bias and racism are based on misinformation and that negative feelings like anxiety, fear, and disgust about other groups can never be extinguished unless contact reveals their unwarranted nature. Referred to as the *contact hypothesis*, it was believed that if you were required to interact with people of different races, much of the prejudice and intergroup hostility would diminish.

This line of thinking was given great impetus in the *Brown* v. *Board of Education* of Topeka, Kansas, outcome.[2] In 1954, the U.S. Supreme Court ruled against the *separate but equal doctrine* in schools in the South. The ruling was founded on evidence that separate was inherently unequal. Up until that time, it was believed that separation of Black and White students in different schools had no adverse impact on Black students and was justifiable and constitutional.

As a result of the decision, great hope was garnered in the belief that prejudiced attitudes and racism among White students and parents would decline. Through court-mandated contacts, students would have stereotypes dispelled, parents would see one another as human beings, and fears associated with interracial conflict would diminish. In the early days of integration, however, studies revealed improvement in race relations in only 25 percent of the cases. Continued conflicts, negative feelings, and distrust characterized the majority of situations. In some instances, racial harmony seemed to decline in a racial backlash. Rather than improved interracial relations, things got worse.

Why do you think interracial contact in some cases seems to increase prejudice and antagonism rather than diminish them? Perhaps the proponents of the contact hypothesis were naïve. Most of you know that having contact with people you dislike may increase your negative feelings. In dysfunctional families, where husband and wife and even the children are in conflict, members can be in contact with one another but experience extreme dislike and antagonism despite their intimate interactions with one another.

So it is clear that some forms of intimate contact may not lead to improved racial harmony. Despite this outcome, however, intimate contact is still a necessary condition, but perhaps not a sufficient one, for improved interracial relations. The question you must ask, therefore, is under what conditions will intimate contact promote interracial harmony and diminish bigotry?

Principle Two—Cooperating Rather Than Competing

Years ago, I was employed as a counselor at the student counseling center at the University of California-Berkeley. The student body consisted of the brightest students in higher education. In those days, only the top 12 percent of the high school seniors qualified for admission, and even fewer would be actually admitted. In other words, the students were among the brightest, those who had excelled in high school and chose Berkeley because of its excellent academic reputation.

Needless to say, there was a very competitive atmosphere on the campus. This was especially true for premed students, who competed with one another in their chemistry classes. Professors at most universities grade on what we call the normal distribution, or bell-shaped curve. Grades would be distributed in such a manner that the majority of students would get C's, with fewer getting B's and even fewer receiving A's. All students knew, however, that good medical schools would select only those students with the highest grade point averages. Because only a very low percentage of students could obtain A's, it was clear that for some to do well, others had to do poorly.

In such an atmosphere, several premed students who were suffering from guilty consciences came to see me as part of their therapy. The stories they told me were quite disturbing. When professors assigned readings from journals, one male client would immediately go to the library, photocopy the articles for his own private use, and destroy the originals so other students would not have access to them. Usually, he took a razor blade and slashed the article into unreadable strips. Another male student told how he would sabotage the lab experiments of other students by dropping small crystals into the flasks of unsuspecting classmates. Still others told about their refusal to share class notes with students who had missed the last session.

In general, these students operated from the assumption that if others did poorly, their chance of getting a good grade was vastly improved. Helping other students and sharing knowledge only served to "raise the curve" and make it more difficult to obtain a good grade. In this case, they saw one another as competitors and not as classmates or friends! As a therapist, I was bound by issues of confidentiality not to reveal the unethical behaviors of the students. I could not, for example, turn them into the dean for disciplinary action. In actuality, I worked and was successful at convincing a few students to stop their behaviors.

The major problem that confronted me, however, was how to change the institution. How does one convince the Berkeley administration that the grading system and climate of extreme competition on the campus contributed to the delinquent behavior of its students? Indeed, the more I worked on the campus, the more I began to entertain another perspective: Is it possible to view the behaviors of students as a healthy response to a "sick system" rather than as a sick response to a healthy system?

But, realistically, I realized that as a single individual, I could not effect major institutional change. My way of dealing with the issue was to conduct group sessions with students about how to survive on a competitive campus (without cheating or sabotaging their fellow students), serve on campus committees on student life, and voice my thoughts to administrators and fellow counselors. Making students, professors, student support personnel, and administrators aware of the broader systemic issues seemed an important first step in effecting a change.

In our society, individual competition is deemed desirable and encouraged. The legendary and much admired coach of the Green Bay Packers, Vince Lombardi, is quoted as saying, "Winning isn't everything, it's the only thing!" Such a statement is used to indicate the importance of winning and the need to avoid losing at all costs. For you to win, others must lose. For you to do well, others must do less well. In our society, competition, winning, and achievement are intertwined and seen as motivationally healthy and desired. The most visible measure of overall success is materialistic possessions or socioeconomic status. The win-lose mentality not only pits you against other individuals but also pits your group against other groups. Little doubt exists that the hierarchical educational, social, political, and economic stratification in our society has a strong racial flavor.

In a competitive atmosphere, in-group and out-group demarcations along racial lines are as old as history itself. Indeed, one of the major explanations of racism is called the *political-economic competition theory*. In situations of limited resources (political, economic, social status, jobs, and desired human symbols of success, like grades, athletic prowess, and promotions), groups compete against one another and become prone to feelings of antagonism and hostility.

Think about it. How competitive are you? Do some situations seem to bring out your competitive spirit? In sports, when you are embroiled in an athletic contest with another athlete or a team, do you tend to see your opponent as a friend or a foe? When you are aware that you are competing with someone for something you prize, like admission to law school, being the valedictorian, making the most sales, or getting that promotion, how do you feel toward potential rivals? When you add a racial flavor into the equation, the hard feelings can truly intensify.

If individual competition fosters and reinforces your existing bias and bigotry, then might not producing a cooperative atmosphere reduce them? Indeed, social psychologists have found this to be the case. In what is called the *jigsaw classroom* approach, educators and psychologists placed young students in six-person learning groups that required them to cooperate rather than compete. Each student possessed exactly one-sixth of the information needed for group success. In other words, success was not defined as superior individual performance but rather as contributing to the group and relying on others to do the same.

The cooperative experience in White, Black, and Latino students had several major effects: the students learned that the old competitive ways were no longer functional for success and that the new norms for solving problems involved valuing others as equal contributors. As a result, liking for one another increased significantly, self-esteem increased among all groups, positive attitudes toward school increased, and although Whites showed no change in academic performance, the minority children showed improved school performance.

Principle Three—Sharing Mutual Goals

It is also clear that when you do not share the same goals, the likelihood of having you work together in fruitful harmony with others of a different persuasion is minimal. Indeed, racial antagonism and conflict may be the result if the goals of your group are incompatible with those of another. People of color who desire to integrate work sites are unlikely to find assistance from those White Americans opposed to it. Attempts to diversify an institution of higher education by increasing minority students, staff, and faculty are met with disapproval when the goals vary among potential consumers. For people of color, affirmative action represents an attempt to level the playing field so that it will ensure minority admission to colleges. If you, however, perceive an affirmative action program as reverse racism and believe that it will decrease your chances of being admitted to the college of your choice, you are likely to oppose it. Worse yet is your tendency to see the other individual in a less favorable light or the other group as an enemy.

Educators of color who desire to change requirements or admission standards so that they would result in greater numbers of minority students being admitted to a university are at odds with White educators who oppose the move because the changes are seen as "lowering requirements." In both cases, the goals are not shared by the two groups and appear antagonistic to one another. Suppose, however, we reframed the situation so that a superordinate goal replaced the group ones? Would it make any difference if the goal was to allow for equal access and opportunity to higher education? Opinion polls suggest that the majority of citizens in this nation, regardless of race, share such a superordinate goal.

In athletic contests, for example, strangers rooting for the same team share a mutual goal: to win! In stadiums or sports bars, they often seem to bond with one another. Divisions along racial lines seem to dissolve as the fans share a superordinate goal: to see their team victorious. Politicians have long known that when an outside force threatens the security of the United States, as in times of war, the nation seems to pull together in a united effort. Defeating a common enemy and securing the safety of the nation become of paramount importance, outweighing past differences and conflicts. Immediately after the September 11 terrorist attacks, a survey conducted by the *New York Times* indicated that racial divisions among Black and Whites had diminished. Many of those interviewed reported that race relations had improved, although the change appears to have been transitory. And who can forget the image of Senate Majority Leader Tom Daschle fondly embracing his nemesis, President George W. Bush, in a show of unity directly after the attacks? Most observers believe that the *common enemy syndrome* provides a superordinate goal that is responsible for submerging racial differences and activating diverse groups to work together.

Principle Four—Exchanging Accurate Information

As I have repeatedly emphasized, most of your knowledge and beliefs about other racial/ethnic groups do not come from personal experience and contact. It is generally provided to you through the mass media, through the messages that family, friends, and neighbors convey to you, and through your educational system. It goes without saying that these sources of information that form the foundations of your belief system are often erroneous and filled with falsehoods and stereotypes. The beliefs that Asian Americans are sly, sneaky, and sinister and may be potential spies usually do not come from direct experience but from other outlets. Images of Fu Man Chu, Charlie Chan, Ghengis Khan, and the sinister Dr. No that are provided in the media; statements by neighbors, family, and friends that the "Chinese are the Jews of Asia"; and history texts that discuss the bombing of Pearl Harbor as an act of deceit and back stabbing all combine to create a stereotypical view of Asians in America.

Although it would be helpful to combat stereotypes, misinformation, and misunderstandings to dispense accurate information through these sources, overcoming racism and bias is not solely an intellectual exercise. Obtaining correct information about the group must come from experiential reality, where the information is personalized into your thoughts and feelings. All thoughts and beliefs that you possess have an affective dimension—that is, they are accompanied by emotions and feelings. A White woman, for example, who is consciously aware that the image of Black men being prone to violence, rape, and crime is a stereotype may still experience apprehension and fear when riding in an elevator alone with a Black male. Accurate information can only be meaningful when the interacting parties dispel the negative nested emotions that are based on stereotypes about one another by counteracting them with new and positive feelings.

Being an Asian American psychologist, my work on multicultural psychology has provided me with much knowledge and information about stereotypes on Black Americans. As a young assistant professor, one of my most meaningful experiences was with a Black colleague, Malachi. We had established a good relationship at the university based on common subject matter interest. We served on committees together and found much in common. Despite my historical knowledge of African Americans, my friend must have sensed my continuing "unease" around Blacks. One late afternoon, he invited me to meet him for drinks at a local bar. I was unaware at that time that the lounge was frequented primarily by Black patrons.

Imagine my surprise as I stepped from the bright outdoor sunlight into the dim confines of the bar and was confronted with a sea of Black faces. Not only did I feel alone and, frankly, anxious but to make things worse, I could not find my friend. I remember the thoughts and feelings that flooded me: Am I safe? Did they notice I'm different from them? Are they upset that I'm here? How will they treat me? Should I order a drink? But I also kept saying reassuring things to myself: Your fears are unwarranted. Don't let stereo-types rule your thoughts. Don't be afraid. Luckily, Malachi soon appeared. He was obviously well-known and liked among the patrons, as many greeted him with great affection. Spying me, he came over, ordered a carafe of wine for us both, steered me over to a table of his friends, and whispered only one word to me: "relax."

After several glasses of wine, being welcomed by Malachi's friends, and listening to their conversations, I began to feel more at ease as the heavy burden of fear lifted from my body. I would listen to them, they would listen to me, as we spoke about sports, work hassles, family, and friends. I came to understand their worldviews, hopes, fears, concerns, and aspirations and their different commu-nication styles. I began to truly understand the Black experience, not only from a cognitive perspective but also from an emotive one. Likewise, they came to understand my experience as an Asian American. That afternoon marked the true beginning of my multi-cultural education.

Principle Five—Sharing an Equal Relationship

Think about *all* the relationships you have ever had with peo-ple of color. How many of them involved a relationship in which they were at least your equal? I would bet that most people of color you meet, know, or interact with are usually in subordinate roles. They are clerks, janitors, sales personnel, your clients, and so on. If this is not the case, then you represent an exception.

It goes without saying that the majority of contacts between majority group members and minority group members are fraught with inequality in the distribution of power and resources. This power imbalance represents a major barrier to improving race rela-tions. The ability to work through disagreements and racial con-flicts is most likely to occur when participants share an equal relationship. An improved interpersonal relationship between a Latino custodian and his White CEO boss, for example, is not likely to happen for several reasons.

First, their roles have already been structured in such a way as to define who has more value and authority, not only in the work situation but in almost all aspects of their societal life. By virtue of social status in our society, the White CEO is more valued, considered more knowledgeable, and treated as having more credibility than the Latino custodian. Placed in a situation where they must interact with each other, the status hierarchy is likely to prevail, with the White executive more likely to be the communicator and the Latino worker the recipient of the assertions of the CEO. Communication is not only likely to be one-way (from those with more power to those with less power), but it may also reinforce stereotypes: persons of color are less competent and capable.

Second, and related to this point, is our understanding of the nature of attributions for success and failure. Though it may be unfair to place worth on occupational roles like that of a custodian and a CEO, society definitely imputes greater worth to the latter and generally views it as a sign of work success. You are likely to attribute traits like intelligence, high ability, and hard work as reasons behind high achievement. Likewise, you are likely to attribute traits like low intelligence, low ability, and laziness as reasons for low achievement or failure.

Studies do reveal that you are more likely to see occupational success as due to positive internal qualities of the person and lower job roles as due to more negative personal qualities. So in a situation where persons of color or the group do not share an equal relationship with their White counterparts, the attribution is likely to be something negative about the racial minority individual or group. Again, negative perceptions of the group lesser in prestige, status, and power are likely to be maintained or increased.

Third, when you possess greater authority, influence, and power, you seldom are placed in a position where you need to listen to someone lower in the status hierarchy. If anything, it appears that those with the least power are more sensitive and aware of the habits and motives of those who can influence their lives for better or worse. This explains why women so often are able to see sexism in the behavior of men, why gays and lesbians can spot heterosexism quickly, and why people of color can discern the racist behaviors and attitudes of their White counterparts. Unfortunately, those who possess power are often oblivious to their privilege and how their unintentional bigotry affects those most disempowered.

It is therefore clear that even with the best of intentions to eradicate racism by placing different groups in contact with one another, societal rules, regulations, and structures continue to oppress people of color by placing them in lesser positions and by placing Whites in superior ones. Inequality in every facet of American life abounds: CEOs continue to be primarily White males, over 90 percent of public school teachers are White, minorities and women continue to encounter the glass ceiling, students of color generally have lower educational attainment and receive inferior education, more persons of color suffer from poverty, and nearly every leadership position in our society is occupied by White males. In our society, unequal status relationships foster greater racial misunderstandings, block our ability to learn from one another, and perpetuate racism.

What our society must do is to somehow redistribute resources and share power. This is a lofty goal, but you can all help by taking small steps in your personal life: helping make sure that committees and groups include people of color, providing feedback to your school about the need to hire teachers of color, and voting for political candidates of color or those who are in favor of social policies that stress equal access and opportunity.

Principle Six—Supporting Racial Equity by Leaders and Groups in Authority

During the early days of court-ordered integration, the success of desegregation varied from community to community and in many cases from school to school in the same community. Social scientists soon discovered that support from community leaders for integration often was the single most important predictor of success. Schools or communities that fared poorly generally did not have the support of leaders. For example, when former governor George Wallace stood at the front of the school to block the entrance of Black students, it sent a loud and clear message to the community: regardless of the law, Blacks are undesirable and unwelcome. In other words, the actions of Alabama's highest-ranking officer continued to model the continuing hatred and bigotry of its White citizens. As a result, improvement in race relations was doomed to fail in such a situation.

In contrast, it was found that when leaders supported court-ordered integration, busing Black students to White schools resulted in less hostility and greater movement toward racial harmony. When community leaders, politicians, superintendents, and teachers expressed support for integration as important to end discrimination and prejudice, both White and Black parents and students seemed to have an easier time accepting one another. In this case, the leaders expressed overarching humanistic values (eradicating racism and stressing our common humanity are desired) and modeled appropriate respect toward all persons of color.

Likewise, it meant much to persons of color and many White citizens to witness a Jack Kennedy or a Bill Clinton, presidents who took active stands against racism and stressed our common belief in equality. Even though our history is replete with political leaders who acted to inflame racism, it is also filled with courageous politicians who fought against discrimination and prejudice. President Truman eliminated racial segregation in the military, President Roosevelt established the Fair Employment Practices Committee, and President Johnson established the Equal Employment Opportunity Commission. It was again Gordon Allport who stressed the need for public and private institutional and organizational support in combating racism. In a recent survey of whom we trust to enhance the national dialogue on race, religious organizations were ranked first and national media last in fostering constructive dialogue on race. The following was the rank order of various organizations and groups:

1. Religious organizations
2. Community-based not-for-profit groups
3. Schools and universities
4. Local government
5. Local businesses
6. National government
7. State government
8. Local media
9. National media—almost never mentioned

In other words, organizations like the National Association for the Advancement of Colored People (NAACP), B'nai B'rith, the Southern Poverty Law Center, and the Anti-Defamation League, along with churches, were perceived as important in fostering racial harmony. Public institutions, usually governmental agencies, can also help because they are empowered by laws to influence the American public on their attitudes and behaviors. Fair employment practices, discrimination in housing, and civil rights protection are all aspects of governmental oversight. Interestingly, the media are seen as the least helpful and trusted.

Principle Seven—Feeling Connected and Experiencing a Sense of Belonging

As we have emphasized, the United States is characterized as an achievement-oriented society, a trait most strongly manifested in the Protestant work ethic. Basic to the ethic are the concepts of separation and individualism: the individual is the psychosocial unit of operation, the individual has primary responsibility for his or her own actions, independence and autonomy are highly valued and rewarded, and one should be internally directed and controlled.

Consistent with this orientation is our nation's heavy reliance on asking and answering questions about the human condition through sensory information as defined by the physical plane of reality (Western science). You are told to be objective, that rationality is the ability to separate yourself from the issues, and not to let your emotions "get in the way." Our worship of science reveals the value placed on symbolic logic, analytical and linear approaches, and the ability to tease out parts from the whole. The results of this overriding philosophy of life are also reflected in our legal system (individual rights), our standards of healthy development and functioning (autonomy, independence, and being your own person), our definition of the family (nuclear family versus extended family), and even our religion (separation of church and state).

Although individualism as a value has many positive components, is it possible that like competition its extreme form may lead to an unhealthy separation between you and others? When you objectify others, see them as distinct from you, and perceive your relationships with people as less desirable than individuality, is it possible that you may also be prone to dehumanize them? Extremes of individualism often result in people becoming self-centered, narcissistic, and selfish. If you are the victim of this unhealthy scourge, you will begin to evaluate everything from the perspective of "me." How does it benefit me? Because your world revolves around you, others are less important. Indeed, you may perceive them as either impediments to achieving your own personal goals or a means to achieve them. In either case, others become objectified and in many cases dehumanized as well. You will have little regard for others, see them as separate from you, and experience little empathy for them.

During World War II and the Vietnam War, for example, referring to the Japanese and Vietnamese in demeaning racial epithets, like Japs, gooks, and slants, frequently dehumanized Asians. They were not seen as human beings but rather as subhuman aliens, evil beings, and animals that should be wiped off the face of the earth and destroyed. They were the true Yellow Peril frequently referred to in our historical relationship with Asians. Such an approach made it easier for our soldiers to kill them.

A similar analogy can be made to that of racial hatred in the United States. Persons of color are perceived as "other beings": sub-human, criminals, untrustworthy, animalistic, uncivilized, aliens, dangerous, lazy, unintelligent, and the dregs of society. Consequently, you have little empathy for them and believe that a civilized society would be better off without persons of color. Such a belief, whether spoken or not, makes it easy for outright racists to enact violence and cruelty on persons of color without guilt or compassion. It also allows the majority of White Americans to sit idly by and bear witness to the cruelty and oppression inflicted on a "subhuman group of beings" without protest. After all, as long as you do not feel connected to the other beings and do not perceive them as part of you, injustice and oppression are not disturbing.

If your disconnection from the other allows racism to thrive, then the solution might lie in becoming connected with one another by viewing humanity as all encompassing and inherently unifying. In that respect, if the "us and them" thinking is replaced by the collective "we," then what happens to one person happens to all. If injustice were carried out against a member of another race, we would all feel the pain and bear the responsibility in rectifying the situation. To achieve this end, however, would require a monumental shift in our philosophies of life. What, for example, would have to exist for you to begin thinking about yourself and others as interconnected? Two aspects of indigenous cultural values and philosophy may provide clues to an answer.

First, most non-Western indigenous cultures possess an interconnected and holistic outlook on life. For example, minimal distinction is made between physical and mental functioning, life forms are interrelated, and the environment and cosmos are linked to life itself. Illness, distress, or problematic behaviors are seen as an imbalance or separation between people or environmental relationships. The seeking of harmony or balance is life's goal. Among

American Indians, for example, harmony with nature is symbolized by the circle, or hoop, of life. Mind, body, and spirit, people and nature, are seen as a single unified entity with little separation between the realities of life, medicine, and religion. All forms of nature, not just the living, are to be revered because they reflect the creator or deity. Illness is seen as a break in the hoop of life, an imbalance or separation between people or the elements.

Likewise, the Afrocentric perspective, with its roots in Egypt and Nubia, teaches that human beings are part of a holistic fabric and should be oriented toward collective rather than individual survival. The indigenous Japanese assumptions and practices of Naikan and Morita therapy, for example, attempt to move clients toward being more in tune with others and society, to move away from individualism, and to move toward interdependence and connectedness (harmony with others).

Second, many cultural groups place strong emphasis on the interplay and interdependence of spiritual life and healthy functioning. Puerto Ricans, for example, may sacrifice material satisfaction in favor of values pertaining to the spirit and soul. The Lakota Sioux often say *Mitakuye Oyasin* at the end of a prayer or as a salutation. Translated it means "to all my relations," which acknowledges the spiritual bond between speaker and all people present, to forebears, to the tribe, to the family of man, and to Mother Nature. It speaks to the philosophy that all life forces, Mother Earth, and the cosmos are sacred beings, and the spiritual is the thread that binds all together. Likewise, a strong spiritual orientation has always been a major aspect of life in Africa and in this country during the slavery era. The African American church continues to play a strong role in the lives of Black people. Spirituality (not necessarily formal religion) is believed to be an intimate aspect of the human condition.

In a recent Gallup Poll, it was found that over 90 percent of Americans expressed a "spiritual hunger." So although I speak about indigenous cultures as possessing clues to our connections with one another, in reality, your early White European forebears were equally collectivistic, communal, and spiritual. One only has to study the early history of European immigrants, who relied on extended families and neighbors for survival. If your early European ancestors were more collectivistic, what moved the generations to come toward a more individualistic focus?

The answers seem to lie in the history of our nation: the industrial revolution, the advent of technology, the increasing reliance on science, and our mobility all served to separate us from one another. According to existentialists, for example, our nation increasingly began to become machine and technology oriented rather than people oriented. Assembly lines minimized people interactions, technology made it easy for us to do our work in office cubicles in isolation from coworkers, and our ability to travel to different parts of the country and away from extended families all served to reinforce our emphasis on individualism.

This analysis is not meant as a condemnation of science, technology, and individualism. What I am trying to say is that in light of these factors, you need to work extra hard to connect with others. It would appear that only if we begin to reconnect with one another and reclaim our humanity will we begin to step away from racism and bigotry.

ERADICATING RACISM MEANS ADVOCATING FOR SOCIAL CHANGE

To achieve these conditions in our society is truly an uphill battle. But just as I have stated that the history of the United States is the history of racism, it is also the history of antiracism. There have always been people and movements directed toward the eradication of racism. Abolitionists, civil rights workers, private organizations (Southern Poverty Law Center, NAACP, B'nai B'rith, other religious organizations), political leaders, and especially people of color have all opposed racism. So there is a critical mass in our society already from which to effect change. How we harness that energy and force is the $64 million question. And I hope you will become an ally for social change.

What I am proposing is a concerted effort by all of you to eradicate bigotry and prejudice by using the channels of socialization (education, media, groups and organizations) to spread a curriculum of multiculturalism and using the seven antiracism principles to help guide your efforts and strategy. An antiracism movement of the massive scale being proposed is indeed a Herculean undertaking, and frankly, I hope you have the courage and fortitude to help implement such widespread changes in your own special way. Your goals would be to substitute a multicultural worldview for a monocultural one, to challenge and change the racial reality of White America, and to make major structural and cultural changes in your social, economic, political, educational, and media systems. To redefine our nation's racial reality requires a shift in the attitudes, opinions, and beliefs of our citizens similar to what has happened in our attitudes toward cigarette smoking.

At one point, smoking was considered desirable and normative in our society. Tobacco companies filled the airwaves with advertisements linking smoking to sophistication, sexiness (masculinity or femininity), maturity, and overall health. Actors and actresses, sports figures, and other role models would light up on-screen, at the ballparks, in restaurants, and in most private and public places. Those who objected to the nuisance of the smoke or its potentially detrimental health consequences were seen as fringe elements in the society. They were perceived as not having a right to impose their standards on smokers.

As we now know, however, attitudes toward smoking have changed dramatically. It is now considered a character weakness and detrimental to the well-being of both smokers and nonsmokers. Smokers are often seen as addicts, sinners, unsophisticated, intrusive, and selfish. They are often accused of having "smoker's breath" and smell, aging poorly from wrinkles caused by the smoke, and causing increased health cost for others due to their greater use of medical services. Rightly or wrongly, they have also been accused of causing medical problems like emphysema and other respiratory problems, not just for themselves but for nonsmokers as well.

As of this writing, five states have banned smoking in bars and restaurants, and most states now do not allow smoking in public places. Indeed, the picture of smokers huddled together outside their work sites in order to have a smoke presents the image of wrong-doing, shame, and guilt. How did society's attitude toward smoking change so dramatically and quickly? It changed because a coalition of groups had the courage and fortitude to use the major channels of socialization to combat the powerful tobacco industry: schooling and education, mass media, and significant human groupings.

Likewise, I believe that if we are to eradicate or diminish racism in a significant manner, we must build multicultural alliances that use these three channels to alter the nature of race relations in this country. Even though mass media, for example, are often guilty of insensitivity to racial/ethnic groups and perpetuate misinformation and derogatory stereotypes, they can also be a powerful means of combating them. Likewise, education and schooling need not be monocultural. It can be used to teach fairness, equity, inclusion, appreciation, and valuing of differences, as well as the many other democratic principles this country was supposedly built on.

What You Can Do to Overcome Racism

In 1999, the President's Initiative on Race produced a publication outlining what they called "promising practices for racial reconciliation," which are consistent with the seven principles of anti-racism.[3] A nation committed to eradicating racism should prioritize activities, programs, and practices that contain these characteristics in all aspects of societal life.

1. *Promoting racially inclusive collaboration*. Our society would benefit from schools, work sites, governmental projects, and other activities that create opportunities for peer-to-peer collaboration in achieving common goals. It must, however, represent meaningful joint tasks among people who vary in racial diversity and are representative of the local population. National, state, city, and local community organizations must build programs that foster cooperative interactions. Several key questions should be asked: Does the program or activity foster peer-to-peer collaboration across racial lines? To what extent do the program participants reflect the full racial diversity of the local community? and To what extent is there full diversity among program managers and board members? Help ask these questions persistently whenever the opportunity arises.

2. *Educating on racial issues*. Participants must interact in such a manner that they become educated about the importance of historical and contemporary facts regarding race, racism, and culture. In this case, accurate information must be dispensed even if it's unpleasant. Schools and significant human groupings can do much in this respect. Several key questions should be asked: Does the program educate participants about the historical contributions of diverse racial and cultural groups and about issues of racism in our society? Does the program educate participants about the personal impact of subtle racial issues such as unconscious prejudice, unearned privilege, and racism against one's own group? and Does the program encourage participants to educate nonparticipants about issues of race?

3. *Raising racial consciousness*. The activity or program goals should be to reduce racism and lessen racial disparities and divisions. Several key questions should be asked: Does the program include the unique perspectives of different racial groups? Does the program encourage participants to become aware of the connection between activities and racial reconciliation? and Does the program raise awareness about the interrelationships between race and other sociodemographic divisions, like gender, class, and sexual orientation?

4. *Encouraging introspection*. The setting should encourage deep and serious reflection about the participants' conscious and unconscious attitudes and beliefs about race and culture. Several key questions should be asked: Does the program result in open examination and dialogue about conscious and unconscious biases? and Are participants encouraged to explore connections between their feelings and race-related issues in society?

5. *Expanding opportunity and access for individuals*. The program should expand and work toward equal access and opportunity for groups that have traditionally and historically been excluded in our society. Several key questions should be asked: Does the program provide resources that help participants, particularly those from historically disadvantaged groups, increase their opportunity to attain success? and Are there follow-up sessions to document gains and to provide additional assistance?

6. *Fostering civic engagement*. The program should encourage participants and leaders to take action in addressing racial reconciliation at all levels of society and government. Several key questions should be asked: Does the program provide the skills needed to recognize racism and constructively engage others who would foster racial reconciliation? Does the program allow for participation in civic causes that promote leadership in racial-reconciliation efforts? and Does the program allow for engagement of established community and civic leaders to address the causes and effects of prejudice and racism?

7. *Working for systemic change*. There should be reform in ways that organizations, institutions, and systems operate to lessen racial disparities and eliminate discrimination. Several key questions should be asked: Does the program provide constituents and consumers tools to hold institutions accountable for practices that undermine racial reconciliation? Does it address discriminatory behavior by people whose decisions may perpetuate racial disparities? and Are there efforts to analyze and change the ways that policies and practices may perpetuate racial disparities and divisions?

8. *Assessing impact on the community*. It should measure the organization's accomplishments, consider the challenges it faces, and reassess the desired future outcomes. Several key questions should be asked: Does the program attempt to assess the breadth and depth of its effect on people and organizations? and Does the program continually adjust its goals and practices to keep pace with changing local needs and racial demographics?

How we operationalize and implement these best practices and the seven antiracism principles in our society is the major challenge confronting our nation. I believe that each and every one of us, at some level, is aware of the choice we must make. If we truly believe in the principles of equity, fairness, and justice, then we cannot allow racism, sexism, and the other "isms" to exist in our society. The choice, I believe, is one of ethnocentric monoculturalism or multiculturalism.

The final questions you must ask are these: As a nation, will you choose the path we have always traveled, a journey that has benefited only a select group? Or will you choose the road less traveled, a journey of multiculturalism that is full of uncertainties but offers benefits to all groups in our society? It would be unfortunate, indeed, to look back one day and echo the words of poet John Greenleaf Whittier, who wrote, "For of all sad words of tongue or pen, the saddest are these: 'It might have been!'"

What Must People of Color Do to Overcome Racism?

A Personal Message to My Brothers and Sisters of Color

I am tired of . . .

Watching mediocre White people continue to rise to positions of authority and responsibility.

Wondering if the White woman who quickly exited the elevator when I got on was really at her destination.

Being told I do not sound Black.

Being told by White people that they "don't see color" when they interact with me.

The deadening silence that occurs when the conversation turns to race.

Having to explain why I wish to be called "African American."

Wondering if things will get better.

Wondering if the taxi driver really did not see me trying to hail a ride.

Being told that I should not criticize racially segregated country clubs because I wouldn't enjoy associating with people who belong to them anyway.

Being followed in department stores by the security force and pestered by sales clerks who refuse to allow me to browse because they suspect I am a shoplifter.

Never being able to let my racial guard down.

Listening to reports about people of color who failed as justification for the absence of other people of color in positions of authority.

Being told that "we are just not ready for a Black person in that position."

Having to explain that my sexual fantasies do not center on White women.

Feeling racially threatened when approached by a White law enforcement officer.

Explaining that not all African Americans are employed to meet some quota.

Being told that I need to openly distance myself from another African American whose words have offended someone.

Having people tell me that I have it made and then telling me that I have "sold out" in order to have what I have.

Explaining why I am tired.

Being tired [Adapted from "Fatigue: An Essay," by Don C. Locke].[1]

———

The police came to our house on a December morning in 1995. They had a search warrant for what they claimed to be stolen property in the possession of my nineteen-year-old son. Because my wife was running a car pool, no one was at home. The police broke down our front door and claimed to have recovered the missing equipment. My son was subsequently arrested and imprisoned on felony charges. These charges were finally dismissed after an outcry from friends, neighbors, and minority group organizations that saw the actions as an example of racism. What our family was forced to endure was extreme, unwarranted, and to me clearly in retaliation for our antiracism work in the community and a reflection of anti-Asian sentiment among certain elements in the city. I was positive that a White family in this primarily White affluent community would never have suffered a similar fate.

I cannot possibly convey to you the anguish and pain this incident has inflicted on my family and me. The pain associated with personal discrimination is different than when a member of your own family is used to strike back at you.

After no less than nine court hearings and countless attempts by the district attorney to have us bargain to reduced charges, the judge finally dismissed the case for lack of evidence. We filed a civil suit against the city for false arrest, false imprisonment, and violation of civil rights.

At that time, I was filled with bitterness and hatred toward the police and select community leaders who seemed to take delight in terrorizing an Asian American family. I equated my hatred with anyone who was White. Although I am still very angry, I no longer experience the blind hatred that briefly ruled my life.

Dear Brothers and Sisters of Color:

I write this last chapter mainly to you and to those White folks who have marched with us against racism and shown that their hearts are in the right place. Throughout our peoples' histories, we have had to contend with invalidation, oppression, injustice, terrorism, and genocide. Racism is a constant reality in our lives. It is a toxic force that has sought to

- Strip us of our identities
- Take away our dignity
- Make us second-class citizens
- Destroy our peoples, cultures, and communities
- Steal our land and property
- Torture, rape, and murder us
- Imprison us on reservations, concentration camps, inferior schools, segregated neighborhoods, and jails
- Use us as guinea pigs in medical experiments
- Blame our victimization on the faults of our own people

Attempts to express these thoughts have generally been met with disbelief and incredulity by many of our well-intentioned White brothers and sisters. We have been asked, "Aren't you distorting the truth? Where is your proof? Where is your evidence?"

When we attempt to provide it, we are interrogated about its legitimacy, told that we are biased or paranoid, and accused of being dishonest in how we present the facts. After all, they say, "Our nation is built on life, liberty, and the pursuit of happiness. It was founded on the principles of freedom, democracy, and equality."

Yet these guiding principles seem intended for Whites only! In the classic book *Animal Farm*, when the issue of inequality arose, the character in a position of power justified the treatment by stating that some are "more equal" than others. Rather than offer enlightenment and freedom, education and healing, and rather than allowing for equal access and opportunity, historical and current practices in our nation have restricted, stereotyped, damaged, and oppressed persons of color.

For too long, people of color have not had the opportunity or power to express their points of view. For too long, our voices have not been heard. For too long, our worldviews have been diminished, negated, or considered invalid. For too long, we have been told that our perceptions are incorrect, that most things are well with our society, and that our concerns and complaints are not supported. For too long, we have had to justify our existence and to fight for our dignity and humanity. No wonder that we are so tired, impatient, and angry. Yet, as people of color, we cannot let fatigue turn into hopelessness nor anger into bitterness. Hopelessness is the forerunner to surrender, and bitterness leads to blind hatred. Either could spell our downfall!

It is important for us to realize that despite these indignities, we have persevered and become stronger. We have survived through our collective strength. We have survived through our heightened perceptual wisdom. We have survived through our ability to read the contextualized meanings of our oppressors. We have survived through our bicultural flexibility. We have survived through our families and communities. We have survived through our spirituality and religion. We have survived through our racial/ethnic identity and pride. We have survived through our belief in the interconnectedness of the human condition.

Unlike many of our White brothers and sisters who are untested, we have demonstrated superhuman resiliency in the face of adversity. Our perseverance in battling the forces of racism comes from our understanding the strengths and assets developed by our ancestors as they fought oppression and from our cultural values, mores, and traditions.

STRENGTHS THROUGH ADVERSITY

As persons of color, we have been subjected to inhuman stressors in our lives: poverty, high unemployment rates, and lower standards of living; conflicting value systems imposed by a White Euro-American society; a history of broad governmental actions that have led to the enslavement of Black Americans, the internment of Japanese Americans, and the colonization of Native Americans; and constant micro-invalidations and micro-aggressions that strike at the core of our group identities.

Indeed, Vernon E. Jordan Jr., attorney and confidant of former President Bill Clinton, speaking at Howard University in June 2002, made that point in startling terms. In making an analogy between the terrorist attack of September 11 and those suffered by Blacks, Jordan stated:

> None of this is new to Black people. War, hunger, disease, unemployment, deprivation, dehumanization, and terrorism define our existence. They are not new to us. Slavery was terrorism, segregation was terrorism, the bombing of the four little girls in Sunday school in Birmingham was terrorism. The violent deaths of Medgar, Martin, Malcolm, Vernon Dahmer, Chaney, Schwerner, Goodman were terrorism. And the difference between September 11 and the terror visited upon Black people is that on September 11, the terrorists were foreigners. When we were terrorized, it was by our neighbors. The terrorists were American citizens.
>
> Now that America is warring on terrorism, it is Black people who remind America that we know terrorism well. We know that dangerous rhetoric can lead to acts of lunacy that kill innocents. And we know that the surest defense against terrorism is affirmation of America's basic values, the values we have learned in our churches, the values we have fought and died for in America's every war, even in segregated armies.[2]

In light of the historical and continuing experiences of oppression, even I marvel at our ability to continue our lives in such a normative fashion. It seems that White America exhibits minimal appreciation for the incredible strength and resiliency that we have shown in surviving and sometimes flourishing in the face of racism. Our experiences of oppression have required us to sharpen and hone our survival skills to such a degree that they now represent assets. We have learned this through the courageous and undefeatable actions of our ancestors who showed us the way. It is ironic that overcoming adversity has led us to develop an ability to understand the minds of our oppressors with astounding clarity.

So when we begin to become tired and discouraged, when hopelessness seems just around the corner, and when we wonder what good our actions are doing, we need to remind ourselves of the strengths and assets we possess, many of them taught to us by our ancestors. We need to take pride in the fact that our heightened perceptual wisdom, our ability to rely on nonverbal and contextual meanings, and our bicultural flexibility have proven to be the keys to our survival. Let me recount them here.

Adversity Strength One—Heightened Perceptual Wisdom

As people of color, we understand White folks better than they understand us. This statement will anger many of our White brothers and sisters, but it is generally an accepted reality for people of color. Although it may not be true with regard to all aspects of life, we know it has great validity in assessing issues of bias, prejudice, and White privilege. Even studies by White psychologists support this finding: the most accurate assessment of bias comes not from those who enjoy the privilege of power but from those who are most disempowered.

Unfortunately, White folks do not realize that possessing unchecked power and control over others often results in the dimming of their own perceptiveness and leads to a distorted reality. This is because their high status and power means they seldom have to worry or even think about people of color, they use one another to validate their sense of false racial reality, and they inaccurately define people of color from a stereotypical template. It deprives them of seeing the world as it really is.

As people of color, however, we have been forced to operate within a predominantly White culture and are taught the history, mores, and language of Western society from the moment of our birth. We have attended their White schools, been exposed to a Euro-American educational curriculum, worked for White-controlled places of employment, and been subjected to a White justice system. In other words, we have been immersed in the prejudices of our oppressors and their biased institutions. Our survival therefore depends on how accurately we are able to discern the truth as it relates to the thoughts and actions of White Americans.

It is often stated that people of color and other oppressed and marginalized groups possess a clarity of vision and truth that is discomforting to those who are most empowered. I believe this is absolutely true. Our power of accurate perception—the ability to see beyond the obvious, to read between the lines, to not be easily fooled, and to intuitively understand the motives, intent, and meaning of others—is an extremely valuable asset that we have developed.

For our survival, we have had to become hypervigilant in discerning the motives, attitudes, and the often unintentional biased contradictions of our White brothers and sisters. Our intuitive insights about White Americans and their biases often cause great discomfort and consternation to those in the dominant group. It is precisely this fear of being unmasked in the eyes of persons of color and in public that creates much of the difficulty that Whites have in speaking about racism and oppression. Yet it is exactly this heightened perception and wisdom that represents a valuable asset and an aspect of optimal human functioning among persons of color. As people of color, we must rely heavily on our intuitive and experiential reality. Never allow White folks to make us doubt our perceptual wisdom!

Adversity Strength Two—Nonverbal and Contextualized Accuracy

"To truly understand White people, don't listen to what they say but how they say it." This saying, often made by my brothers and sisters of color, refers to our ability to discern the biased attitudes and stereotypes that many Whites possess but that are intentionally or unintentionally concealed. We have always known that nonverbal communication is a more accurate barometer of what White folks truly intend than the words they use. In communication theory, these are generally accepted principles: people communicate on both verbal and nonverbal levels, only 30 to 40 percent of what is communicated occurs verbally, nonverbal behavior is least under conscious control, and nonverbal communication is likely to be more accurate than verbal messages.

If one of the attributes of healthy functioning is the ability to accurately read nonverbal communication and discern the truth, then we must conclude that many people of color possess strengths unmatched by our White counterparts in this arena. Our ability to read nonverbal cues accurately and efficiently has long been important for the survival of persons of color. Clues to conscious deceptions and unconscious biases can be seen more readily through facial expressions, bodily movements, hesitations in speech, and so forth.

My Black brothers and sisters, for example, frequently give examples of the need to be vigilant when traveling in unknown parts of the United States. Not only must they be alert to possible dangers to their physical survival, but their psychological survival is also at risk. They must be able to discern the double messages being sent to them by both intentional and unintentional racists. That is why Black Americans and many persons of color place so much value on genuineness.

Adversity Strength Three—Bicultural Flexibility

Because persons of color in the United States inherit two different cultural traditions, we are often placed in a situation of not only having potential cultural conflicts but also experiencing the press to become bicultural, a valuable asset to our ability to function optimally. I am not advocating that people of color "become White" but rather that we foster our ability to be bicultural without losing our sense of integrity. Because White Americans are seldom placed in such a position, one might characterize them as disadvantaged when it comes to bicultural development. One of the major advantages to being bicultural or multicultural is the ability to see multiple worldviews, both sides of an issue, and to understand more readily the other's point of view.

The second advantage entails the concept of bicultural or behavioral flexibility. The saying "When in Rome, do as the Romans do" speaks to the issue of adaptability. When I testified before President Clinton's Race Advisory Board in 1997, I outlined some of the advantages of being bicultural: broadening one's horizons in viewing the world; increasing appreciation for the strengths and limitations of all people; becoming less afraid and intimidated by cultural differences; feeling more self-fulfilled; being able to communicate more openly and clearly with family, friends, and coworkers; experiencing increased effectiveness in relating to diverse cultural groups; and feeling connected to social justice. Interestingly, our White brothers and sisters would also benefit immensely if they became more bicultural.

STRENGTHS THROUGH OUR CULTURAL VALUES

Our cultural values have also been a major source of strength in allowing us to function adaptively in a very oppressive environment. We must cherish and not lose touch with the very values that have allowed us to persevere in the face of invalidation. Ironically, our society has often viewed our customs, values, and beliefs as pathological, non-normative, and deficient.

Many White Americans fail to realize that it is our culture that has allowed us to survive and oftentimes flourish in a toxic environment. We must also remind ourselves of this point. Five important cultural resources have immunized us against racism and have allowed us to function adaptively throughout our history: collectivism; racial and ethnic pride; spirituality and religion; the interconnectedness of mind, body, and spirit; and family and community.

Cultural Strength One—Collectivism

As people of color, we have always seen ourselves from what psychologists call a *collectivistic* orientation—that is, our identities are seen as inextricably tied to and defined in relation to our social networks, such as family members, friends, and cultural groups. In many cases (for example, Native Americans), the collectivistic orientation may also extend to the social environment, Mother Earth, all living and nonliving forms, and the universe. This is in marked contrast to the Western individualistic orientation, where the psychosocial unit of operation is the individual rather than the group. In such a case, ties between many of our White brothers and sisters are loose, and they are expected to function autonomously and to look out for their own welfare.

Collectivistic groups like those of African Americans, Asian Americans, Latino/Hispanic Americans, and Native Americans, however, integrate the individual from the moment of birth into strong, cohesive in-groups that continue to shield or protect the individuals throughout their lives. It can truly be stated that White society has historically attempted to destroy our family systems and to wipe us off the face of the earth. We have learned that near and distant relatives, neighbors, friends, and acquaintances are important and valuable allies by forming an extended family support network. We have learned to replace and make our personal goals to be consistent with benefiting the group. We have learned that in this society, what is good for groups of color is ultimately good for us. In an oppressive and invalidating environment, collectivism has allowed people of color to prosper, despite the hostile forces directed against us.

Cultural Strength Two—Racial and Ethnic Pride

Developing healthy cultural identities and self-esteem is challenging for many people of color, as we continually combat an oppressive society that equates our differences with deviance and pathology. However, despite our exposure to racism and discrimination, many people of color continue to have positive racial and ethnic perceptions of themselves (that is, racial and ethnic pride) and subsequently high levels of well-being. Again, our collectivistic orientation has allowed us to internalize a positive racial or ethnic identity.

Strangely enough, our group identities have been reinforced by what many of my African American brothers and sister describe as the sense of "peoplehood" developed as a result of the common experience of racism and discrimination. The Black Power movement, the Yellow Power movement, other racial/ethnic identity movements, and the civil rights movement were the result of our collectivistic orientation and strength. It appears that collective self-esteem or the degree to which we positively assess our social or cultural groups is intimately related to psychological adjustment. Interestingly, psychological studies reveal that many persons of color are able to separate how we privately feel about our groups and how we believe others may evaluate us. Our ability to separate public and private evaluations may represent an important survival strategy for many people of color. I believe that as a parent of color it is important to raise our sons and daughters with a strong sense of racial/ethnic identity and pride.

Cultural Strength Three—Spirituality and Religion

Spiritual valuing rather than material valuing has been one of the mainstays of persons of color, immunizing us against the forces of racism and allowing us to continue in the face of oppression. African Americans, Asian Americans, Latino/Hispanic Americans, and Native Americans have always placed a strong emphasis on spirituality. I define spirituality as the animating force in life and the cosmos, the force that gives us meaning, hope, growth, and love. It can be manifested in a belief of a creational force or some higher Supreme Being. Spirituality is not religiosity, but it can be manifested in religion. Religion is the routine and pragmatic demonstration of spirituality reflected in formal theological beliefs and activities (for example, church attendance and rituals). Religion and spirituality may each represent important coping and social support mechanisms for many people of color. In the context of community structures, religion and spirituality have been particularly salient for many people of color throughout their histories in the United States.

The Black church, for example, is one of many manifestations of African American spirituality and represents a social, psychological, political, familial, and healing institution for African Americans. During the slavery era, a strong spiritual orientation through highly emotional religious services helped my Black brothers and sisters persevere in the face of oppression. Indeed, many spirituals sung by congregations during those times contained hidden messages and a language of resistance, and they allowed those who were enslaved outlets for expressing pain, anger, and action (for example, "Wade in the Water," "Steal Away," "Nobody Knows the Trouble I've Seen").

Likewise, many American Indian, Asian American, and Latino/Hispanic American groups believe religion and spirituality to play vital roles in their overall well-being. For instance, although

American Indians vary according to tribe, level of acculturation, and other personal characteristics, many of these individuals believe that mental health is spiritual and holistic in nature. Spirituality has been vital in helping us cope with hopelessness, identity issues, and feelings of powerlessness.

Cultural Strength Four—Interconnectedness of Mind, Body, and Spirit

My Native American brothers and sisters are the epitome of this cultural strength. It is symbolized by the circle, or hoop, of life, where mind, body, spirit, and nature are seen as a single unified entity with little separation between the realities of life, medicine, and religion. All forms of nature whether living or non-living are to be revered because they reflect the creator or deity. Life must be lived in a harmonious and balanced fashion with nature. That is why environmental pollution and land ownership are considered travesties to Mother Earth. The concepts of separation, isolation, and individualism are hallmarks of Euro-American society but are alien to that of Native Americans. Based on these assumptions, it follows that people of color believe that illness, distress, and problematic behaviors may be seen as imbalances in human relationships, a disharmony between individuals and their group, or individuals being out of synchrony with internal or external forces. More important, however, is the belief that functioning as a group against the forces of racism is the key to survival.

In many ways, this holistic outlook on life, the belief in interconnectedness and harmony, is shared by other groups of color as well. The ancient Chinese use of acupuncture and references to *chakras* (points of physical or spiritual energy in the human body) in Indian yogic texts involve the rebalance and healing of mind and body. Concepts of balance between *yin* (cold) and *yang* (hot) in the body are still much in vogue among many Chinese Americans.

Buddhist practices often stress the importance of moving people to being more in tune with others and society, to move away from individualism, and to move toward interdependence and connection with others. Likewise, the Afrocentric perspective teaches that human beings are part of a holistic fabric, are interconnected, and should be oriented toward collective rather than individual survival. In other words, working for the group ultimately benefits the individual.

Cultural Strength Five—Family and Community

Consistent with my earlier points, an interdependent cultural value orientation exists in the extended family structure of many African Americans, Asian Americans, and Latino Americans as a source of both psychological and instrumental support for coping with adversity. Extended family systems continue to serve as sources of personal empowerment for many African Americans, and these variables frequently act as cultural resources that may facilitate coping schemata, cognitive strategies, and adaptive responses. The presence of ethnic communities and their roles act to buffer people of color against a hostile society and provide cultural nourishment that validates their worldviews and lifestyles.

Such resources have enabled many of us to adjust our outlooks and subjective interpretations of the environment in the face of adversity or hardship. Our connectedness with family members, friends, and neighbors is evident in the ways we cope with problems. Coping practices that include social activities with family members and friends are collective coping strategies that highlight kinship ties, concern and responsibility for others, and self in relation to others within communities of color. Such relational coping practices not only provide further evidence of strong interdependent emphases in many populations of color but also often serve to bring about optimal mental functioning in many people of color.

WHAT PEOPLE OF COLOR CAN DO
TO OVERCOME RACISM

Some of you may already sense that much of what I have written in this chapter is for me as well. After years of antiracism work, I have gone through periods of anger, bitterness, doubt, and hopelessness and feelings of inadequacy. Each time when the picture appears most bleak, I have called upon the lessons of my ancestors and recounted the blessed cultural strengths that have helped my people through the bitterness and bleakness born of racism. Before I close, however, I would like to share with you some further lessons I have learned about combating racism.

1. *It's important for people of color to experience racism.* I am aware that this is a sad statement. The advice may also sound illogical and strange, but it is important to understand. What I am suggesting is that we live in a racist society, and facing incidents of racism is a common everyday occurrence. If our sons and daughters are to survive, they must learn to develop the ability to deal effectively with it. Trying to protect them or insulate them from all the perils of prejudice and discrimination will only lead to a false sense of security and deprive them of developing the necessary survival tools. Our task as parents and as a community of color is to help our children develop the resources to face the challenges of a racist system. The desire to protect our loved ones from the forces of prejudice and our need for them to experience invalidation require a delicate balance.

2. *We will never eradicate or eliminate racism.* Although there is no way to prove or disprove this statement, for me the answer is clear. Racism is as old as history itself. It will always be with us. Whining and complaining about it, however, doesn't help. Yes, we will always need to deal with racism. Yes, what we are asked to endure is unjust. Yes, life for persons of color is unfair. The important question, however, is, What do we do about it? Whine? Com-

plain? Give up? Each of us must find the answer to that question. Fighting racism and oppression for me is a personal matter linked to my sense of integrity. To me, the process of standing for social justice and combating racism is as important as the outcome (elimination of racism). Spike Lee's film title *Do the Right Thing* says it all for me.

3. *People of color will always be primarily responsible for combating racism.* This is not fair, but it is a reality. If you study the history of racism, you will find that the struggle for equal rights has always come from those who are oppressed. Granted, we have had valuable White allies, and they have played a major role in the struggle for civil rights and antiracism. But it is also clear to me that it is people of color who have been always at the forefront and have given their lives to speak out against injustice. Without our ability to prick the conscience of White America, it is doubtful that changes would occur. So even though we may resent it, we will always play the role of educator to our White brothers and sisters about racism. We will always be placed in a position of teaching them about our people, our history, and our worldviews. Don't let this unfair position and responsibility get you down.

4. *White people can be valuable allies.* We need to acknowledge and appreciate the fact that many White Americans are eager to help and represent powerful allies. It is important for us to realize that our enemy is not White Americans but White supremacy. As a group, Euro-Americans are decent and fair-minded. Once they begin to understand themselves as racial/cultural beings, take responsibility for their roles in the perpetuation of racism, and connect back with their humanity, they become eager allies with people of color. Some of the greatest friends of people of color have been White folks.

5. *Don't write off people's racially insensitive remarks without a chance for rectification.* Realize that we all need an opportunity to learn and grow, so making insensitive remarks or racial blunders cannot be the sole test of a person's value. There have been times

in which my comments or actions reflected bias or insensitivity to another group. And even though my immediate reaction was one of defensiveness, I very much appreciated the opportunity afforded me by others to be educated about my offensive remarks. All of us are born and raised in a highly racist and sexist culture. As a result, many of us have taken on many of the biases of our society. Helping one another understand the meaning of our words and actions must also be one of our primary responsibilities.

6. *We must form multicultural alliances.* Recognize that we also need to reach out to one another to form multicultural alliances and realize that race, culture, and ethnicity are functions of each and every one of us. Race is not just an Asian American thing, an African American thing, a Latino American thing, or a minority thing. White folks must begin to see that they are also racial/ cultural beings and have an equal investment in racial/ethnic matters. We must allow them to enter into our world if we are to build bridges of mutual understanding. Any one group, alone, cannot achieve the struggle for equal rights.

7. *Remember that our achievements are not attained without the help of many.* There is an old African proverb that states, "We stand on the shoulders of those who have gone on before us." As I have repeatedly emphasized, we would not be here without the wisdom, commitment, and sacrifice of the many who have gone before us. Their inspiration, courage, and dedication have made our journey easier. Our individual and group achievements are the result of a collective effort, not just an individual one. As we are a collective people, it is also important to acknowledge that family, friends, neighbors, and our communities have made us who we are. Don't hesitate to ask for help from those who have nourished us through the troubled times. Our strength lies in the group. In some respects, united we stand, but separated we fall.

8. *We are not immune from having biases and prejudices.* Most of this book has been directed at the biases and prejudices of White folks. However, people of color also inherit the biases and stereo-

types of the larger society. So even though I have been speaking against White supremacy and White racism, we need to "confess our sins" as well. I have met Asian Americans who possess strong stereotypes and prejudices against not only Whites but also other racial minorities. Likewise, I have encountered brothers and sisters of color who expressed negativism toward my racial group.

9. *Avoid the "who's more oppressed" trap.* Because all oppression is damaging and serves to separate rather than unify, playing the "I'm more oppressed" game is destructive to group unity and counter-productive to combating racism. There is little doubt that each group, whether Native American, African American, Latino/Hispanic American, or Asian American, can claim that it has suffered immensely from racism. If we understand our own group's oppression, it should make it easier to recognize the oppression of another. But to use one group's oppression to negate another group's is to diminish, dismiss, or negate the claims of another. It leads to separation rather than mutual understanding.

10. *Don't let interethnic/interracial conflicts destroy our unity.* We must face the fact that there is also much misunderstanding and bias among and between groups of color. It goes without saying, for example, that in some parts of the country, friction between Asian Americans and African Americans is greater than that between Blacks and Whites. We must learn to validate one another's experiences and to credit and appreciate how each has struggled to survive in a racist and oppressive environment. In some respects, we have avoided dealing with one another for political reasons. We have functioned under the common-enemy dictum in dealing with White society. We have submerged our differences with one another, avoided airing our dirty laundry in the eyes of White society, and been wary of the divide-and-conquer ploy used against us. Though this is a source of strength in dealing with racism, it also belies the need to work on our group misunderstandings and differences. It is time for us to truly have a dialogue with one another and to build bridges of mutual understanding.

11. *Not all bad things that happen to us are the results of racism.* I have repeatedly emphasized that we cannot let White supremacy strip us of our perceptual wisdom. Although we need to trust our intuitive or experiential reality, it is equally important that we do not externalize everything. Although blaming the victim is detrimental to our psychological well-being, it is equally destructive to attribute all negative events in our lives to racism! I have borne witness to brothers and sisters who tend to find fault in everything but themselves. Sometimes it is easier to blame others and attribute negative outcomes to external forces in our lives rather than accept responsibility for our own actions. Regardless of race, all of us have faults, limitations, and weaknesses. Owning up to them is a source of strength.

12. *Learn to take care of yourself.* As persons of color, we experience everyday lives that are filled with invalidations that tend to deplete our energies. The drain is even greater for those who choose to actively confront racism and oppression. Working for social justice as an educator, community worker, or civil rights advocate means that we are constantly swimming upstream, or against the White supremacy current. Studies continue to show that those who advance and press for social justice in our society are more likely to experience an extreme backlash or punitive measures from the establishment. It is because we challenge the prevailing norms and the status quo. The constant work for social change can cause burnout and feelings of isolation, alienation, and psychic drain. All of us need an opportunity to replenish our resources. Learning how to take care of us is very important. Again, being validated and nourished by our group is an important activity. After all, we are no good to our people if we have burned out.

13. *Don't allow yourself to be co-opted by the system.* It goes without saying that our lives are often better if we support the status quo. One of the ways the system maintains control over persons of color is to punish us if we challenge it but reward us for cooperation. If you work for a multinational corporation, for example, there is

much the company can do to reward you when you toe the company line and don't rock the boat. Increases in salary, promotions, and keys to the executive suite are used to seduce us into complicity with the biased policies and practices of the organization or society. Often these incentives are insidious because we like to believe we are valuable to the company. In contrast, if we push for social justice, organizations can punish us by isolation, lack of promotions, and making life difficult for us. All persons of color understand the meaning of the phrase *sell out*. Again, being firmly grounded in your own values and connected to your community serve as deterrents to being co-opted.

14. *Being bicultural or multicultural is not selling out.* We cannot confuse our bicultural assets with the myth of the melting pot. Being able to function in White society is different from "acting White." We need to realize that there are acceptable and unacceptable things in all cultures, and it is important for us to be able to examine and accept or reject aspects of cultures based on their merits, not just because they come from the dominant group. We need to own and accept those aspects of U.S. culture that are healthy and stand against those that are toxic (racism, sexism, and oppression). There is a major difference between our reactions related to forced compliance (cultural oppression via assimilation and acculturation) and freedom of choice in adopting functional values in all cultures. I have emphasized how an asset of persons of color is our bicultural flexibility. I believe that the issue before us is not whether to maintain one way of life but how we can function in a bicultural manner without losing our sense of integrity.

15. *Don't allow the current "terrorist atmosphere" to blind us to civil rights issues.* Since September 11, we need to be more vigilant in protecting the civil rights of all. The seeds of prejudice, stereotyping, and discrimination have been planted against our law-abiding Muslim brothers and sisters. We must stick together in combating ignorance and prejudice and not allow hysteria to dictate our lives. As people of color, we know how unwarranted fears can stereotype

a whole group of people. The recent Wen Ho Lee fiasco was the result of hysteria about the perceived threat to our country from an international power. And one does not have to look far back to see the devastating consequences of the internment of 120,000 Japanese Americans (two-thirds were U.S. citizens by virtue of birth) during World War II. The lessons from the past cannot be forgotten: we cannot continue to allow this nation to view racial/ethnic minority groups as disloyal aliens in their own country; as people of color, we must constantly step forward to voice opposition to prejudice and scapegoating; and our actions must be guided by values of social justice and civil rights.

16. *Being who you are is the best way to combat racism.* In some ways, just being a person of color is to combat racism. How we look, what we stand for, and our desire to be true to ourselves force society to consider race, racial differences, and racism. We are a constant visible reminder to White America about the disparity between its values of equality (respect, inclusion, freedom, and civil rights) and its racist policies and practices (disrespect, exclusion, oppression, and White privilege). That's why our visibility (racial, ethnic, and cultural differences) is enough to engender feelings of guilt, anger, hatred, and discomfort among many of our White brothers and sisters. Until our nation begins to see the racial and cultural mosaic of our society as something beautiful and valued, our presence will always represent a stand against racism.

In closing, we should all take pride in being people of color. No one or no system should ever rob us of our self-pride and collective group esteem. So let us work with one another, including our White brothers and sisters, to create a truly multicultural society by overcoming our biases and prejudices.

Epilogue

Congratulations on finishing this book, confronting your biases and prejudices, taking a long but honest look at yourself in the mirror, gaining insight and understanding, and making a commitment to change yourself and to fight for change in this society. If you have traveled to this point and accept the basic premise of unintentional bias and discrimination, you are well on your way to overcoming your racism and becoming a valued ally to people of color. You should feel proud of yourself.

Although you have traveled a long and difficult journey with me, it is far from over. The road to liberation has just begun, but you should feel good about making it through to this stage of your life. It has not been easy, has it? At times, you have felt angered by my assertions, defensive about my accusations, guilty about your role in the perpetuation of racism, and overwhelmed by the magnitude of the problem. But your persistence in working through these feelings is nothing short of admirable.

Let me briefly summarize some of your accomplishments.

First, you now realize how you have contributed to the racism problem. Although that insight is painful, you no longer need to allow it to go on. You have the awareness and insights to prevent it from continuing and to help others do likewise.

Second, you no longer need to deny your Whiteness because of defensiveness. You can actively define your Whiteness from a nonracist framework that incorporates a commitment to combat racism. You can now stand against White supremacy and fight shoulder to shoulder with people of color against its toxic effects.

Third, you are no longer paralyzed by negative emotions that prevent you from making a commitment to overcome racism. When these feelings arise, you are able to monitor them, analyze them, and make sense of them. They no longer prevent or block you from taking personal and collective action to combat racism.

With these insights about yourself, I hope that you will never turn back to the days of ignorance, denial, and the inability to see yourself as a racial/cultural being. The words of Pastor Martin Niemoller express the dangers we all face should that occur:

> In Germany, they came first for the Communists, and I didn't speak up because I wasn't a Communist. Then they came for the Jews, and I didn't speak up because I wasn't a Jew. Then they came for the trade unionists, and I didn't speak up because I wasn't a trade unionist. Then they came for the Catholics, and I didn't speak up because I was a Protestant. Then they came for me, and by that time no one was left to speak up.[1]

Overcoming your racism is a lifelong process. Though "a journey of a thousand miles begins with but a single step," there are many more to take. The road to liberation is filled with potholes, quicksand, fallen trees, and inclement weather. But with each step that we take together, we come closer to overcoming racism and reclaiming our humanity.

For you to continue the journey, however, means that you must travel it with others. You cannot let yourself and others falter on this important quest. You must rely on them for strength and nourishment, just as you give them strength to go on. The road to liberation must be a collective effort. Whether Red, Yellow, Black,

Brown, or White, as a family, we will ultimately call one another brothers and sisters, and we will overcome!

People of color have a saying that is appropriate to use here: "Keep on keeping on!"

Notes

Chapter One

1. Southern Poverty Law Center, *Intelligence Report* (Montgomery, Ala.: Southern Poverty Law Center, winter, 2000).

2. R. A. Serrano, "Study Counts Record Number of Hate Groups, 20 Percent Jump in Year," *San Francisco Chronicle*, March 4, 1998, p. A5.

3. U. S. Bureau of the Census, *Profiles of General Demographic Characteristics 2000* (Washington, D.C.: U.S. Government Printing Office, 2001).

4. D. W. Sue and D. Sue, *Counseling the Culturally Diverse: Theory and Practice* (New York: Wiley, 2003).

5. President's Initiative on Race, *One America in the Twenty-First Century* (Washington, D.C.: U.S. Government Printing Office, 1998).

Chapter Two

1. B. L. Whorf, *Language, Thought, and Reality: Selected Writings of Benjamin Lee Whorf,* ed. John B. Carroll (Cambridge: MIT Press, 1956).

2. G. W. Allport, *The Nature of Prejudice* (Reading, Mass.: Addison-Wesley, 1954).

3. L. Festinger, A *Theory of Cognitive Dissonance* (New York: Harper-Collins, 1957).

4. S. Lee, *Do the Right Thing* (Universal, 1989), *Jungle Fever* (Universal, 1991), *Malcolm X* (Warner Brothers, 1992), and *Bamboozled* (Forty Acres and a Mule Filmworks, 2000), films.

5. J. Jones, *Prejudice and Racism* (New York: McGraw-Hill, 1997).

6. Bureau of the Census, *Profiles of Demographic Characteristics 2000*.

Chapter Three

1. T. F. Pettigrew, "The Mental Health Impact," in *Impacts of Racism on White Americans*, eds. B. P. Bowser and R. G. Hunt (Thousand Oaks, Calif.: Sage, 1981), 97–118.

2. President's Initiative on Race, 1998.

3. J. F. Dovidio, S. L. Gaetner, K. Kawakami, and G. Hodson, "Why Can't We Just Get Along? Interpersonal Biases and Interracial Distrust," *Cultural Diversity and Ethnic Minority Psychology* 8 (2002): 88–102.

4. Center for Community Change, "Study of Racial Disparities Found in Costs of Mortgages," *New York Times*, April 2002.

5. S. G. Stolberg, "Racial Disparity Is Found in AIDS Clinical Studies," *New York Times*, May 2, 2002.

6. Jones, *Prejudice and Racism*.

7. M. Zhou and J. V. Gatewood, "Mapping the Train: Asian American Diversity and the Challenges of the Twenty-First Century," in *Contemporary Asian America: A Multi-Disciplinary Reader* (New York: New York University Press, 2000), 5–29.

8. W. H. Lee, *My Country Versus Me* (New York: Hyperion, 2001).

9. Ibid., 2, 7.

10. C. M. Steele, "Institutional Climate and Stereotype Threat" (keynote address at the National Multicultural Conference and Summit, Santa Barbara, Calif., January 2001).

11. F. J. Hanna, W. B. Talley, and M. H. Guindon, "The Power of Perception: Toward a Model of Cultural Oppression and Liberation," *Journal of Counseling and Development* 78 (2000): 430–446.

Chapter Four

1. R. V. Guthrie, *Even the Rat Was White: A Historical View of Psychology*, 2nd ed. (New York: HarperCollins, 1998).

2. E. Omori, *Rabbit in the Moon* (PBS Television Race Initiative, 1999), television film.

3. Letter to the Editor: "Internment Films Lack Perspective," *Piedmonter* (Piedmont, Calif.), June 25, 1999.

4. D. W. Sue, Letter to the Editor: "Dissecting the Flawed Thinking," *Piedmonter* (Piedmont, Calif.), July 2, 1999.

5. D. K. Tamaki, Letter to the Editor: "Government Knew It Was Wrong, *Piedmonter* (Piedmont, Calif.), July 2, 1999.

6. Sue and Sue, *Counseling the Culturally Diverse*.

7. A. Thomas and S. Sillen, *Racism and Psychiatry* (New York: Brunner/Mazel, 1972).

8. F. Riessman, *The Culturally Deprived Child* (New York: Harper-Collins, 1962).

9. Children Now, *A Different World: Children's Perceptions of Race and Class in the Media*, www.childrennow.org, New York, 1998.

10. Harris Poll, commissioned by a national conference on minority mistrust and perceptions, 1994.

Chapter Five

1. R. Kipling, "The White Man's Burden," *McClure's Magazine*, February 1899.

2. W. Ryan, *Blaming the Victim* (New York: Pantheon Books, 1971).

3. T. A. Parham, "Beyond Intolerance: Bridging the Gap Between Imposition and Acceptance" (keynote address at the National Multicultural Conference and Summit, Newport Beach, Calif., January 28, 1999).

4. Pettigrew, "Mental Health Impact," 97–118.

5. Jones, *Prejudice and Racism*.

6. D. Gregory, *The Light Side: The Dark Side*, Poppy Industries Album, 1969.

Chapter Six

1. D. Keltner and R. J. Robinson, "Extremism, Power, and Imagined Basis of Social Conflict," *Current Directions in Psychological Science* 5 (1996): 101–105.

2. R. Terry, *For Whites Only* (Grand Rapids, Mich.: Eerdmans, 1970), 2–3.

3. B. Wehrly, *Pathways to Multicultural Counseling Competence* (Pacific Grove, Calif.: Brooks/Cole, 1995), 24.

Chapter Seven

1. P. McIntosh, "White Privilege: Unpacking the Invisible Knapsack," *Peace and Freedom* (July/August 1989): 8–10.

2. P. Freire, *Pedagogy of the Oppressed* (New York: Continuum, 1970).

3. R. Ellison, *Invisible Man* (New York: Random House, 1972).

4. R. Jensen, *White Privilege Shapes the U.S.*, http://uts.cc.utexas.edu/~rjensen/freelance/whiteprivilege.htm, 1998.

5. *Off Balance: Youth, Race, and Crime in the News.* (April 2001).

6. T. Wise, "School Shootings and White Denial," *AlterNet*, March 6, 2001.

7. McIntosh, "White Privilege"; S. Winter, "Rooting Out Racism," *Issues in Radical Therapy* 17 (1977): 24–30; R. Jensen, *More Thoughts on Why the System of White Privilege Is Wrong*, http://uts.cc.utexas.edu/ ~rjensen/freelance/whitefolo.htm, 1999; R. Jensen, *Fleeing Whiteness: A Memoir About Achieving Humanity*,

http://uts.cc.utexas.edu/~freelance/rothenbergreiview.htm, 2000; M. Maier, "Invisible Privilege: What White Men Don't See," *Diversity Factor* 1, no. 3 (1997): 28–33.

Chapter Eight

1. C. R. Ridley, *Overcoming Unintentional Racism in Counseling and Therapy* (Thousand Oaks, Calif.: Sage, 1995).

2. J. E. Helms, *Black and White Racial Identity: Theory, Research, and Practice* (Westport, Conn.: Greenwood Press, 1990).

3. McIntosh, "White Privilege," 8.

4. Winter, "Rooting Out Racism."

5. Ibid.

6. Ibid.

7. Ibid.

8. M. S. Kiselica, "Preparing Anglos for the Challenges and Joys of Multiculturalism," *The Counseling Psychologist* 26 (1998): 10–11.

9. Winter, "Rooting Out Racism."

Chapter Nine

1. Harris Poll, commissioned by a national conference on minority mistrust.

2. S. Cisneros, *The House on Mango Street* (New York: Vintage Books, 1989), 28.

3. P. Pitts, *The Shadowman's Way* (New York: Avon, 1992), 34.

4. E. Gaines, *A Lesson Before Dying* (New York: Knopf, 1993), 46.

5. American Psychological Association, *Racism and Psychology* (Washington, D.C.: American Psychological Association, n.d.).

Chapter Ten

1. Allport, *The Nature of Prejudice*.

2. *Brown v Topeka Board of Education* (D. Kan. 1954).

3. President's Initiative on Race, *Pathways to One America in the Twenty-First Century: Promises, Practices for Racial Reconciliation* (Washington, D.C.: U.S. Government Printing Office, 1999).

Chapter Eleven

1. D. C. Locke, "Fatigue: An Essay," *Asheville (N.C.) African American News*, October 1994, p. 30.

2. V. E. Jordan (speech given at Howard University's Rankin Memorial Chapel, June 2002).

Epilogue

1. Widely disseminated quote by Pastor Martin Niemoller.

About the Author

Derald Wing Sue is professor of psychology and education at Teachers College, Columbia University. He was past president of the Society for the Psychological Study of Ethnic Minority Issues, was cofounder and first president of the Asian American Psychological Association, and is currently president of the Society of Counseling Psychology. He is the author of several best-selling textbooks on multicultural psychology and education and has been described as a pioneer in the field of multicultural psychology, multicultural education, and multicultural counseling and therapy.

Sue's services have been widely sought by many groups and organizations. He was invited to address President Clinton's Race Advisory Board on the National Dialogue on Race and participated in a congressional briefing on the psychology of racism. He is frequently sought as a spokesperson on issues of racism, multiculturalism, and diversity by the press and other media outlets. He has been interviewed on many television specials and is frequently quoted in the press.

As evidence of Sue's stature in the field, a national Fordham University study of multicultural publications and scholars concluded that "Impressively, Derald Wing Sue is without doubt the most influential multicultural scholar in the United States."

Index

A

Acculturation, 129–132. *See also* Assimilation

Accuracy, nonverbal and contextualized, 263

Acosta, O., 221

Action, commitment to antiracist, 185–187. *See also under* White identity, development of nonracist

Acton, Lord, 103

Acupuncture, 268

Adler, A., 103

Adversity, strengths through, 259–264

Afghanistan, 61

African American church, 267

African American Heritage Month, 224

Afroasian, 35

AIDS, 56

Alabama, 244

Alexie, S., 222

Alien Land Law (1913), 79

All the Way Home (film), 226

Allende, I., 221

Allport, G., 24, 232, 244

Alvarez, J., 221

America, diversification of, 10

American Counseling Association, 203, 225

American Indian Heritage Month, 224

American Me (film), 228

American Psychological Association, 216–217, 225

Anaya, R., 221

Andrews, M., 212–213

Angelou, M., 220

Anglo, 39

Animal Farm (Orwell), 258

Anti-Defamation League, 218, 223, 245

Antiracism, principles of, 232–251. *See also* White identity, development of nonracist

Arizona, 11

Arkansas, 151

Asian American, 38

Asian American Heritage Month, 224

Assimilation, 58, 129–132, 175–176

Association of American Indian Affairs, 223

Assumptions: biased, 68–69; possible, inherent in items, 112

Atlanta Braves (baseball team), 113

Attitude, as component of racism, 24, 30

Autobiography of a Brown Buffalo (Acosta), 221